MORE
FORENSICS
AND FICTION

MORE
FORENSICS
and FICTION

Consultant to the writers of
Law & Order, CSI: Miami, and *House M.D.*

D. P. LYLE, M.D.

MEDALLION
P R E S S

Medallion Press, Inc.

Printed in USA

INTRODUCTION

The first book in this series, *Murder and Mayhem: A Doctor Answers Medical and Forensic Questions for Mystery Writers*, appeared in 2003, and the second, *Forensics and Fiction: Clever, Intriguing, and Downright Odd Questions from Crime Writers*, in 2007. Once again I've attributed each question to its author, if he or she chose to be identified. Some preferred to remain anonymous, and others I simply could not reach because their contact information was no longer valid.

You will see questions from professional, multipublished, award-winning authors alongside those submitted by writers who are still searching for a home for their stories. What do these disparate groups of writers have in common? Each is a storyteller. Each possesses the same driving curiosity and the desire to get it right. Each settles before that annoying blinking cursor with the same questions. Can I write a believable and publishable story? Can I transfer the images in my head to paper in a coherent manner? Can I make the reader turn the page?

Many of the questioners have books in publication and personal websites. Visit their sites and read their books. Your effort will be rewarded.

This book is intended to inform and entertain not only writers but anyone who enjoys books, movies, or a good story. The questions and answers inside will offer some insight into how writers think and how they construct their stories. I am confident that readers will find many interesting, educational, humorous, and downright odd things in these pages.

As was the case with the earlier books in the series, this book is not solely mine. It belongs to many people. To each writer who submitted a question, I thank you for your curiosity, your imagination, and your dedication to accuracy. I have learned as much from researching and answering your questions as I hope you have from my answers.

To all the readers out there, I hope this book answers some of your own questions, raises your level of understanding of medical and forensic issues, causes new questions to sprout within your own mind, and, most of all, stirs your creative juices. Maybe you'll ask yourself the question that starts every writer's journey into a new story: What if? Maybe you'll pick up pen and paper and join us in this often maddening—but always rewarding—profession.

In answering each question, I have attempted to give enough background to add context to the particular medical or forensic issue at hand as well as to address the nuances of the specific scenario. The goal is to allow the writer to use this newly gained understanding to craft a more believable scene or story. I have tried to make each question and answer stand alone, while minimizing unnecessary repetition of information contained in other questions.

What this book is not:

In no way should the material contained in this publication be used for diagnosis or treatment of any medical disorder. Even the simplest question and answer would require decades of education and experience before it could be applied in a real-life situation.

Although I have endeavored to make the information accurate and scientifically correct, many subjects are too complex to explain in detail while addressing the nuances and controversies of modern medical knowledge. Such is the art of medicine. The answers are provided for use in the context of fiction writing and storytelling and should not be used for any other purpose.

This book is not to be used for any criminal activity or to bring harm to anyone.

TABLE OF CONTENTS

PART I: TRAUMATIC INJURIES, ILLNESSES, DOCTORS, AND HOSPITALS

PART II: POISONS, TOXINS, MEDICATIONS, AND DRUGS

PART III: THE POLICE, THE CRIME SCENE, AND THE CRIME LAB

PART IV: THE CORONER, THE BODY, AND THE AUTOPSY

PART V: ODDS AND ENDS, MOSTLY ODDS

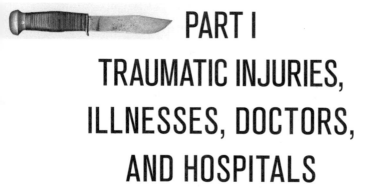

PART I
TRAUMATIC INJURIES, ILLNESSES, DOCTORS, AND HOSPITALS

WHAT INJURIES MIGHT MY CHARACTER SUFFER IN AN AUTO ACCIDENT THAT WOULD REQUIRE HOSPITAL TREATMENT FOR AT LEAST THREE DAYS?

 My protagonist gets into a car accident. I need him to be kept in the hospital for at least three days to leave his partner alone to get into trouble. Nothing life threatening but rather something that requires ongoing medical attention. Someone suggested a blood clot could show up after an accident and would require treatment with anticoagulants. Would this work? What kind of anticoagulant would he be given? How long would he be in the hospital?

P.A. Brown
Author of the L.A. Shadows series
Ontario, Canada
www.pabrown.com

A There is a wide array of injuries that can occur in an automobile accident, but a blood clot is not one of them. Not that it can't happen, just rarely in the period immediately following the accident. Blood clots can form a day or more later when the victim is in the hospital and confined to the bed. This is particularly likely with injuries to the legs or pelvis. We call this thrombophlebitis or deep venous thrombosis (DVT). If one of the clots breaks free and travels through the right side of the heart and into the lungs, this is called a pulmonary embolus (PE), which can be immediately deadly. DVT and PE typically do not occur for several days after an accident and usually only if the person is severely traumatized and confined to bed rest. The anticoagulant treatment is heparin for several days followed by coumarin for many months.

Since you want your character to survive, I suggest something less serious. The fracture of a rib or two could easily occur under these circumstances. This is extremely painful, and he would likely be kept in the hospital for two or three days. In accidents such as this, rib fractures are often associated with contusions (bruises) of the lung, which could further complicate and delay his complete recovery.

In either circumstance, the treatment is limiting mobility, pain medications, and oxygen by mask or nasal prongs to make breathing easier. He could be released from the hospital after a few days but would have a great deal of pain for the next two or three weeks. Ribs heal slowly. He would not likely return to work until he could function off the pain meds. There is no specific treatment for a simple rib fracture except for pain medications and time. I think this injury would fit your plot needs quite well and would not require much scientific explanation for the reader to understand the situation.

CAN MY SERIAL KILLER NURSE USE INJECTED AIR TO KILL HER VICTIMS?

Q In my story, a nurse becomes a serial killer. I have heard that injection of a bolus of air into the vein or artery will kill the intended victim, mimicking a heart attack. If this is true, how much air should be injected? Where can the injection needle be placed, so it will not be detected or cause the medical examiner to suspect anything but a natural cause of death? How long will it take the victim to die?

Linda F. Ames
Columbus, Georgia
http://thoughtsalongtheway-lizabeth.blogspot.com

A It could work if enough air is given. A simple bubble injected into a vein or the IV of a hospitalized patient would not cause problems. The bubble would simply pass through the right side of the heart and into the lungs where it would be filtered out and go completely unnoticed by the victim. But if a large amount was given, that would be a different story.

This is called an air embolus. To kill, the bolus (wad or mass) of air would need to be 100 to 200 cc's or more. For reference, a cup is about 240 cc's. When injected rapidly this air bolus would travel into the right side of the heart and block its pumping action. How does this work? Blood is a liquid and is not compressible. When the right ventricular heart muscle contracts (squeezes), the liquid blood is forced out and into the lungs. Air is compressible. If the right ventricle is filled with air, the air bolus will not be squeezed forward, but rather it will simply be compressed into a smaller volume and stay where it is. Sort of a vapor lock. This stops blood flow and can lead to cardiac arrest and death in a minute or two.

The air would have to be injected into a vein, any vein since all eventually lead back to the right side of the heart, and not an artery, which carries blood away from the heart. Your deadly nurse could also use any IV line the victim might have in place.

Such a death would indeed look like a heart attack (myocardial infarction or MI for short). But if the ME did an autopsy, which would be likely in such an unexpected hospital death, he would see the mass of air in the right ventricle and know that air had been injected. Since hospitalized patients often have needle marks and IV lines, he might not know where it had been injected, and of course, this would not tell him who injected the air or whether it was done on purpose or by accident. Your sleuth will have to figure that one out.

CAN AN AIR EMBOLUS CAUSE A STROKE IN MY CHARACTER WHO HAS HAD RECENT OPEN-HEART SURGERY?

 How would someone get an air embolus in the brain? Could this be caused by recent coronary artery bypass surgery or a viral infection?

AG

An embolus is any foreign object or substance that travels through the circulation. Usually they are blood clots, but they can be air, plastic IV lines, catheter tips, dirt and cotton from the IV use of heroin, and almost any small item that can be injected.

The circulatory system is divided into the venous and the arterial systems. The venous system gathers blood from the body and returns it to the right side of the heart, where it crosses through the lungs to the left or arterial side. The left ventricle (main pumping chamber of the heart) then pumps it into the arteries and out to the entire body, including the brain.

Any embolus that enters the body through a vein will travel through the right side of the heart and into the lungs. Here it is filtered by the tiny capillaries of the lungs and will not reach the arterial side. This means that in a normal individual anything injected into the right or venous side can't reach the arterial side and the brain.

For a clot or a mass of air to reach the brain, it must be

introduced into the arterial side of the circulation. During cardiac catheterization, coronary angiography, or an angioplasty procedure, a catheter is passed up the femoral artery (the main artery to the leg on each side) and into the main aorta and the heart. If any air is accidentally injected during these procedures, it can travel up the carotid arteries (one on each side of the neck) and into the brain. This can lead to a stroke. During open-heart surgery, air can enter the arterial circulation through the heart-lung machine or more directly if the heart is opened for a valve replacement. Either can serve as an entry point for air and lead to an air embolus and a stroke.

Either of these would have to happen during the procedure and not at a later time. In the case of surgery where the patient is anesthetized, this event might go unnoticed until the patient wakes up later. So it depends on what you mean by recent. The air embolus and the stroke won't happen later, but the stroke might not be recognized until later. People who suffer strokes several days after bypass surgery usually have underlying atherosclerotic disease of the arteries in the brain.

Air emboli will not follow a viral infection.

CAN MY SEVERELY ALCOHOLIC CHARACTER SUFFER BLACKOUTS AND LOST MEMORIES?

Q Is it credible to imagine a severely alcoholic character who loses hours or days at a time and has no recollection of what she did, including a murder of passion?

A Chronic alcoholics often have memory lapses from alcoholic blackouts or one of the various alcoholic encephalopathies. *Encephalopathy* is a big word meaning brain damage or dysfunction.

Delirium tremens (DTs) is one type of alcoholic encephalopathy. It typically occurs during alcohol withdrawal. The person will become confused and might forget who she is, where she is, and when severe she might talk nonsense and understand little of what is said to her. She could become delusional and think she's Jesus, Napoleon, or maybe even Bill Gates. She might hallucinate. The famous pink elephant is an example. Often these hallucinations are tactile in that the victims feel things crawling on them. People who have lost this degree of contact with reality can be dangerous to themselves and others. She might see another character as a monster coming to harm her and protect herself by killing her "assailant." She might remember none of this.

Alcoholic blackouts are similar. Here the brain does not register what is going on. What data gets through is chaotic and of little use in reconstructing what happened while she was out. This type most often occurs during intoxication rather than during withdrawal. She might talk to people, drive her car, go to a party, or kill someone and have no recollection of the events.

There are other types of encephalopathies associated with alcohol, but they are more complex, and I think either DTs or an alcoholic blackout will work well for you.

One other point to consider is that severe alcoholics are constantly intoxicated or withdrawing. There isn't much in between. When they are drinking, they are becoming increasingly intoxicated. When they pass out and sleep all day, they are undergoing withdrawal. That's why many wake up nervous and short-tempered. As soon as they get up they reach for the hair of the dog to dampen the withdrawal symptoms, and then they're off and running. Another twenty-four-hour binge. Tough life. Tough to treat.

WHAT HAPPENS WHEN SOMEONE IN A COMA WAKES WITH AMNESIA?

Q In my story, a patient comes out of a coma with full-blown amnesia. She can't remember anything. Later in the story she regains her memory. Is this possible? What would it feel like to come out of a coma? Would her personality change? What questions would the doctors ask her? How could the memories come back? How long would she remain in the hospital, and what treatment would they give her?

SG

A With comas and amnesia virtually anything can happen. A comatose person might remain so for days or months or years and then wake up gradually in fits and spurts or suddenly. After awakening, your character could be disoriented for minutes, hours, days, or weeks. She could return completely to normal or be left with all sorts of mental deficits and could definitely have personality changes. She could be withdrawn, talkative and outgoing, paranoid, angry and combative, quiet and passive, or anything else. All is possible.

She would have no memory for the time she was comatose and might or might not remember what came before. This is called retrograde amnesia. Her memory of previous events could be absent, partial, spotty, or complete. Her memory could return slowly over days, weeks, or months or might return quickly. Again, all is possible.

Comas and amnesia are poorly understood, and each comes in a thousand flavors. This is good since you can craft your story any way you wish and it will work.

Once she woke up, her physician would perform a mental status exam. This is designed to assess orientation, memory, and cognitive function. He does this with a series of questions. She might be able to answer all, some, or none of the questions. This is a complex procedure, but here are a few things he might do.

Orientation is knowing who she and others are, the date, her location, and her situation. The doctor might ask: What's your name? How old are you? Who is this? (While indicating someone she should know.) What is today's date? Who is the president? Where are we? What type of building are we in?

Memory would be tested by asking: What do you last remember? What street do you live on? The doctor might say a series of numbers or object names and then ask her to repeat them.

Cognitive function means the ability to understand concepts and connections. He could ask her to subtract 7 from 100 and 7 from that number and so on. (Answers: 100, 93, 86, 79, etc.) He might ask her what the phrases "cry over spilt milk" or "a penny saved is a penny earned" mean. Such questions test her ability to reason and use abstract thinking.

It's more complex than this but it should help.

Your victim might need little treatment other than time, or she might need psychiatric counseling and physical therapy (PT). If the coma was prolonged, her muscles would become weak and small (atrophy) from disuse, and it could take weeks or months of PT for her to regain the strength to sit and walk and bathe and feed and clothe herself. Again, you have great leeway here.

IS IT POSSIBLE FOR SOMEONE TO BE RELATIVELY IMMUNE TO ANESTHESIA?

Q Is it possible for someone to be relatively immune to anesthesia? My character undergoes anesthesia for facial cosmetic surgery (scar removal), but the anesthetic doesn't take and she freaks out. I imagine she'd be able to communicate this to the anesthesiologist, who'd then try a different form of anesthesia, but it would scare her in any case. A few years later could the same character be given a shot of morphine by the bad guy and again be relatively unaffected by it (maybe woozy but not out cold)? I figure he gives her what he thinks is enough to render her unconscious or even kill her, but she comes to eventually. I want the earlier operating room experience to give credence to the later morphine experience.

Harley Jane Kozak
www.harleyjanekozak.com

A Yes, this would work. Drugs of all types affect each of us in very different ways. Alcoholics can tolerate alcohol in quantities that would kill the normal person. Same for heroin in those addicted to that drug. Similarly, some people require a small dose of an anesthetic, while others take ten times as much. This is also true for morphine sulfate (MS in medical lingo). Just 2 or 3 milligrams might put one person out, while 20 might not sedate another. It's extremely unpredictable.

In addition, some people have the exact opposite response to anesthetics and sedatives than what was intended. Rather than sedating or rendering them unconscious, the drug makes them hyperexcitable. They become disoriented, agitated, even combative. These are called idiosyncratic reactions. This is a general term for any reaction that is different from what is expected with a particular drug.

Your character could have a hyperexcitable reaction to the anesthetic, and the anesthesiologist would have to use a different one. Or she could simply not be affected by it as much as expected and still feel what was going on. Here a larger dose of the same anesthetic would finally put her out. She could then later have either of these reactions to the MS.

So, yes, your character could easily require more than the usual amount of either or both meds to be sedated. Or she could have an idiosyncratic reaction to either or both. She could even be resistant to one and hyper with the other. Anything is possible.

CAN NASAL TRAUMA CAUSE MY CHARACTER TO LOSE HIS SENSE OF SMELL?

Q I want my character to lose his sense of smell after a blow to the face. My research suggests that this is possible if he has damage to his cribriform plate. Would blunt trauma be sufficient to crack the plate and sever his nerves? What other injuries would be likely? Would he be knocked out? Could a blood clot or hematoma cause a temporary loss of his sense of smell?

George Day
Austin, Texas

A Anosmia is the loss of the ability to smell. It can be temporary as in a simple cold or permanent as can occur in various neurological disorders. Any form of trauma to the ethmoid bone (cribriform plate) at the base of the skull in the nasal area can damage the nerve endings of the olfactory system and lead to anosmia. A blow to the nose or face can do it. This could be from a fist, a metal pipe, an auto accident, a fall, basically anything.

The sense of smell is the most primitive of our senses and is a combination of chemical and electrical reactions. A flower or an open bottle of ammonia releases molecules into the air. These contact the nerve endings in the cribriform plate, which in turn transmit a signal to the brain. The brain identifies the molecules, and the person recognizes the odor. Any damage to the nerve endings can interrupt this process and reduce or obliterate the sense of smell. This loss can be permanent or temporary in that the sense of smell might return as the injury heals.

Other injuries from a blow to the face would include fractures of the periorbital bones (the bones around the eye sockets) or the zygomatic arch (cheekbones) as well as hematomas (collections of blood), bruises, damage to the eyeball, loss of teeth, and a concussion, with loss of consciousness for a brief period. Or the injury could be to the nasal area alone.

So your character could suffer severe nerve damage and have a permanent loss of his sense of smell, or he could simply have a nasal fracture and bleeding within the nose and sinuses, and once healed his sense of smell could return. In either situation, the initial treatment would be the evacuation of blood or hematomas, sometimes surgical repair of any fractured bones, though this is not always necessary, pain medications, ice applied to the area of injury, and time. Whether his sense of smell returned or not would be unpredictable. It could or it could not. This means that you can construct your plot either way.

CAN A STROKE LEAVE MY CHARACTER PARALYZED FROM THE WAIST DOWN AND UNABLE TO SAY WHAT HE WANTS TO SAY?

Q A sixty-four-year-old character in my novel suffers a stroke that causes below-the-waist paralysis and the inability to vocalize. I want him to be able to formulate thoughts, just not vocalize them. What kind of stroke would make this possible?

LF
White Lake, Michigan

A Let's look at the communication issues first. What you describe is called aphasia. With strokes, some infections, and certain types of brain trauma, aphasia can occur. It can be receptive, expressive, or both.

A receptive aphasia is where the individual does not understand what he hears or sees written or is not able to recognize objects. These defects can come in any combination. For example, he might be able to look at a wristwatch and not recognize it but be able to write the word *watch* on a piece of paper. Or he might see *watch* written and not be able to speak it yet point one out. And almost any other combination.

An expressive aphasia is one where he knows what he wants to say but can't say it. Words and concepts will form in the victim's mind, but he can't speak what he is thinking. This can be extremely frustrating for him.

Both receptive and expressive aphasia can occur separately or together.

A stroke in the parietal area and the temporal area of the dominant hemisphere could cause this. These two lobes of the brain are located just above and behind the ear. The dominant hemisphere is the one opposite to the dominant hand. In other words, the left hemisphere is dominant in a right-handed individual. So in a right-handed person, a stroke that involved the left parietal and temporal lobes could result in aphasia.

Your paralysis is a little more problematic. What you are describing is paraplegia. This is paralysis of the lower half of the body. It can occur with certain spinal cord injuries and illnesses such as tumors and infections and some really odd diseases that cause damage to the spine in the lumbar (lower back) area. In this case, none of the neurologic transmissions that normally go through that area can get by the damaged area. Motor impulses, the ones that cause movement, can't go down the spinal cord to the legs, resulting in paralysis. Sensory impulses, the ones that allow us to feel, can't get from the legs up the spinal cord to the brain, resulting in numbness.

A stroke can't cause this. The reason is that the left side of the brain controls the right side of the body, and the right side of the brain controls the left side of the body. If the individual had a stroke in the left side of the brain, he could have right-sided paralysis, and if the stroke was on the right side, left-sided paralysis. But he could not develop paraplegia from either.

If your character was right-handed and suffered a stroke in the left parietal area of his brain, he could have his right leg or the entire right side of his body paralyzed and either receptive or expressive aphasia or both since his left brain would control the right side of his body and would also be his dominant hemisphere.

HOW WAS LOCKED-IN SYNDROME TREATED IN THE 1880s?

Q I am writing a murder mystery that takes place in the 1880s in America. I want a character to suffer from locked-in syndrome after a severe head injury. As I understand it, this would leave him fully conscious yet unable to move or communicate. How long could he live given the state of medicine at that time? Would the doctors be able to tell that he was still aware? He is a wealthy man and can afford the best medical care available for that time period.

J. Sharon Smith
Santa Cruz, California

A Locked-in syndrome is when the victim's muscles are paralyzed, yet he is alive and awake. Most sufferers of this syndrome can breathe without assistance, and often eye movements are spared, which allows communication through blinks and movements. Some victims will have no eye movements, but that's not the norm. It can be caused by trauma, as in your scenario, but also by infections, strokes, and several different types of neurological diseases.

The victim would not need life support, which was unavailable in the 1880s anyway, but he would have to be fed and cared for. The doctors, his family, or others might be able to communicate with him as described above. Or not. He might be completely unresponsive. They would of course know he was alive since he would breathe and have a pulse.

There was no specific treatment in the 1880s and little today. Most victims die from lung or kidney infections or pulmonary emboli—blood clots that form in the legs and travel to the lungs. These clots are common in immobilized individuals such as your unfortunate character.

How long could he live? Days, weeks, months, or years. In the 1880s it would depend on diligent care and luck more than anything else.

Locked-in syndrome is also called the Monte Cristo syndrome after the title character in *The Count of Monte Cristo*, the 1844 novel by Alexandre Dumas. Since this book would have been around by the 1880s, your doctors could use that term to describe the condition.

HOW WOULD MY CHARACTER WITH ADULT RESPIRATORY DISTRESS SYNDROME BE TREATED?

Q I have a character with ARDS caused by trauma to the chest during a car accident. I'd like her to be in a coma for about three weeks. Is this realistic? Would they do a tracheostomy or some other form of ventilation? How long would she be in the hospital once she was breathing on her own and oxygen levels were staying normal?

JB

A Adult respiratory distress syndrome (ARDS) has many causes, one of which is indeed chest trauma. After such trauma, the lungs can become inflamed, probably from an immunologic reaction that is poorly understood, and once inflamed they can weep fluids and become very stiff. This interferes with the transport of oxygen from the air sacs to the bloodstream and the oxygen concentration in the blood drops, sometimes to dangerously low levels. The treatment for this is to place the victim on a ventilator and then adjust the ventilator to supply pressure throughout the cycle. We call this PEEP or positive end-expiratory pressure. In English this simply means that the pressure inside the airways and air sacs is kept higher than normal through the entire breathing cycle. This forces more oxygen across the damaged barrier between the air sacs and the bloodstream and increases the level of oxygen in the blood.

Also, the oxygen that flows through the ventilator is increased dramatically. Normal room air contains approximately

21% oxygen. Here the percentage of oxygen will be raised to 80, 90, or even 100%. The victim would also be given steroids to lessen the lung inflammation and antibiotics to prevent a secondary infection.

The outcome depends upon this type of aggressive supportive therapy and good luck. Some people get better and some don't. Some people survive and some don't. It is a treacherous medical condition.

Your victim could be in a coma for three weeks if she also suffered head trauma during the accident. A cerebral (brain) contusion (bruise) or one of several other forms of brain injury could easily cause this. Add very low oxygen concentrations from the ARDS, and you have a recipe for a coma. In addition, some people with this condition do not tolerate being on a ventilator and fight it. It simply means that they cough or strain against it. Some of this fighting is involuntary, and some is out of fear and anxiety. This is critical since if the breathing cycle is not controlled and in a rhythmic to and fro motion, the oxygen transport from the ventilator through the lungs to the bloodstream is not ideal. Many of these patients will be maintained in an induced coma by giving them morphine or another sedative to keep them relaxed and asleep. It's probably the best way to go through this ordeal anyway. So you can also use an induced coma for two or three weeks while her ARDS repairs itself.

Initially an endotracheal (ET) tube would be placed. It's passed through the nose or the mouth and into the trachea, where a balloon cuff is inflated to seal it in place and allow the passage of air into the lungs. But if someone is going to remain on a ventilator longer than five to seven days, a tracheotomy (trach for short) is usually performed. The trachea does not like having a tube and a balloon in place, and it can become damaged from the balloon's pressure, even to the point that it can erode through the wall of the trachea. This creates a whole other set of medical problems. A tracheotomy decreases the likelihood of this. It is simply a hole cut into the trachea just beneath the larynx (Adam's apple). A curved hollow tube called a cannula is passed through the opening and into the trachea, and the ventilator is attached to it.

If your victim was kept in a coma for three weeks, there would likely be another week or so of weaning her from the ventilator. When you are supported by a ventilator, the muscles used for breathing become weak and lose their conditioning and must be reconditioned. The patient is removed from the ventilator for a few minutes every hour, then for an hour out of every three or four hours, then for several hours at a time, and ultimately taken off the ventilator completely. After that process is completed and the patient is stable for a day or two, the tracheostomy cannula is removed.

The problem then is one of rehab, not only of her lungs but of all the other injuries that occurred during her accident. It is impossible to give you exact numbers as to how long this would take, how long she would be in the hospital, and how long she would require physical therapy. I suggest you have her in a coma for three weeks, going through the weaning process for another week, then remaining in the hospital for at least one more week before she would be strong enough to go home. These times are highly variable, which means that you can create your plot in almost any manner as long as you stay within these broad parameters.

HOW WOULD MY CHARACTER WHOSE ARM IS TRAPPED BENEATH AN OVERTURNED VEHICLE BE TREATED ONCE RESCUED?

Q In my novel, a young college boy is in the Ozark National Forest when a portion of road breaks away and his vehicle turns over, pinning his arm to the ground. He can wiggle his fingers but can't free himself. He has several beers, a candy bar, and a Slim Jim. He is trapped from Saturday evening until Monday evening near the edge of a logger-made swamp and is eaten alive by mosquitoes. When he is found, what kind of first aid would he receive? What would happen at the hospital? Is there a chance he could lose the arm? I prefer that he didn't.

BR
London, Arkansas

A There are several medical issues involved here. The first is his level of hydration and nutrition. The latter would be no problem since the beer and food items would feed him for the forty-eight hours you need for your plot. The same can be said for his hydration status, though alcohol serves as a diuretic and beer is not exactly the best thing to maintain hydration, but after only forty-eight hours this should not be a problem.

The second would be the multiple mosquito bites. These would be uncomfortable but not a major problem. They might be in the early stages of infection when he is found but would only require cleaning and perhaps a topical antibiotic.

The likelihood of any long-term problems is very small.

By far the most important health issue is his arm. The fact that he is trapped means that the arm is under a great deal of pressure. Otherwise he would be able to get free. If he can wiggle his fingers, the nerves and the blood supply are intact. Therefore, the tissues of the arm would survive the forty-eight hours, and he would not likely be in danger of losing his arm. However, he could have cuts and abrasions and fractured or even crushed bones, which might require surgical repair. It could be simply setting and casting a fracture or a more involved surgical intervention with rods, screws, and metal plates to put fractured or crushed bones back together. The bones injured could be the humerus, which is the upper arm bone, or the radius or ulna, which are the larger and smaller lower arm bones, respectively.

So your scenario works. He could be trapped for forty-eight hours and yet his arm be okay, though surgical treatment of bony fractures and any tissue injuries might be needed.

First aid would be prying him from beneath the vehicle, controlling any bleeding this might stir up, placing his arm in a sling, and getting him to help. An ambulance could be called, or he could be taken in a vehicle to the local hospital.

Once at the hospital they would do X-rays of the arm and clean and examine any cuts or abrasions. They would be cleaned but would not likely be sutured since a wound that has been left exposed for forty-eight hours has a high incidence of infection and this could be made worse by closing the wound. It would be treated with antibiotic ointment and dressed, and he would be given intravenous or oral antibiotics for the next several days or a week or two. If these were the only injuries and the bones were intact, he would probably go home in a day or two and be treated on an outpatient basis. If he required an orthopedic surgical procedure, his hospitalization would be prolonged for five days or so, and he would be on intravenous antibiotics after the surgery. Here he would require three or four weeks of healing and several months of physical therapy to regain full use of his arm. He could be left with no long-term problems, issues with the use of his arm forever, or anywhere in between.

WHAT DOES THE VICTIM OF AN ARROW TO THE HEART LOOK LIKE, AND HOW WOULD HE DIE?

Q The victim in my story dies from an arrow through his heart. I would like to include the gory details of exactly what is happening to his body from the moment of the arrow piercing his heart until he dies. How long until death occurs? Do his lungs fill with blood? Does his mouth fill with blood, and can he choke on his own blood if lying on his back?

A An arrow to the heart might or might not be deadly. Usually yes, sometimes no. If the arrow penetrates the muscle of the ventricles (the right and left pumping chambers), the muscle might contract around the shaft, there might be little or no bleeding, and the victim can survive for hours, maybe days. Once the arrow is pulled out, bleeding might be brisk and death can quickly follow. If such a person came to the hospital, he would be taken to the operating room, his chest would be opened, a "purse-string" suture would be placed around the entry wound, and the arrow would be removed while the suture is pulled tight to close the wound.

Obviously, this is not the norm.

An arrow that enters the heart can kill by several mechanisms. The arrow might cause a deadly change in heart rhythm, resulting in almost instantaneous death. In this case, the victim would grab his chest, collapse, and die. Sudden and dramatic.

The arrow might damage the heart muscle and/or heart valves, so the heart no longer functions well as a pump, which is basically all it does, and the victim will slip into shock (low blood pressure, weak or absent pulses, a pale and dusky appearance) and die.

The punctured heart muscle might bleed into the pericardium, the sac around the heart. The pericardium is a nondistensible (doesn't stretch) sac, and as it fills with blood it compresses the heart and results in shock and death. Blood in the pericardium is called a hemopericardium. Hemo means "blood" and pericardium means "heart sac," so the word literally means "blood in the heart sac." When it compresses the heart and interferes with its function, the condition is called cardiac tamponade.

In these latter situations, the victim would have chest pain and shortness of breath. His blood pressure would drop, his pulse weaken, and he would become pale and cyanotic (a bluish-gray hue to the skin). He would go into shock, stop breathing, and die.

Blood would not fill the lungs or come from his mouth unless a lung was also penetrated, which of course could easily happen. If so, blood would fill his lungs and mouth, and if he coughed, blood would spray from his mouth. Yes, he could drown in his own blood.

CAN WITHHOLDING OR TAMPERING WITH AN INHALER LEAD TO DEATH IN AN ASTHMATIC, AND CAN THE ME DETERMINE THAT ASTHMA WAS THE CAUSE OF DEATH?

Q In my story, a man in his late sixties is asthmatic. If he suffers a severe attack caused by extreme stress (an attack on him or his property) and his inhaler is withheld or had been switched with an empty canister, would he die? Could an anaphylactic death look like an asthma death?

B.J. Silberman
Germantown, Tennessee

A Stressful situations can indeed trigger asthmatic attacks in asthmatics. If the victim is unable to reach his inhaler or if it had been tampered with as you describe, he could die from the attack. After death he would simply look dead, and there would be no external evidence that he died from an asthmatic attack. However, at autopsy the medical examiner might find inflammation of the airways and mucus and other fluids collected within the airways and the air sacs of the lungs. This would suggest that the victim had died from an asthmatic attack.

Anaphylactic shock includes asthma as part of its complex of symptoms and signs, along with skin rashes and swelling of the face, hands, and feet in many individuals. The rashes, which are often blister-like (we call them bullae), tend to resolve at death so they might or might not be visible by the time the autopsy is done. There could be some residual redness in a splotchy pattern over the skin, or the skin might appear normal. So an anaphylactic death can look very much like an asthmatic death, and it is often impossible for the medical examiner to distinguish between the two.

WHAT INJURIES COULD MY CHARACTER SUFFER IF STRUCK BY A CAR?

Q I have written a mystery based on the hit-and-run death of a female jogger. She has been hit from behind. I assume she would have been thrown some distance. How far? Several feet, yards? What type of injuries would she most likely have sustained?

Sue Parker
Author of *Foul Play*
Yorba Linda, California

A This is very unpredictable. In an auto versus pedestrian accident virtually everything in the body is subject to injury. The factors that dictate what happens include the size, age, and health of the victim, the speed and size of the vehicle, the nature of the contact (head-on, at an angle, glancing, etc.), and other things, including luck.

There is an adage in medicine that says, whatever happens happens. Your victim could die instantly, suffer no injuries whatsoever, and anything in between. She could fly two hundred feet, roll under the wheels, or simply be knocked down. Anything is possible so there are no rules.

The injuries she could suffer are many and varied and include:

Contusions and abrasions of the entire body.

Bone fractures: legs, arms, ribs, back, skull, and neck. Arms and legs could be simple fractures or what we call comminuted (fractured in several areas or crushed) or compound (where the skin is broken and the bone protrudes).

Ruptured internal organs: The spleen is most likely but also the liver, kidneys, intestines, and the stomach. These would cause varying degrees of internal bleeding, and if enough blood is lost she would slip into shock and die.

Lung and heart damage: Rupture of the heart or the aorta would be almost instantly lethal. A bruise or tear of the lung could lead to its collapse (we call this a pneumothorax) of one or both lungs or severe bleeding where she could essentially drown in her own blood.

Head trauma: This can be with or without a skull fracture. There could be a contusion (bruise) of the brain or bleeding into or around the brain. This can be deadly very quickly, or she could survive and require brain surgery. This type of injury, like all the ones above, come in many flavors from minor to deadly.

COULD A DOCTOR SAVE AN UNBORN CHILD IF THE MOTHER IS SHOT AND KILLED?

Q In my screenplay, a thirty-seven-week pregnant woman is shot and killed. Could a doctor successfully deliver her baby? What would the medical response time need to be in order to save the baby, and what would be a likely entry area for the bullet? Could the cause of death be from blood loss and still allow for the survival of the baby? Would it be possible to hide from the public and the police that the infant has survived?

RS
Cameron Park, California

A If the mother is shot and killed instantly, the doctors have maybe five minutes to get the baby out by Cesarean section. This is not a difficult procedure if the mother is dead, but it must be done very quickly. With the mother dead, the child gets no blood and thus no oxygen through the placenta. Death comes soon after.

If the mother is shot and slowly bleeds to death, then the rescuers have more time. The child would be okay until the mother went into shock from blood loss. The low blood pressure associated with shock would reduce the blood flow to the placenta, and the baby would be in increasing jeopardy as her blood pressure declined. The removal would have to be done before or immediately after the mother reached a stage of profound shock or death.

For the police and the public not to know would require that any witnesses, police on the scene, and/or the doctor be involved in the conspiracy. Otherwise the doctor has a moral and legal obligation to notify the police of the shooting.

CAN MY AUTOMOBILE ACCIDENT VICTIM BE BLINDED BUT OTHERWISE UNINJURED?

Q Is it possible for a person to suffer an injury in a car crash that would sever the optic nerve but still allow full brain function otherwise? What kind of injury would it be, and how would it happen?

Douglas L. Perry
Author of *Lost in the Sky*
Livermore, California
www.douglasLperry.com

A Yes, this can work in several ways. The optic nerves stretch from the back of the eyeball to the base of the brain. One comes from each eye, and they partially cross in a complicated fashion that is not necessary to understand for your story. Once in the brain the optical impulses travel to what is known as the optical cortex, which lies at the very back portion of the brain.

Injuries that involve either of the victim's eyes or the bones around the eyes, called the periorbital bones, could also damage either or both of the optic nerves, resulting in complete or partial blindness. That is, one optic nerve could be damaged and the other not, in which case blindness would be on one side and not the other.

Trauma to the back of the head could damage the occipital cortex, and this could cause blindness. We call this cortical blindness since it results from damage to the cortex of the brain and not the optic nerves themselves. This can happen with a direct blow to the back of the head, a direct injury, or from a blow to the forehead such as when the head strikes the dashboard. Here the damage to the back of the brain is what we call a contrecoup injury. Basically, the brain floats inside the skull, tethered by certain membrane coverings and by spinal fluid. When the blow is delivered to the front of the head, the brain is propelled backwards and bounces off the back of the skull. This contrecoup injury can damage the optical cortex and produce blindness.

So you have two ways of causing blindness in your victim: direct frontal head injury with damage to the optic nerves or blunt head trauma, resulting in either a direct or a contrecoup injury to the optical cortex.

WHAT COULD BE USED TO KILL A HOSPITALIZED PATIENT WHO HAS HAD A RECENT BONE MARROW TRANSPLANT?

Q In my story, a minister visiting a member of his congregation in the hospital wants to kill him without getting caught. The patient had a recent bone marrow transplant and is still in the transplant unit. He has little or no working immune system. What would be available, easily delivered (maybe put in a glass of ice water), and lethal?

Warren Bull
Award-winning author of
Abraham Lincoln for the Defense
and *Murder Manhattan Style*
Kansas City, Missouri
www.warrenbull.com

A There are numerous methods for doing someone in while he is confined in a hospital. A range of poisons such as arsenic or cyanide could be brought in and administered. Even standard medications including digitalis and narcotics and sedatives of all types can be lethal if given in large doses. Also, your character might have an intravenous line, which opens up a host of other options. Intravenous medications that could do the job include insulin, digitalis, potassium chloride, quinidine, any of the beta-blockers, and hundreds of other medications.

But I get the impression you wish to use his immuno-suppressed state as part of your murder scenario. Perhaps some overwhelming infection that would kill him. There are many options for that also. The simplest would be for the killer to mix a small amount of fecal material with water and inject it intravenously. This would cause an overwhelming multiorganism blood infection that could be deadly. If this is a little too crude, then your murderer could have access to the Bacteriology Department of the hospital lab and simply steal some growing organisms. Such labs always have incubators filled with growth plates that contain all sorts of nasty organisms. Any of the so-called gram-negative organisms or perhaps methicillin-resistant Staphylococcus aureus (MRSA) could be stolen and used.

Symptoms of the infection would not appear for twenty-four to forty-eight hours, giving your killer time to be far away. Fever and chills would be the first symptoms followed by shortness of breath, a low blood pressure, a rapid heartbeat, sweating, and finally the victim would slip into shock and die. We call this type of infectious shock septic shock. Deadly in someone with a compromised immune system.

CAN A HEATED BRANDING IRON APPLIED TO MY VICTIM CAUSE DEATH?

Q Is it possible to kill someone by application of a branding iron to the top of the head? The abdomen? If so, would it take repeated reheatings and applications? Would such a procedure on the head cook the brain? Would it leave a permanent burned impression in the skull?

DW

A The major factors determining the nature of the injuries that might occur are the temperature of the iron, the pressure with which it is applied, and the duration of the application. Very painful third-degree burns of the skin, muscles, and other tissues in the area would be a given. To be lethal, the burning would have to penetrate the skin and other tissues and reach vital organs. Unless the victim died of shock induced by the severe pain, that is.

Burning through the abdominal wall and into the abdominal cavity would be easier than burning through the skull, but with enough heat, pressure, and time, the skull could be penetrated. Then the brain damage would be severe and potentially deadly. Even if the skull wasn't penetrated, enough heat could be applied to cause thermal damage to the brain, and this could also lead to death. Either of these would likely take several applications of the glowing iron.

Yes, this would leave a permanent charred area wherever the iron was applied, whether the victim lived or not. Third-degree burns always leave scars.

WHAT INJURIES CAN RESULT FROM DEPLETED URANIUM BULLETS?

Q I have a character who is shot with depleted uranium ammunition. What would be the main characteristics of the entry and exit wounds? If the bullet is found, what would be the telltale signs that depleted uranium was a factor (considering they are not known bullets but rather homemade)?

RB

A Depleted uranium bullets (DUBs) are much more dense than regular ammunition. This means that they travel farther with greater accuracy and are capable of piercing armor plate. If such a dense bullet struck a human, it would probably pass through with clean entry and exit wounds. Exit wounds from standard bullets are large and irregular due to the expansion and/or distortion of the bullet as it passes through flesh or strikes bones. The softer the bullet (lead versus jacketed lead), the more it is distorted and the more internal damage and the larger the exit wound. A dense DUB would most likely pass through unscathed. At least relatively. So it would leave smaller entry and exit wounds.

If it struck a bony structure, it would do more damage to the bone than a standard bullet. If the bullet or fragments of the bullet remained within the victim, radioactivity could be detected. Depleted uranium has very low radioactivity, but it is detectable.

The effect of such a bullet or fragment that remained within a victim for a long period of time (maybe it can't be removed because the victim couldn't withstand the surgery or the bullet was in such a location that removal was too dangerous) is unknown, but it probably would have little long-term effect since the level of radioactivity is low.

If the bullet was found fairly well intact, an educated examiner should be able to distinguish between one manufactured by the military and one that was homemade. First of all, the military bullets are metal jacketed, while a homemade one would not likely be.

COULD A TWELVE-YEAR-OLD BOY SUFFOCATE A SMALLER CHILD BY SITTING ON HIM?

Q I am submitting a television script for a mystery/crime series that airs on the BBC. My question is whether a twelve-year-old boy of average weight and height would be able to crush and suffocate a six-year-old child by kneeling on the child's chest. Approximately how long would it take?

Chrinda Jones
Plano, Texas

A Yes, this could happen. It would depend on the weight difference between the two as much as anything else, but the strength of the older boy would also play a role. This is a form of asphyxia known as mechanical asphyxia. It also carries the moniker burking, a name derived from William Burke and William Hare, two seventeenth-century criminals.

William Burke was a merchant in Edinburgh, Scotland, in the early 1800s. He bought old shoes and refurbished and sold them. He also trafficked in clothes, skins, and human hair. In 1827 he hooked up with William Hare, who ran a beggars' hotel in the village of Tanners Close. In December a resident of the hotel named Donald died, and Burke arranged to sell his body at Surgeons Square to Dr. Knox, who needed corpses for his dissection demonstrations.

To pull off their scam, the two men loaded Donald's

coffin with bark, and it was buried in front of many witnesses. They then delivered the body to Dr. Knox and received seven pounds and ten shillings in return. A business was born. Burke and Hare became grave robbers, supplying pilfered corpses to the doctor for eight pounds in summer and ten in winter. Must have been more difficult to dig them up when the ground was cold.

Greed did them in. The local populace refused to die fast enough, so they resorted to kidnapping and killing people who were not likely to be missed. Burke would sit on them and hold their mouth and nose closed until they suffocated, after which they would deliver the corpse and collect their fee. Over the next year, sixteen people died at their hands.

Finally, a lodger at the hotel notified authorities when she discovered their sixteenth and last victim beneath a bed. Apparently the two men had stashed the body there while awaiting an opportunity to transport it to Surgeons Square. The two men were arrested. Hare then turned King's evidence on Burke and testified against him. Burke was convicted and hanged on January 28, 1829, an event attended by as many as forty thousand people.

In your scenario, if the older boy lay on top of the smaller boy and concentrated his weight over the boy's chest, he could prevent the younger child from taking complete breaths. His ability to breathe would be greatly diminished, and as he struggled against his attacker he would consume much more oxygen. This imbalance between supply and demand would result in his death from mechanical asphyxia. The time required is highly variable since it would depend upon the exact amount of crushing force applied and whether the force was somewhat intermittent. By that I mean if the struggling child was able to twist one way and then the other enough to catch a breath from time to time, the struggle could go on for maybe twenty or thirty minutes. But if the older boy maintained complete control and was able to apply continuous pressure, the younger child could die in as few as three or four minutes. He would likely lose consciousness before that, perhaps in a minute or two.

HOW WOULD MY CAR FIRE VICTIM BE TREATED IN A SPECIALIZED BURN CENTER?

Q I've just given one of my characters first-, second-, and third-degree burns from an automobile accident. The character is treated in a specialized burn center. I want him to survive. Beyond IV fluids and high-flow oxygen, what type of treatment might he receive? I suspect that infection and pneumonia are issues. Is he allowed visitors?

Norm Benson
Freelance writer and writer for the
"Green Chain" environmental column
in the *Lake County Record-Bee*
http://timberati.com

A He would be placed in strict isolation and allowed no visitors. At least not until the healing process was well under way. Each physician, nurse, lab tech, or other medical personnel who entered his room would wear sterile gowns, masks, and gloves.

He would receive broad-spectrum antibiotics by IV, and his burns would be dressed using Silvadene. This is a thick white ointment that looks and feels similar to Crisco. It is applied thickly on the burns, which are then dressed with gauze. This dressing is changed once or twice a day. Morphine, Demerol, or some other powerful analgesic would be liberally used to control pain, particularly with each cleaning and dressing since this process is very painful. Many third-degree burns are less painful than second-degree ones since the deep burn damages the nerves in the skin, blunting sensation. This is not always the case, however. Your character, as you pointed out and as is the case with most burn victims, would have burns of varying degrees.

If the wounds began to heal and no infection was present, skin grafting of the third-degree burns would begin. Wound healing is heralded by the appearance of granulation tissue, which is red, moist, and rich in blood supply. It appears in the burned areas after one to two weeks in most victims. Many third-degree burns will not granulate. Either way, grafting could be done from several days to a couple of weeks after the burn. Sometimes longer. Infection sets everything back and increases eventual scarring.

Infection and pneumonia are the most common causes of death in severe burns.

WHAT TYPE OF CANCER IS DEADLY BUT HAS NEITHER OUTWARD SIGNS NOR SYMPTOMS THAT WOULD ATTRACT ATTENTION?

Q In my story, I have a guy who is murdered, but before he's killed he takes out a life insurance policy on himself naming his wife beneficiary. During his autopsy he is found to have had terminal cancer. Further investigation reveals that he was being treated by a physician and he knew he was dying.

What kind of cancer could he have that would be untreatable, quickly fatal, and produce few, if any, identifiable symptoms that his wife and coworkers might have seen and questioned? I want him to have known he had terminal cancer, but I want the illness to have been unknown to others.

M. Diane Vogt
Author of the Judge Willa Carson mysteries
and *The Little Book of Bathroom Crime Puzzles*
Tampa, Florida
www.mdianevogt.com

A Though there are many options, your best bet might be melanoma—a nasty little malignancy that can kill in a few months. It is often discovered as a dark and irregularly shaped mole on the arms, legs, back, scalp, or almost anywhere, though most often in sun-exposed areas. It is initially biopsied, and when the diagnosis of melanoma is confirmed, it is removed by what is called a wide margin excision. This simply means that the mole is removed along with a fair portion of the surrounding tissue.

The real danger with melanoma is that by the time it is diagnosed it has often already metastasized (spread) throughout the body. A favorite location of these mets (metastatic lesions) is the brain, and when it spreads there it is uniformly fatal. Chemotherapy is of little help. Death can occur in weeks or months after spreading to the brain.

Some common symptoms of melanoma with brain mets are: headache, blurred or double vision, weakness or paralysis of one or more limbs or one side of the body, nausea, vomiting, seizures, disorientation, delusional or irrational thinking, erratic actions, and coma. These symptoms can occur in any degree or combination. He could have essentially no symptoms, or they could be minor enough that he could cover them.

So your victim could have metastatic melanoma, know he was dying, exhibit few outward symptoms or signs, and set up the insurance policy to protect his wife financially after his death.

HOW WAS OVARIAN AND CERVICAL CANCER TREATED IN THE 1870s?

Q I need some information on the treatment of ovarian or cervical cancer in a small Midwestern town in the early 1870s. How readily might it have been diagnosed, and what would have been done to treat it? The victim is the wife of a young and inexperienced doctor, and my thought is he would likely not have the experience or facilities to do a proper job of it himself, so he would take her to a hospital in a larger city for surgery. How long would she stay in the hospital following surgery? Would they even attempt surgery, or would her treatment be purely palliative?

A By today's standards, cancer treatment was nonexistent in the 1870s. There was no radiation therapy or chemotherapy, and treatment was mostly comfort measures such as opium and alcohol to lessen pain. Surgery, itself a risky proposition in the 1870s, was intended to be curative, and at times it probably was, but for the most part it was an exercise in futility. Cancers were seldom discovered until they were well advanced.

Yes, your character could undergo surgery and could survive it and even the cancer itself. Her recovery would be much as it is today: a few weeks of discomfort, a few weeks of regaining strength, and then full recovery and a return to a normal life. But there are many pitfalls between points A and B.

First was anesthesia. There were several choices in the

1870s. Opium, alcohol, and mandrake root were all used but were marginally effective. Ether and chloroform were available, with ether having been first used by Dr. Crawford Long in Atlanta in 1842 and the first public demonstration of its use at the Massachusetts General Hospital in 1846. By the 1870s it was administered in many hospitals but not all.

The second problem would be the surgery itself. Most surgical deaths came from blood loss, shock, and secondary infections. There were no blood transfusions and no antibiotics. Hand washing by surgeons and the wearing of masks and gloves in surgery were relatively new. Surgical deaths and death from post-op infections were common.

Your character could be treated with opium and comfort measures or with surgery. She could sail through without problems or could bleed and/or become infected, and she could either survive or die from these complications. Anything is possible, so you can construct your story as you wish.

CAN A BLOW TO THE HEAD CAUSE
CAPGRAS SYNDROME?

 I'm writing for a new police procedural show for A&E. It is set in western Florida and is titled *The Glades*.

Would it be possible to get subjective Capgras syndrome from a brain injury, like falling down stairs and hitting concrete? Could this syndrome manifest itself ten hours later? Could it resolve in a few days as the brain swelling goes down? Basically I'm hoping somebody can come into the ER, injured, at midnight, then tell the nurse and the cops the next morning that he has a doppelganger who killed somebody last night.

Matt Witten
Writer, producer
Los Angeles, California

Yes, I think it's possible, though most brain injuries that are associated with this syndrome are more severe than a simple concussion. I suggest your character suffer from a cerebral contusion—a brain bruise. The swelling could take a few hours to develop, and therefore, the neurological and psychiatric defects might require several hours to occur. Later when the swelling improved he could return to normal. This would be more likely to occur if your character had underlying schizophrenia. It could be mild or what we call functional schizophrenia, meaning he could function in society without anyone knowing he was schizophrenic.

Capgras syndrome is in the class of psychiatric disorders called delusional misidentification syndromes. It is the delusional belief that a friend, spouse, or another person has been replaced by an identical-looking impostor, a doppelganger. It is most commonly associated with schizophrenia but can also follow certain brain injuries, particularly those involving the back (posterior or occipital) area of the right brain hemisphere. This is where facial recognition takes place, and the loss of this ability seems to be one of the generators of Capgras syndrome. So simply have your victim injured in that area.

Once he entered the emergency room, he would undergo a complete neurologic examination and a brain scan, either a CT or MRI. The scan would likely be completely normal, but later as he began to develop delusional beliefs, the concern would be that brain swelling or bleeding into the brain had occurred. A repeat scan might show some swelling in his right posterior hemisphere. The treatment would be rest, steroids to lessen the swelling, and sometimes diuretics to dehydrate the entire body, including the brain. The steroids might be 16 milligrams (mgs) of dexamethasone, and the diuretic would most likely be 40 mgs of furosemide, each given intravenously every twelve hours for a couple of days.

Once his brain swelling resolved, he could return to normal with no neurological or psychiatric problems down the road. If he did have underlying schizophrenia, he would see a psychiatrist and begin treatment.

HOW LONG WOULD IT TAKE MY ASSAILANT TO KILL HIS VICTIM IF HE USED A CHOKE HOLD?

Q How long does it take to kill someone with a choke hold? The assailant is standing behind or is on the victim's back while applying pressure with the forearm to cut off blood flow. There are substantial weight and height differences between the two; the victim is five eleven and weighs 140 pounds, the assailant six two and 205 pounds.

MF

A The various types of choke holds work not by blocking the airway but as you pointed out, by compressing the carotid arteries. The two carotid arteries supply approximately 90% of the blood to the brain, so collapsing them greatly reduces blood flow and leads to loss of consciousness followed by death. The time required is unpredictable and depends on how aggressively the hold is applied, how completely the carotid arteries are compressed, whether the arteries are continuously compressed or if the victim "breaks" or at least lessens the hold briefly from time to time, the thickness of the victim's neck, and other things. It could take as little as twenty seconds for the victim to lose consciousness and as little as one to two minutes to die, or the struggle could continue for many minutes, allowing the victim to damage the attacker before succumbing. And anywhere in between. As we say in the South, it ain't the size of the dog in the fight but the size of the fight in the dog.

HOW IS A CASTRATION PERFORMED?

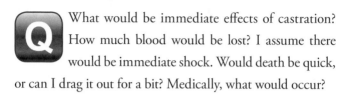 What would be immediate effects of castration? How much blood would be lost? I assume there would be immediate shock. Would death be quick, or can I drag it out for a bit? Medically, what would occur?

P.A. Brown
Author of the L.A. Shadows series
Ontario, Canada
http://www.pabrown.com

Castration is removal of the testes and is actually a simple and safe procedure. It requires opening the scrotum, tying off the artery and vein to each testicle, and snipping these just distal to the tie. There is very little bleeding. The scrotal wounds are then sutured and dressed. This is in a medical setting. If done elsewhere? That's another story.

It would be painful if no anesthesia was used and would bleed if the vessels weren't tied off first, but the bleeding would not likely be life threatening. These arteries and veins are small. The vein would clot fairly quickly. The artery would spasm (constrict) the body's normal response to an arterial injury, which would slow the blood flow and hasten clotting. The person would not go into shock and would not die from this procedure except under unusual circumstances or bad luck. A secondary infection could easily occur if this was done under nonsterile conditions, and it could be deadly. If you haven't already, watch the movie *Hard Candy*, which deals with this very scenario. Ellen Page (of *Juno* fame) is spectacular in it.

WHAT FACTORS DETERMINE WHETHER A CHILD CAN RECEIVE A BLOOD TRANSFUSION FROM A PARENT?

Q What disease could a baby have that would require a transfusion or other "donation" from the father but not the mother? In other words, the mother is disqualified from providing the blood or other necessary tissue.

Twist Phelan
Winner, Thriller Award
www.twistphelan.com

A Your question touches on two important issues. Why would the child need a transfusion or some form of transplant, and what factors would exclude one parent from being the blood donor?

The child could suffer an injury such as an automobile or other accident, which led to severe blood loss, and thus a transfusion of blood. In most cases the blood used would be banked blood and not a direct donation. So neither parent would give the blood. Possible, just not likely.

To require a direct transfusion or other tissue donation from a parent, the child would need a more sophisticated medical problem. Something like leukemia.

Leukemia is essentially a cancer of the bone marrow cells. These cells produce our red blood cells (RBCs) and white blood cells (WBCs) among other things. The WBCs produced by a leukemic individual are abnormal and in massive quantities. The WBC count in the blood can reach levels that are ten, twenty, or more times normal. These leukemic WBCs are abnormal and usually don't function as they should. WBCs are our main defense against infections, but leukemic cells don't perform this duty properly, so even though the victim has plenty of WBCs, he is prone to infections. In fact, most leukemia victims die from infections.

Anemia (low RBCs) occurs because the overproduction of leukemic WBCs "crowds out" the bone marrow cells that make RBCs, so fewer are made and fewer are released from the marrow into the bloodstream. This can be severe enough to require a transfusion.

Also, the chemotherapeutic agents used to treat leukemia damage or destroy most of the cells within the bone marrow, not only the leukemic cells but also the "good" WBCs as well as the cells that make RBCs. These cause severe anemia and a very low WBC count, which can lead to infections. Here there aren't enough good WBCs to fight an infection.

Often the chemotherapy will completely "wipe out" the bone marrow. The theory is to kill all the cells, good and bad. Then a transplant of fresh, healthy bone marrow is given, which repopulates the marrow, and the leukemia is cured. Most leukemias have a 90% or more cure rate.

Your child character could have leukemia and need a transfusion due to severe anemia or could undergo chemotherapy and need a bone marrow transplant. The parents would be considered as possible donors in either situation.

Now, the second part. Why would the mother not be a good donor of either blood or bone marrow?

Parents do not necessarily have the same blood type as their offspring, and it is the blood type that in part determines whether a donor and a recipient are compatible. The child and the father could be A positive, while the mother is B negative. She could not be a donor for the child, but the father might be. Since compatibility is determined by more than simply blood type, the father would have to be "crossmatched" against the child to determine if he could be a donor or not. So the mother could not give blood or bone marrow, while the father might be able to.

Or the mother could have a disease that excluded her as a donor regardless of compatibility. The most common problem here would be acute or chronic hepatitis.

WHAT CHILDBIRTH COMPLICATIONS COULD LEAD TO MATERNAL DEATH IN A THIRD WORLD SETTING?

 I have a character serving in the Peace Corps who witnesses a fifteen-year-old girl die during childbirth. She's serving in a country where prenatal and medical care are virtually nonexistent. What could cause her death during delivery, and what would someone witnessing the event see?

JP
Georgia

There are many possibilities. Maternal and fetal deaths happen all too frequently in remote areas where hospitals and health care are scarce.

One situation is called cranio-pelvic dissymmetry, meaning the baby's head (cranium) is too large for the mother's pelvic opening. In an ideal situation, the child would be delivered by C-section, but this might not be possible in the situation you describe. The mother would suffer increasing and prolonged contractions and pain. She would become exhausted and sweaty and experience shortness of breath. She'd scream and moan and beg for help. Eventually the baby would die as the uterine contractions continued and compromised the placental blood vessels that supply blood to the fetus. The uterus might rupture, which would be very painful immediately. There could be considerable vaginal bleeding, and the mother would go into shock and die.

Or the baby could be a breech (butt first), a footling (a foot comes out first), or a shoulder (shoulder comes first) presentation. These can be dangerous situations as the child often can't pass through the pelvic opening or the birth canal in this position. Again, in ideal circumstances, the OB doc would reach in and turn the child to the proper headfirst position and complete the delivery, or a C-section would be done. If no one knew how to do these procedures, the same sequence of events as above would unfold.

Another might be a placenta previa. This is a true medical emergency and is treated by an immediate C-section. The placenta, which usually attaches along a side or back wall of the uterus, attaches over the cervical opening. This usually isn't a problem until labor begins. As the cervix opens and the uterine contractions force the fetus toward that opening, the placenta is in the way. It will rupture and lead to severe pain and vaginal bleeding. The fetus will die since the placenta can no longer supply it with blood, and the mother will die from massive hemorrhaging and shock.

IS IT POSSIBLE FOR A WOMAN TO BE IN A COMA FOR SIX WEEKS AFTER CHILDBIRTH AND THEN AWAKEN?

Q I'm working on the next season of *Judging Amy* and want to give a birthing mother something like preeclampsia. She gives birth to a healthy baby but then suffers a cardiac arrest and, though successfully resuscitated, is left in a coma. Can she remain in this coma for six weeks? Once she wakes up, what kind of rehab or care would she need?

Paul Guyot
Supervising producer of the TNT series *Leverage*
http://paulguyot.net

A Preeclampsia would work. It can cause high blood pressure, edema of the hands, feet, and face, seizures, coma, and rarely a cardiac arrest, as in your scenario.

After a cardiopulmonary arrest (CPA), even with successful cardiopulmonary resuscitation (CPR), the victim could suffer brain damage that can be temporary or permanent. This is called anoxic encephalopathy, which is injury to the brain resulting from lack of oxygen.

After such an event, she could be in a coma for six weeks and then wake up. She would first begin to move her limbs or fingers, not purposefully but movement nonetheless. These movements would become more purposeful such as tugging at the sheets, pulling at IV lines, and grasping at objects. When she awakened, she would be lethargic and confused. She might not recognize where she is, what is going on, what day or month or year it is, who she is, and who the people around her are. We call this disorientation to person, time, place, and situation. She might talk nonsense or even show signs of paranoia, thinking she is being held prisoner and that her family and the doctors are out to get her. Gradually, these defects would resolve. This might take hours, days, weeks, or months. Typically, days or weeks.

Or she could simply wake up and be almost immediately normal. Either is possible.

She would require physical and psychiatric therapy and could return to normal or be left with memory, cognitive, mental, or emotional problems that could last for months or forever. This gives you great leeway in how you handle the sequence of events.

HOW WERE COMAS TREATED IN THE 1500s?

 How were comas dealt with in the late 1500s? To keep victims alive, how did they feed them or give them water? How were they cared for?

Throughout most of the world in the 1500s, medical thinking was dominated by the great first-century Greek physician Galen. Much of his thought was in turn a by-product of the writings of Aristotle. Galen believed in good and bad humors as the cause of health and disease and in various herbs and ointments for the treatment of all types of illnesses. He also believed in bloodletting. Galen's influence over medicine continued into the 1700s and even beyond. Most herbal-based medications from the time of Galen until modern medicine took over were called galenicals. They would be mixed up by a local apothecary according to the physician's instructions. These medications might be oral preparations, ointments that were spread over wounds or various body parts, or concoctions that were steamed or burned so the released vapors could be inhaled. Few actually worked but that's all they had.

In the 1500s medicine was predominately practiced by priests (or their equivalent), and churches often served the role of the modern hospital. Medicine was rudimentary at best, almost nothing was known about the workings of the human body, the germ theory still four centuries away, and surgical procedures were dangerous, bloody, and painful.

With the exception of wound treatment, amputations, Cesarean sections, and the removal of kidney stones from the bladder, few surgical procedures were of benefit.

Most illnesses were felt to be either punishment from God for sinful activities or the evil act of some witch or sorcerer that had cast a spell on the individual. The general thinking was that good, pious people did not become ill. This good versus evil attitude dictated almost all medical care. Chants, ceremonies, and other rituals often accompanied the application of the ointments and taking of the herbs.

Since no one knew what caused a coma and no one knew how to treat it, the standard treatment for all other illnesses applied. Your coma victim would likely be considered to have fallen under an evil spell or afflicted by a vengeful God. Oral medicines could not be given to your comatose victim, so treatment would revolve around ceremonies complete with chanting and other activities, the burning of herbs and oils to create vapors and smoke, and the application of herbs and ointments to various body parts. These could be done by a local physician or a member of the church. Bloodletting would probably be part of the treatment. The rationale was that illness led to the buildup of foul humors within the body, and removing some of the blood would remove these toxins and the person would get better. It usually didn't work out that way, though.

The bottom line is: there was no effective treatment at that time, and any treatment offered would be wrapped in the religious dogma.

UNDER WHAT CIRCUMSTANCES WOULD SOMEONE BE PLACED INTO AN INDUCED COMA?

Q I have a character who suffers blunt force trauma to the head. Would the doctors put him into an induced coma, and if so, why? What is the benefit of an induced coma? If not, under what circumstances would doctors use this treatment method? Essentially, I'm using an induced coma to keep a character on ice for a few chapters.

Simon Wood
Author of *Paying the Piper*
Bay Area, California
www.simonwood.net

A In a head injury with loss of consciousness, any form of sedative or narcotic is usually avoided. The reason is that the victim's neurological and mental status must be continually assessed, so any complications from the injury can be recognized before permanent damage is done. Sedatives of any type will depress brain function and interfere with these evaluations.

However, there are circumstances when a medically induced coma is desirable. These are when the patient cannot be controlled, and this lack of control is causing a worsening of his situation. One example would be uncontrollable seizures, which we call status epilepticus. It's a series of powerful and recurrent seizures that can last for minutes or hours. They can occur after head injuries and with other conditions and when present can interfere with the person's ability to breathe, which can be deadly. Seizure medications such as phenobarbital and phenytoin might be given intravenously to control the seizures, but sometimes it takes hours to work or doesn't work at all. If so, it is best to completely paralyze the patient and put him on a ventilator until the anticonvulsant medications take effect.

Also, some brain injuries are associated with depression of the breathing drive, and the victim must be placed on a ventilator to prevent death from asphyxia. Sometimes these victims are disoriented and constantly fight against any form of treatment. This combative behavior can manifest as attempts to remove IVs and ventilator tubes and everything else they can get ahold of. Restraints will help, but the person might fight the ventilator, and this can interfere with breathing. The doctor would use morphine and perhaps a neuromuscular paralytic agent such as curare or succinylcholine to completely paralyze the patient, so respiratory control can be maintained.

Either of these situations can result from blunt head trauma. The injury would not be a simple concussion but could be a slightly less simple cerebral contusion. This is basically a brain bruise. More sinister things could also cause it such as bleeding into and around the brain. It's much more sophisticated and would require surgery and a long recovery period. From your question, I get the sense that this is not what you want. I would go with a cerebral contusion and either seizures or combative behavior or both.

WHAT ARE THE SYMPTOMS AND SIGNS OF A MISCARRIAGE?

Q In my story, a young woman undergoes in vitro fertilization. The procedure fails and she miscarries. What are the symptoms during the miscarriage? Would she require hospitalization?

Rebbie Macintyre
www.rebbiewriter.blogspot.com

A The symptoms and signs of a miscarriage (also termed a spontaneous abortion) are the same regardless of how the pregnancy came about, natural or through in vitro fertilization (IVF).

In any pregnancy if the fetus is defective in such a way that is incompatible with survival, if there are defects in the uterus or placenta, or if certain drugs are taken, the fetus will die. The uterus will then expel the dead fetus and the placenta. It does this by contracting and forcing blood and fetal placental tissues out through the cervix.

The symptoms are lower abdominal cramps (similar to menstrual cramps), bleeding, and the passage of tissue. The cramps can begin as mild discomfort for a few hours, even a few days, but they will ultimately become severe. The bleeding may be acute and severe or may be several days of spotting before the severe bleeding appears. The tissue passed will depend upon how far along the pregnancy is. If only a couple of months, the placenta and a small amount of fetal tissue will appear. If several months along, the placenta and formed fetus will be expelled.

Many women undergo this and never tell anyone or see a doctor. Once the fetal placental materials are passed, the bleeding will stop, and over a few days she would return to normal. At least physically.

Or after she thought the ordeal was over, she could become increasingly ill with continued bleeding and cramping. She might develop an infection with fevers, chills, nausea, vomiting, and severe abdominal pain. This usually occurs when all the materials are not passed. We call this a retained fetus. The uterus will continue attempting to expel what remains, and if an infection arises it becomes very dangerous and potentially lethal. In this case, she would require an emergency dilatation and curettage (D&C) to evacuate the retained tissues as well as blood replacement and antibiotics.

HOW WOULD A PREGNANT WOMAN AND HER CHILD BE TREATED IF SHE WAS IN A COMA FOR A YEAR?

Q I have a character who is in a coma for a year. Her husband attempted to murder her and was unsuccessful but left her in a prolonged coma. Is there a drug or some sort of trauma that could have done this? Unknown to her and her murderous husband, she was pregnant. What kind of problems would the unborn child experience? What physical problems would the mother experience in this situation?

Connie Whipple
Portland, Oregon

A Comas are caused by a severe derangement of brain function. This can be due to trauma, infection, tumors, drugs, shock, drowning and cardiac arrest (from which they were resuscitated but suffered a permanent brain injury due to lack of oxygen during the event and re-suscitation), and some other serious illnesses. Sedatives and narcotics can cause the victim's blood pressure (BP) and breathing to drop to very low levels, and this can lead to a marked reduction in oxygen to the brain. We call this anoxic encephalopathy, meaning brain damage due to lack of oxygen. Insulin can drop the blood sugar level so low that brain cells die from absence of sugar. This would be another type of encephalopathy. Bottom line is that anything that damages the brain can lead to a prolonged coma. A narcotic or insulin would work well for your scenario.

Also, blunt head trauma can cause bleeding into or around the brain, and this can lead to a prolonged coma.

People in prolonged comas almost never recover. In the situation you describe we would use the term *permanent vegetative state*. This means that the victim is in a coma and unresponsive to any stimulus such as noise or touch. She would require continuous supportive treatment to survive. Some are ventilator dependent, meaning they can't breathe for themselves and must have a ventilator attached to survive, but many require no such support, only feeding and general care. They could survive for decades with proper care, so a year would work. She could die anytime from one of the many complications that arise in this situation, but the chances of her waking up and being anywhere near normal would be remote.

Some of the major complications are:

Bedsores: They are called decubitus ulcers and are due to pressure from the body lying in one position for extended periods. These sores can be deep and become infected, and if they do they can be difficult to treat and lead to septicemia (infection in the bloodstream) and death.

Pneumonia: This is common in comatose persons. They don't breathe as deeply as a normal person, the lungs collapse slightly, and an infection sets in. Again, deadly and difficult to treat. Also, pneumonias can occur after aspiration of liquid foods, which are typically given by a feeding tube passed through the nose and into the stomach and left there. This is called aspiration pneumonia and is treacherous. The acids from the stomach and the foods actually burn the lungs and the bronchial (breathing) tubes and set the stage for infections with some pretty nasty bugs. One way to lessen this is with a gastrostomy tube, which would likely be done to your young lady. Here the plastic feeding tube is passed into the stomach directly through the abdominal wall. This requires only a minor incision and can stay for years. Since the tube does not pass through the throat, the incidence of aspiration is greatly reduced.

Urinary tract infections: Many coma victims have a Foley catheter passed into the bladder to collect urine and prevent them from soiling themselves. This tube can allow bacteria to enter the bladder and then travel upstream to the kidneys. These types of infections can spread to the bloodstream and cause deadly septicemia.

Pulmonary embolus: This is a blood clot that forms in the veins of the legs or the pelvis, breaks off, and travels through the right side of the heart and into the lungs. It can lead to death very quickly. People who are immobile for any reason—coma, after an operation, stroke, or auto accident—are prone to this development.

The fetus could also be damaged from the original insult. That is, if the mother suffered low oxygen levels from the administration of narcotics or low blood sugar from insulin, the fetus could also suffer brain damage. And could die and be aborted. Or not. The child might survive all this unscathed. Anything is possible, so if you want a normal child, that'll work. If you want a damaged child, that'll work too. If you want the mother to miscarry, that's also common. The mother would receive supportive therapy as described, and the pregnancy would be allowed to progress. Then near term she could deliver naturally, but most likely a C-section would be done.

WHAT COMPLICATIONS FROM A PREGNANCY COULD CAUSE MY FEMALE CHARACTER TO BE UNABLE TO BEAR CHILDREN IN THE FUTURE?

Q I have a sixteen-year-old character who is gang-raped. She becomes pregnant, miscarries, and is unable to conceive another child. What would be plausible? Might she get a pelvic infection from the rape that caused her to miscarry and then be unable to conceive?

Hallie Ephron
Award-winning author of
Never Tell a Lie and
Come and Find Me

A She could get pregnant from the rape and could also contract a venereal disease such as gonorrhea. This could damage and scar the fallopian tubes and render her incapable of getting pregnant. The infection could also involve the uterus, a very dangerous situation. It would possibly require a hysterectomy as a life-saving measure. Infections within the uterus can be deadly if not treated aggressively, up to and including uterine removal.

As she miscarried she would have abdominal pain and bleeding. At the hospital she would undergo a dilatation and curettage (D&C) and during this procedure could suffer uterine damage, making her unable to conceive in the future. Or the miscarriage could be complicated by severe bleeding, requiring an emergency hysterectomy.

One point: it would be best if she didn't report the rape

for several days, so any infection she contracted would have time to do its damage. Two or three days could work. Why? Because part of any treatment for a rape victim includes the use of prophylactic antibiotics to clear up any infectious venereal disease such as gonorrhea and the use of an abortive to prevent pregnancy. The proper use of these would stop any infection or pregnancy in its tracks. Of course, she could refuse this treatment. Maybe on religious grounds or whatever fits her character. But a delay of a few days, which is common with rape victims, might be best. She could decide not to report the rape, but when she became ill with gonorrhea she would have no choice. Her symptoms would be fever, chills, lower abdominal pain, and perhaps a cream-colored, foul-smelling vaginal discharge.

HOW WAS CPR PERFORMED IN 1949?

 My story takes place in 1949. Was CPR done then? If not, what steps would a medical professional take to resuscitate a victim of cardiac arrest?

RD

In ancient times, some very odd techniques were employed whenever someone collapsed into unconsciousness. Things like stretching, bending, and pumping the arms, as if these might "pump" life back into the victim. Of course, none of them worked.

In 1903 Dr. George Crile first used external chest compressions successfully to save someone who had suffered a cardiac arrest. Mouth-to-mouth breathing, which has recently been removed from the CPR protocol, was first demonstrated by Peter Safar and James Elam. Safar described the procedure in his 1957 book, *ABC of Resuscitation*. It is interesting that mouth-to-mouth breathing is mentioned in the Old Testament, and in 1797 the Dutch Humane Society published resuscitation guidelines for drowning victims that included mouth-to-mouth ventilation. But it was never used in a medical setting for CPR due to a cardiac arrest until Safar and Elam demonstrated its usefulness.

So in 1949 they would have used chest compressions only and no breathing techniques. Exactly as it is now since the mouth-to-mouth part of CPR is no longer recommended. Why this change? It doesn't help survival in cases of out of hospital cardiac arrests and is very difficult for a layperson to do properly.

HOW WOULD MY CHARACTER PERFORM CPR IN A HELICOPTER?

Q I have a medic working on a patient in a medevac chopper. The patient goes into cardiac arrest. If he's wearing a Kevlar vest pierced by shrapnel, where would the medic attach the defibrillator electrodes?

Michelle Gagnon
Best-selling author of *The Gatekeeper* and *Kidnap & Ransom*

A Performing CPR in a helicopter would not be easy, and the Kevlar vest wouldn't help. It might not interfere very much, though. Modern Kevlar vests are more flexible than the old vests with metal or ceramic plates, which would have made chest compressions impossible, so with Kevlar the compressions could be done. This would be done initially while the defibrillator was prepped and ready to go.

A defibrillator is often needed during CPR to correct abnormal cardiac rhythms, particularly ventricular tachycardia or ventricular fibrillation. The pads or the handheld contact plates (paddles) that are part of most defibrillators must make contact with the skin more or less on opposite sides of the heart. This allows the current to pass through the chest and heart as it travels from one pad to the other.

Typically one paddle or pad is placed on the upper right side of the chest, while the other is placed on the lower left side. In your scenario, since the vest would get in the way of the typical placement areas, one of the paddles/pads could be placed on the right shoulder or neck area and the other one on the left upper part of the abdomen. It would allow the electrical current to pass through the heart, and this is really all that's necessary to accomplish the cardioversion (the conversion of the cardiac rhythm from an abnormal one to a normal one). The medic could work around the vest and still do his job.

HOW COULD MY KILLER MURDER A MAN WITH SEVERE EMPHYSEMA AND MAKE IT LOOK LIKE A SUICIDE OR AN ACCIDENT?

Q I have a character, a seventy-year-old man, who has severe emphysema and spends his days in a wheelchair plugged into an oxygen bottle. If my bad guy wanted to kill him and make it appear to be a suicide or an accident, how could he accomplish it? Could he simply remove or tamper with his oxygen bottle?

Simon Wood
Author of *Paying the Piper*
Bay Area, California
www.simonwood.net

A It is true that many emphysema sufferers require full-time oxygen and carry around small oxygen tanks or oxygen concentrators. Either way the amount of oxygen in the inspired air that the individual receives is slightly higher than it would be if he was just breathing room air. Removing his tank or concentrator or emptying his oxygen tank could indeed cause death, and it would be indistinguishable from an accident or a suicide.

Another way would be to increase the amount of oxygen he is breathing. Let me explain. People with emphysema and other forms of chronic obstructive pulmonary disease (COPD) are highly sensitive to oxygen inhalation. The physiology is extremely complex, but in a person with this medical condition, a very high oxygen level in the inspired air will severely depress the respiratory center in the brain stem. The person would become lethargic, sleepy, lapse into a coma, and die from asphyxia. This would be a more pleasant way of committing suicide since reducing the oxygen intake would cause extreme shortness of breath and distress before death, while increasing the oxygen intake would cause him to fall asleep, lapse into a coma, and die quietly.

If the villain returned to the scene and turned the oxygen tank back to a normal flow rate, there would be no way of determining the exact manner of death. That is, homicide, suicide, accident, and a natural death from COPD would look identical. The normal flow rate for oxygen tanks in this type of patient is around two liters per minute. Increasing it to four or five liters per minute could cause death in a few minutes or up to an hour.

WHAT TYPE OF INSANITY WOULD MY CHARACTER HAVE IF HE HEARS VOICES TELLING HIM TO KILL?

 My villain sees and hears Hitler telling him to kill Jews and other people. He also kills people who get in his way, with no conscience or feeling about his crimes. He is building a private gas chamber and plans to kill a couple of people he hates, and he sees his own powers as omnipotent and has no remorse about his crimes. How would I explain the psychology of his insanity? Is he psychotic, narcissistic, delusional, or what?

TS

What you're describing is an individual who suffers from narcissistic, grandiose, paranoid schizophrenia with delusional and psychotic components. A little sociopathy too. Because the gurus in every field of medicine argue over terminology, it varies depending on who you read. What those in the ivory towers of academia call a disorder often has little relationship to the language doctors in the trenches use. But something like the above description is what your psychiatrist might say when speaking about this individual.

He is schizophrenic because he has a severe mental disorder that has caused a break with reality. He is delusional in that he believes he is omnipotent and all-important. He is psychotic because he is hearing voices that do not really exist.

A delusion is merely a misinterpretation of something

in the environment. An individual with a paranoid delusion might see someone looking at him and believe the person is a threat. If he sees two people talking, he might believe they are talking about him. These are simply misinterpretations of actual events. In a psychosis, the things perceived by the individual are made up in his head. He hears voices or sees pink elephants or feels bugs crawling over him when none are actually there. He believes things to be true that have no basis in reality.

Since your character has no remorse, he has some sociopathic tendencies. He sounds like an interesting character, but I hope you off him by the end of your tale.

WHAT COULD CAUSE DISORIENTATION IN MY MIDDLE-AGED MALE CHARACTER?

Q My murder victim is modeled after a man who wandered away from his outdoor job and got lost. He was said to have a mental condition that made him appear to be disoriented, but the condition was not identified in news reports. What could cause disorientation in a middle-aged male?

Glenn Ickler
Hopedale, Massachuesetts

A There are many reasons that someone could become disoriented. Physical causes would include brain trauma, infections, and tumors. He could have suffered a blow to the head, which can cause confusion and memory loss. There does not need to be any external sign of injury for this to happen. He could have an infectious process like viral meningitis. If so, he might have fever, chills, sweats, a stiff neck, and photophobia (an aversion to light). He could have a brain tumor. Depending on the type and location, it can cause headaches, seizures, paranoia, hallucinations, and the list goes on. They can occur in any combination and any degree of severity.

He could have a psychiatric disorder such as schizophrenia. Schizophrenics can be high or low functioning, the difference being whether they can navigate society or not. Some have odd emotions or reactions to others and say things that are just a little off, while others sit on a park bench and talk to pigeons or themselves. Some know who and where they are, and others have no clue what is going on. And anywhere in between. This diagnosis would give you much leeway in constructing your character since almost any behavior is possible.

Drugs could be involved. Chronic users of alcohol, heroin, and other downers can be lethargic, disoriented, and forgetful, and withdrawal can lead to delusions. Chronic amphetamine and cocaine users can be excitable, paranoid, and psychotic. They can attack people or run from them screaming. Disorientation is far from rare in chronic alcohol and drug abusers.

He could suffer from one of the many types of dementia, including Alzheimer's. True Alzheimer's is dementia in a younger person, usually beginning in the forties and fifties, but it has evolved to mean dementia at any age, including old age of senile dementia, which usually doesn't begin until after age sixty. Dementia is a widespread loss of brain function due to the death of or damage to neurons. Memory loss, slow speech, slow movements, confusion, crying jags, temper tantrums, and more are all part of dementias from any cause.

Your character could suffer from any combination of these.

IF A KILLER HAS HAD A BONE MARROW TRANSPLANT AND LEAVES BLOOD AT A CRIME SCENE, WILL THIS BLOOD MATCH HIM OR THE BONE MARROW DONOR?

 If my main character has donated bone marrow to a murderer who has left blood at the crime scene, will the DNA of the blood match my main character, or will it match the killer?

ET

 Bone marrow transplants are often part of the treatment regimen for various leukemias and a handful of other medical problems. In this procedure the bone marrow of the recipient is first obliterated with chemotherapeutic drugs. This wipes out all the marrow cells that produce the various types of blood cells. Bone marrow from the donor is then infused intravenously. These materials migrate to the recipient's bone marrow, set up housekeeping, and begin producing cells, which are then dumped into the recipient's bloodstream. The blood cells would have the DNA of the donor, so blood left at the scene would indeed match the donor. Not good for him. Fortunately, the ME has other options.

If the killer left behind semen, saliva, skin, or hair, the DNA in those would not match the donor. Only the DNA in the blood would. The transplanted bone marrow only affects the blood of the recipient and has no relationship to the DNA in other bodily tissues. So if the ME had any of these other materials, he could show that they came from the killer and not from the bone marrow donor. If the suspect is arrested, his blood would show the donor's DNA pattern, while DNA obtained from a buccal smear would reveal the suspect's own native DNA profile. This would allow the ME to unravel the mystery.

With hair, there must be a follicle attached in order to obtain nuclear DNA. This usually occurs when hair is pulled out rather than naturally shed as happens all the time. But if no follicles are attached to any hair found at the scene, all is not lost. The hair shaft can yield mitochondrial DNA (mtDNA). This type of DNA is passed down the maternal line unchanged for many generations. The killer and the donor would have different mtDNAs. Unless they had the same mother, that is.

WHAT HAPPENS WHEN MY CHARACTER CONTACTS AN ELECTRIFIED FENCE?

Q In my story, a sixteen-year-old boy contacts an electric fence that surrounds a cabin on a ranch near Hamilton, Montana. The fence was constructed to contain the people in the cabin. Later a forty-year-old doctor also contacts the same fence. How would they physically fare after this contact, and what steps are reasonable for a doctor to help the victims? Do they pass out? Is CPR necessary?

Sue A. Lehman
http://www.suealehman.com

A What happens when someone contacts an electric current depends upon many variables and luck. In general, the smaller the person, the higher the voltage, the longer the contact, and the damper the ground, the more dangerous it is.

The possible outcomes are numerous. Either of your characters could be knocked backwards, breaking the contact, and except for being dazed and confused for a minute or two would otherwise be okay. Or he could suffer a period of unconsciousness that lasted for several minutes and awaken disoriented. Or the current could cause seizure activity for a minute or so. In any of these situations he would likely be normal once his head cleared.

If the electric shock was more powerful, it could affect the heart, causing a deadly change in the cardiac rhythm, which could result in instantaneous death. If immediately applied, CPR could be life saving. This would of course mean that someone qualified to do CPR was readily available and that it worked. CPR in an out of the hospital situation such as this is successful only 10% or less of the time.

The electric shock could cause the brain to shut down, leading to a cessation of breathing, and the victim could die from asphyxia in a few minutes.

But if none of these life-threatening events occurred and your character survived, there are other injuries that could result from the shock. Electric current travels through the body from the point of contact to the point of grounding. Let's say the victim grabbed the fence with his left hand, and the electricity flowed through the body and out the right foot. Charring of the tissues could occur at both the entry and exit points or one and not the other. It would be most likely to occur at the entry point, but it could be isolated to the exit point. The current could be powerful enough to weld metal buttons or jewelry or a watchband to the victim's skin.

Such an electrical current can also damage other body tissues with the liver and the bone marrow being most susceptible. This could lead to temporary or permanent damage to these tissues and organs, and it might require long-term medical therapy.

So electrical shocks come in many flavors and with many possible outcomes. They give you a broad range of events from which to construct your plot. Almost anything—from a minor shock to a sudden death—is possible.

HOW WAS EPILEPSY TREATED IN THE 1940s?

 How were active epileptic seizures treated in the 1940s? Would a doctor give any medications to calm them down?

Simon Wood
Author of *Paying the Piper*
Bay Area, California
www.simonwood.net

The standard treatment for epilepsy for the first half of the twentieth century was barbiturates and other sedatives, but the barbiturate phenobarbital was the best. In fact, it is still used today.

In 1937 and 1938, H. Houston Merritt, MD and Tracy J. Putnam, MD published several papers on their work with diphenylhydantoin (marketed now as Dilantin) and its positive effects in seizure control. Taking either diphenylhydantoin or phenobarbital would control and help prevent seizures, and both were used in the 1940s.

For treatment of an active seizure, your doctors most likely would have used phenobarbital, given either IV or IM (intramuscular) injection. Since at that time diphenylhydantoin was new while phenobarbital had a long and successful track record, the latter would have been the drug of choice in most situations. If this didn't work to break the seizure, the new "experimental" diphenylhydantoin would then be used.

WHAT TYPE OF EYE INJURY COULD REQUIRE MY CHARACTER TO BE HOSPITALIZED WITH HIS EYES BANDAGED FOR SEVERAL WEEKS?

Q For my story I need an injury or operation that would require my hero to be hospitalized for several weeks with his eyes bandaged most of that time. He can have other complications/injuries that could extend the hospital stay, but I need to have him sightless for as long as possible yet still able to function in terms of conversation, eating, etc. Can you think of anything I might be able to use?

Bev Huston
Tumbler Ridge, British Columbia, Canada

A There are a few possibilities that come to mind.
The best would be any form of thermal or chemical burn to the face and eyes. A fire or an acid such as hydrochloric acid or sulfuric acid could burn his face and injure his corneas. It would require hospitalization and treatment of the burns. He would be unable to see through his damaged corneas, and his eyes could be patched for a couple of weeks. He might heal without problems or might require a corneal transplant to regain his vision. His facial injuries could heal without residual effects, leave scars, and/or require skin grafts. Through all of this, a secondary infection, which is common in burns of all types, would greatly complicate the problem, lengthen the course of treatment, and lead to more long-term complications with both his vision and any scarring.

Retinal injury from a bright light could lead to temporary or permanent damage. This is what happens to people who watch a solar eclipse directly. The darkness tricks the pupil into opening widely, allowing the coronal light to enter and damage the retina. The same is true for people who witness nuclear explosions without protection. Any very intense light can do the same. He could be close to a flash explosion. He might be hospitalized and his eyes "rested" with bandaging for a week or two. He could recover completely or suffer some degree of permanent loss of vision up to and including complete, permanent blindness.

Another possibility is a retinal detachment or bleed. It can result from a blow to the eye or the head. A fight, fall, or auto accident would work. The jolt of the trauma could cause bleeding beneath the retina of the affected eye. This could require several weeks of patching and maybe laser surgery to correct. The problem here is that it would not likely affect both eyes. He would be on strict bed rest but would be able to see with the unaffected eye, so this might not fit your needs.

WHAT INJURIES MIGHT MY CHARACTER SUFFER WHILE ESCAPING FROM A BURNING HOUSE?

Q I have a character who escapes from a burning house. It takes him ten to twenty minutes to find his way through thick smoke and flames. What sort of injuries might he sustain, and how would they be treated?

Dawn Brown
Author of *The Curse of Culcraig* and *Living Lies*
www.dawnbrown.org

A There are three areas of concern.

He could suffer first-, second-, or third-degree burns to his skin. Often there are areas of each. I'd keep any third-degree burns to a minimum since these are the ones that scar and often require skin grafting. First-degree burns are like a bad sunburn, and second are when blistering of the skin occurs. Hair on his head and arms and his eyebrows could be singed away.

His eyes, particularly the corneas, might be damaged. This could cause visual defects and require a corneal transplant to correct.

His lungs and bronchial tubes (airways) could be affected by the fire and smoke. This could be a minor irritation or a significant degree of damage that requires hospitalization, placement on a ventilator, and several weeks of treatment. And anywhere in between.

I'd suggest your character suffer only a moderate degree of lung and bronchial injury, which would cause coughing, shortness of breath, and chest pain for several days. The pain would burn when he breathed or coughed, much as if he had an acute bronchitis from a flu. He would be treated in the hospital for a couple of days with oxygen, antibiotics, and corticosteroids. The antibiotics might be one of the cephalosporins given IV twice each day for a few days and then orally for maybe ten days. The steroids might be something like methylprednisolone 8 milligrams IV twice a day for two or three days. After a few days to a week he would be okay.

WHAT TYPES OF INJURIES WOULD OCCUR IF A WOMAN WAS STRANGLED BY A CELLO STRING?

Q I have a character who has looped a steel cello string around his victim's neck as he stands behind her. He likes to prolong this act so he applies just enough tension to scare her, and then when he's ready, he gives a good jerk and finishes things. So what happens? Would a cello string sever something vital in the neck or simply cause asphyxiation? I'd like to have blood spurting but only if it is realistic. Could the ME determine the weapon used? Maybe find bow rosin in the wound?

P.J. Parrish
Shamus, Thriller, Anthony award–winning
author and Edgar nominee
Fort Lauderdale, Florida, and Petoskey, Michigan

A A cello wire would function as a garrote rather than a ligature such as a cord. A garrote wire is typically wrapped around gloved hands or handles made of wood or metal or whatever. It works differently than a ligature in that it cuts into the flesh where a rope or cord would not. The bruises and cuts left on the victim's neck would be horizontal and deeper in the front than the back, and this would tell the medical examiner that the killer was standing behind her.

Since he tortured her by strangling her a few times before killing her, each of these episodes would leave a bruise line that would roughly match the thickness of the string.

When he delivered his final pull on each handle, the string could cut into the flesh and sever the carotid arteries and/or jugular veins. At least it could. If an artery was cut, the bleeding would be massive and pulsatile with blood spraying several feet. If the vein was cut, the bleeding would be profuse but not pulsatile. He could cut one artery and one vein and not the other or any combination you want.

The medical examiner could determine the size of the garrote used by looking at the width of the bruises and cuts. If a suspected murder weapon was found, he could then determine whether it was consistent with the wounds or not. If the widths matched, he could not say that this particular garrote was the murder weapon but rather that it was this one or one similar. On the other hand, if he found traces of the victim's blood on the string and DNA matched it to the victim, he could say that this weapon was indeed the murder weapon.

Yes, it is possible that the ME might find a foreign substance on and in the wound, test it, and determine that it was bow rosin.

MORE FORENSICS AND FICTION

COULD MY CHARACTER SUFFER AN ABDOMINAL GUNSHOT WOUND AND SURVIVE FOR TWELVE TO TWENTY-FOUR HOURS BEFORE REACHING MEDICAL HELP?

Q I am the writer's assistant for the TV show *Medium*, and our writers want to have someone shot in the gut, not be able to seek medical attention for twelve to twenty-four hours yet not die. How long could someone survive a gut shot without receiving medical attention if no organs were pierced by the bullet?

Erica B. Peterson
Los Angeles, California

A For an abdominal gunshot to be immediately fatal, a major blood vessel such as the aorta or the inferior vena cava would need to be damaged. This would cause massive bleeding and a quick death. If an organ such as the liver, the spleen, or a kidney was damaged, the bleeding could still be very serious and deadly but not immediately so. Death could take many hours. But neither of these options fit your scenario.

If no blood vessels or organs were damaged, the bleeding would be minimal and the major risk of death would come from infection. This would take a few days to develop and many days or even weeks for death to occur.

A gunshot to the abdomen is excruciating. The lining of the abdomen, which is called the peritoneum, is webbed with nerves, and they are sensitive to pain. This is why appendicitis hurts so much. Even the small amount of blood that would follow the type of gunshot injury in your scenario would irritate this lining, and any movement would be followed by severe, sharp pain throughout the abdomen. The victim would avoid movement, and even breathing would hurt as the diaphragm went up and down and moved the organs within the abdomen. If someone touched his abdomen or pressed on it, it would be extremely painful. Sitting, standing, rolling to one side, and almost any activity would be difficult to tolerate. He would sweat profusely and could have nausea and vomiting, the latter being very painful.

So your character could survive for the time frame you outlined. He would be in great pain, and when he was finally rescued and reached medical help, he would need surgery, aggressive antibiotic treatment, and pain management.

HOW LONG COULD MY CHARACTER SURVIVE AFTER A GUNSHOT TO THE FEMORAL ARTERY?

 In my story, a man is shot in the femoral artery. How long would it take him to bleed out? Would tourniquets help stop the bleeding?

Lisanne Harrington

Award-winning short story author and novelist
Yorba Linda, California

The time it would take for him to bleed into shock and die depends on the exact nature of the injury to the artery (simply nicked or a chunk is blown out), the size and general health of the victim, and luck. If the injury is severe, the blood loss is rapid and comes in great pulsing gushes. As the victim's blood pressure declines, the distance, force, and volume of the spurts will steadily decrease. Ultimately the victim will slip into shock, lose consciousness, and die. Once he is in shock the blood will only trickle, and once he dies it will stop altogether. This entire process could take two minutes or ten minutes, depending on many factors.

If he held pressure on the wound or applied a tourniquet above the wound to slow the bleeding, he could survive for hours. The leg would be okay for an hour or so but much longer than that and he would risk doing irreparable damage, even to the point that an amputation might be required. He could use any strong flexible material for the tourniquet: a belt, rolled shirt, stockings, jumper cable, electrical cord, etc.

CAN MY HERO BE SHOT IN THE HEAD AND BLEED SIGNIFICANTLY YET SURVIVE WITHOUT MAJOR INJURY?

Q I have a brief struggle between a good guy and a bad terrorist type, which ends with a .22-caliber pistol discharging. The good guy goes down with severe bleeding, so the terrorist thinks he's delivered a killing shot. I want the bullet to glance off the good guy's skull, perhaps cause a concussion but otherwise no real injury, so he can be out of the hospital in two or three days. Is this possible?

Philip Donlay
Author of *Category Five* and *Code Black*
www.philipdonlay.com

A Yes, this will work.

A small caliber bullet like a .22 can easily penetrate the skin but not the skull. It can burrow beneath the scalp and travel all the way around the head, even coming to rest on the opposite side of the skull. Or the bullet could deflect off the skull and exit the scalp. There would be both entry and exit wounds, and they could be close to one another or again on opposite sides of the skull. Or the bullet could flatten against the skull and remain just beneath the entry wound. Any of these could cause a concussion with or without loss of consciousness.

Once he reached the hospital he would have a skull X-ray to look for any fractures as well as to locate the bullet or bullet fragments if the bullet fragmented. They would appear bright white on an X-ray film. Treatment would then be to remove the bullet and fragments if still present, clean and dress the wounds, and give the victim antibiotics. He might stay in the hospital for two or three days, then be discharged on pain meds and antibiotics. The wounds would heal over the next few weeks.

COULD MY CHARACTER BE SHOT IN THE HEAD AND SUFFER NO REAL BRAIN INJURY YET DEVELOP IMPAIRED MEMORY?

Q I'm hoping I might be able to pick your medical brain again for the latest book. I have a character who receives a gunshot wound to the head. I want this wound not to kill him but to put him in a coma from which he will ultimately wake with impaired memory and possibly some personality change.

Is it feasible that such an injury would have these kinds of effects? Would they be permanent or improve over time? Is there any particular area of the brain that the round should damage to produce these effects?

Zoë Sharp
Author of the Charlotte "Charlie" Fox crime thriller series
Middle-of-Nowheresville, United Kingdom
www.ZoeSharp.com

A There are several possibilities for your scenario.

The bullet could strike the skull and flatten against it and never enter the cranial cavity. Or the bullet could strike the skull, bounce off and exit the scalp or burrow beneath the scalp, and end up on the opposite side of the entry wound. Any of these could cause a concussion or a brain contusion (bruise), loss of consciousness but only briefly, and could indeed alter memory and personality. This would happen with or without an underlying skull fracture.

The bullet could penetrate the skull and do a varying

amount of brain damage. Here the extent of the damage and the success of any repair would determine the course and the eventual outcome of the injury. The victim would need surgery to remove the bullet and repair the damage as best the surgeon could. Your victim could then be in the intensive care unit on a ventilator and unconscious for a variable period of time. It might be a day, several days, several weeks, or even months. He would be treated with antibiotics and ventilatory and nutritional support.

He could awaken and be completely normal or have significant movement, memory, and cognitive problems. Or he could never awaken at all and remain in a prolonged coma or die from the brain injury or a secondary infection, particularly pneumonia or a urinary tract infection.

Personality and interaction with others are somewhat controlled by the frontal lobes, so an injury to the front part of the brain might alter his ability to understand and interact with others. Motor functions are mostly controlled by the parietal lobes, which are located on the sides of the head just above the ear. An injury here could result in permanent or temporary paralysis, either complete or partial, on the opposite side of the body. That is, damage to the right parietal area would result in motor difficulties on the left side. The individual could require extensive rehab in order to learn to walk and be stable on his feet again. This might take many weeks, months, years, or he might never return to normal.

Memory is a little more difficult since it is unknown exactly what parts of the brain are involved in memory formation and recall. But a gunshot wound to either the frontal or the parietal lobes could easily result in memory loss. It could be permanent or temporary, major or minor, complete or spotty, and his recovery of memory could be quick or prolonged, partial or complete.

So a gunshot wound to the front or the side of the head that penetrated the skull and did brain damage would result in emergency surgery and at least several days or weeks in the intensive care unit. After this he could recover over any time frame you need, and require any amount and duration of physical rehab you want. His recovery could be complete or partial. His memory loss could be in any form, degree, and duration as outlined above.

WHAT WOULD A GUNSHOT TO THE LIVER LOOK LIKE, AND COULD THE VICTIM DIE IN THIRTY MINUTES?

Q I have an adult male character who is shot in the liver with a handgun at a range of three or four feet. He's far from a hospital or anything other than rudimentary first aid. I want him to die in about thirty minutes but be ambulatory for the first ten minutes or so. Feasible?

Where exactly should he be shot? Front or back? Does the caliber of bullet and whether it is jacketed or a hollow point make a difference? What would the wound and the blood look like?

Grant Blackwood
Author
www.grantblackwood.com

A Your scenario will work quite well. The distance between the gun and the victim or the type of ammo used makes little difference since almost anything is possible. A jacketed, high-velocity bullet would in general do less damage to the liver than a softer lead bullet and particularly one that was hollow point, but either can do the damage you need for your story.

In either case, the entry wound would be small and round, and with the muzzle more than two feet away, there would be no stippling or tattooing around the wound. It would simply be a round hole surrounded by the dark ring of an abrasion collar. The exit wound would be larger and more irregular and ragged in appearance, and this would be particularly true with the softer or hollow-point bullets.

The liver sits in the right upper portion of the abdomen tucked beneath the diaphragm and partially protected by the ribs on that side. The gunshot could come from the front, the back, or the side and remain within the body or liver or pass completely through and exit the body. We call this latter situation a through-and-through gunshot wound. The jacketed bullet would more likely go through, whereas a hollow point would more likely remain embedded in the liver or somewhere in the abdomen.

The liver is a highly vascular organ, meaning it is filled with blood and loaded with blood vessels, and when injured it will bleed profusely. In the case of a gunshot wound, some of the bleeding would be external, particularly through the exit wound, but most would be internal into the abdomen. The blood in the liver tends to be very dark and purplish in color. In a poorly lit room or at night it can appear almost black.

As your victim lost blood he would go through a series of symptoms, most of which would be related to blood loss and hypotension (low blood pressure). The wound would be painful as would his entire abdomen as he bled internally.

He would experience fatigue, weakness, shortness of breath, and thirst, and he would feel cold and even shiver. At first he might be able to stand and stagger short distances, but as the blood loss continued and his blood pressure declined, he would become dizzy and might have to sit or lie down to keep from fainting. Then as he bled more, blood flow to his brain would decrease, and he could develop disorientation and even delusions. Finally, he would slip into a coma and die.

This entire sequence could take a few minutes, a half hour, several hours, or even a day or so. It depends upon the rate of blood loss. This means that you can construct your sequence of symptoms and signs and stretch out the victim's death for as little or as much time as you need.

HOW WOULD MY CHARACTER TREAT A SUSPECT'S GUNSHOT WOUND, AND WHAT WOULD SHE USE TO SEDATE HIM?

Q I have a question about how my detective would treat a suspect's shoulder wound. She's dressed as a doctor to fool the suspect, has a crash cart at her disposal, and has been briefed by the hospital staff on what to do, up to a point. I have her using bandages from the cart and applying pressure to stop the bleeding. Is that okay?

Then she's going to give him a shot of something to knock him out. I'm thinking Versed, which the medical personnel would have already put in a syringe for her. I'll have the nurse on the scene inject it into his veins. Am I on the right track?

Paula L. Woods
Author of the award-winning
Charlotte Justice Mystery series

A This is all perfect. She would first grab a handful of sterile 4 x 4 gauze pads and apply pressure to the wound, while someone opened a pressure bandage. This is an elastic bandage with adhesive on one side. Once stretched over the gauze on the wound and pressed into position, it would stabilize the wound until more definitive treatment could be given.

Several medications could be used to sedate him, and Versed (Midazolam) is certainly one of them. Also, Valium (diazepam) or morphine sulfate (called MS by MDs and nurses) would work. Doses would be around 2 to 5 milligrams for Versed, 2 to 10 for Valium, and 5 to 15 for MS. Each can be given IV, and their effects would come on in less than a minute and would peak by three to five minutes.

Any of these would likely be part of the crash cart and could be in ready mixed syringes. Your detective or the nurse would simply need to open the packaging, remove the syringe, pull off the needle cover, and stick the needle in a vein. The syringe is graduated, so she could give the amount necessary to sedate the victim.

WHAT DAMAGE TO MY CHARACTER'S HANDS WOULD LIMIT THEIR USE?

Q I want one of my characters to have impaired use of his hands after an accident. A heavy object falls on his hands, breaking bones and doing other damage. I want him to slowly recover from the injuries but not fully in that he will be left with decreased strength and mobility. What kind of damage would do this?

Simon Wood
Author of *Paying the Piper*
Bay Area, California
www.simonwood.net

A Injuries in the bones, tendons, or nerves would lead to long-term disability. Damage to the arteries of the hand or wrist could also produce problems, but it would be more acute and less likely to cause long-term problems if properly treated.

Any severe damage or crush injury of the bones of the wrist (carpal bones), the hand (metacarpals), or the fingers (phalanges) would fit your needs. An orthopedic or hand surgeon would repair the bones as best he could. This might require the insertion of metal rods, plates, and screws. The hand could then return to mostly normal function, or it could be deformed in such a way that he had very little function and anywhere in between. Most likely the hand would be stiff, and there would be a decreased range of motion and grip strength.

The tendons that move the hands and fingers are of two varieties. The flexor tendons run along the palm of the hand and connect the muscles of the forearm to the wrist, hand, and fingers. They're used to flex the fingers, close the hand, and flex the wrist. The extensor tendons run along the back of the hand and again connect the muscles of the forearm to the wrist, hand, and fingers. These tendons extend or stretch out the wrist, hand, and fingers. Damage to these can usually be repaired, but sometimes the repair is incomplete or the healing process is imperfect, and the individual is left with a decreased range of motion and strength. His ability to open and close his hand, grip things such as a pencil or some other work-related item, and perform fine motions like writing, buttoning clothes, or tying shoelaces could be impaired.

The nerves that supply the hand and fingers run from the spinal cord, down the arm, and all the way to the tips of the fingers. Damage to these nerves could leave the hand paralyzed, weak, uncoordinated, and/or numb.

These injuries can occur in any combination and in any degree of severity. The injuries could cause something as simple as mild numbness of the fingers or could lead to an inability to perform fine motions. They could leave the hand and fingers weak or completely paralyzed. Almost any limitation is possible.

Regardless of the type and severity of the injuries, he would undergo medical and if necessary surgical treatment followed by rehab. Interestingly, this type of hand rehab is called occupational therapy or OT for short. His response to treatment could be excellent, and he could regain normal or near normal function, or the injuries could be so severe that the treatment is ineffective and the rehab not beneficial to the point that he could be left with almost any hand disability you want.

His recovery timeline would depend upon the exact nature of the injury, how well any repairs were done, how well rehab went, the victim's general age and health, and luck. For an injury severe enough to leave him with long-term disability, his recovery period would be measured in months. It could be anywhere between two and twelve months. This gives you great freedom in plotting your story.

HOW LONG DOES THE HEART BEAT AFTER DEATH FROM HANGING?

Q In my story, a man is executed by hanging. The drop is a little over six feet. During my research I found an 1885 newspaper on a hanging that said there was no muscular twitching or respiration, yet it was seventeen minutes before the victim's heart stopped. Why? If his neck was dislocated at the axis, did the spinal cord rupture or break? Wouldn't there be brain activity of some sort?

LD

A In hangings such as this where the bones of the neck crack or fracture, the spinal cord is damaged. This damage is typically a tearing or cutting followed by bleeding into the cord. The victim will immediately go into what is called spinal shock. This occurs whenever the spinal cord is abruptly injured, torn, or transected (cut in half). If this occurs, the nerve impulses to the body—particularly the blood vessels—are suddenly interrupted. The blood vessels dilate (open up), which causes the blood pressure (BP) to drop rapidly and severely. This is a state of shock and leads to immediate loss of consciousness. Also, with the damage to the cord and the interruption of the nerve impulse, the muscles become flaccid (relaxed). Like a puppet whose strings are cut. Thus, no movement is possible. This is why the victims of hangings in which the cord is injured do not seize or move or jerk or struggle for breath. If the neck does not break and the victim dies more slowly from strangulation, then he will struggle for air, and his body will jerk against the rope.

The heart has what is called intrinsic automaticity. This means that it beats on its own. It requires no nerves to send it a signal. The heart will often continue beating for many minutes after the brain is dead. In a hanging of the type you describe, the victim is actually dead immediately, but the heart continues beating. The victim would not be pronounced dead until the heart stopped, however. Why? This is an easily measurable indicator of death, so the doctor on duty would await this before declaring the victim dead.

WHAT UNUSUAL METHOD OF MURDER COULD MY AVANT-GARDE WOMAN USE IN THE EARLY 1800s?

Q My story takes place in Vienna in the early 1800s. I have a female character who murders her lover to stop him from stealing something she herself is trying to steal. I want her to kill him in a way that is disturbing but not bloody or gruesome. I know that poison was popular, but I was wondering if there was something more interesting. She's a bit of an avant-garde woman and often dresses as a man to go out at night on horseback.

M.J. Rose
Best-selling author of *The Hypnotist*

A Guns, knives, swords, crossbows, and poisons were all available then. Arsenic, deadly night-shade, foxglove (digitalis), opium, and many other toxins were used to kill in the 1800s.

But what about a hat pin? It was common then, six or more inches long, made of metal, and pointed, and it would make an odd weapon for murder. She could stab the victim in the chest and damage the heart, the lungs, or both. She would need to aim the weapon between the ribs on the left side of the chest to hit the heart. This could kill him in a few seconds to several minutes.

Or she could drive the hat pin into the victim's ear canal. It would enter the brain and could kill him instantly or over several minutes or hours as he bled into his brain.

In either of these situations there would be little external bleeding as the wound would be very small.

HOW WAS HYPOTHERMIA TREATED IN 1975?

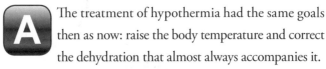 What would have been the usual hospital procedure for treating hypothermia in 1975? The scenario: Two cops are ambushed in the upper Michigan woods during a snowfall. One is beaten and then tied and suspended in a tree, naked. She frees herself, puts on wet clothes, and calls for help within an hour or less of the ambush. The second cop, who is wearing a parka, takes a shotgun blast to the shoulder and goes down in the snow. The other cop finds him barely alive, and help arrives about fifteen minutes after her distress call.

I'm guessing she is relatively okay the next morning and able to give a statement in her hospital room. I am assuming she is hooked up to IVs. Anything else?

Her partner is critical. She visits him later in his hospital room. I'd like to paint an accurate picture of what he would look like, IV wise and stuff. I'm guessing he might have even gone into cardiac arrest. He needs to survive.

P.J. Parrish
Shamus, Thriller, Anthony award–winning author
and Edgar nominee
Fort Lauderdale, Florida,
and Petoskey, Michigan

The treatment of hypothermia had the same goals then as now: raise the body temperature and correct the dehydration that almost always accompanies it.

Her situation would be easy. They would change her into dry, warm clothes, wrap her in a wool blanket or whatever else they had, and give her fluids, preferably warm liquids. They would put her in a vehicle and crank up the heater, then treat her injuries. She would likely be able to talk at the scene because she was able to walk and call for help. They would probably not give her IV fluids since she could rehydrate herself by drinking. Only if she had severe hypothermia would she not be able to talk or take oral liquids, and then of course she could not have escaped and called for help. If her injuries weren't serious, she would be home in a day or two and would do fine.

His situation is more complex and variable, depending upon the severity of his injuries, the amount of blood he lost, and other factors. Yes, he could have a cardiac arrest, but if so, his survival in your scenario would be less than 1%. I'd avoid that unless you want him dead.

They would control any bleeding with pressure over the injury and wrap him in warm materials. Once in the hospital he would be given IV fluids. They would not let him drink since he would likely need emergent surgery. They would give him blood and take him to surgery to repair his gunshot injuries. He would have IV lines for fluids, blood, and medications for pain as well as antibiotics. He would be in the hospital for many days and maybe a week or two. His wounds could get infected, his hypothermia and blood loss could permanently damage his kidneys, or he could develop pneumonia and a few other things that would lengthen his recovery period. If so, he might or might not recover completely.

CAN MY CHARACTER WITH A HYSTERICAL CONVERSION DISORDER TAKE CARE OF HERSELF?

Q The heroine in my book is in a wheelchair, unable to walk due to conversion disorder (hysterical paralysis). She is wealthy, has domestic help in her home, and is independent and active in her daily life with her power chair and service dog. She also works out to build up her strength. But how much of her personal physical care would she be able to attend to without assistance? I see her wanting to do everything for herself, but can a paraplegic manage transferring from the wheelchair to and from the bed, the shower, and the toilet without assistance? Will an aide be required for her to manage her personal care, or will she be able to do it all herself? If she is pulled out of her wheelchair, would she be able to pull herself back into her seat?

Diane M. Downer
Shallotte, North Carolina

A A hysterical conversion reaction is a psychiatric disorder and not a physical one. It is not paraplegia, which is paralysis below the waist and results from damage to the spinal cord. The victims of a conversion reaction have no such neurological defect and can do anything—run, jump, shower, and feed and dress themselves. They just choose not to. Or more accurately, their mental disorder causes them to make that choice.

People with this disorder tend to sit and stare and not acknowledge those around them. They don't travel around in a motorized wheelchair or work out. They look depressed and disinterested. She would not have a service dog since she would likely ignore him too. She could crawl back into her chair and indeed could do anything she wanted to do. Remember, this is a psychiatric disorder, not a physical one.

These types of reactions are seen in schizophrenia and some other mental disorders and often appear after a severe psychological trauma. In the latter case they are usually self-limited, meaning that the reaction resolves on its own without any specific treatment. Usually in a few days or weeks but the syndrome can last for many months or years in unusual circumstances.

So your character can do anything, but she may choose not to. She might need someone to help with her personal care if she refuses to do so. But if she wanted to, she could do all this for herself.

WHAT TRAUMA COULD MY CHARACTER SUFFER THAT WOULD MAKE HIM STERILE BUT NOT IMPOTENT?

Q My story takes place fifteen years after the Civil War. I want my male character to suffer an injury that would make him unable to father children but still be a "husband" to his wife. What trauma could he have suffered during the war that might cause this?

AP

A The testes (testicles) produce two major products: sperm and male sex hormones. Low or no sperm can lead to sterility, and low or no sex hormones can lead to impotency. Sperm produced within the testes must pass up the vas deferens (tubes that connect the testes to the urethra) and into the urethra before exiting during ejaculation. The sex hormones do not pass this way but rather enter the bloodstream directly.

If the testes were severely damaged by a bullet or shrapnel or a direct blow, the battlefield surgeon might remove them. Removal of the testes removes the source of both sperm and male sex hormones. If only one was damaged he would have no problem, but if both were injured and removed, he would be sterile and at least partially impotent. Maybe not completely so this could work for you.

If both of the vas deferens were injured, they could scar and close up, preventing the passage of the sperm from the testes to the urethra. This would have no effect on the production of sex hormones or on their passage into the bloodstream. He would then be sterile but not impotent. This would be ideal for your scenario.

WHAT HAPPENS TO SOMEONE WHO IS CONFINED IN TOTAL DARKNESS FOR AN EXTENDED PERIOD OF TIME?

Q What would be the physical effects on a healthy person who is confined in a small, totally dark room for an extended period of time? How long would it take for any appreciable physical effects to show up? The person's basic needs are provided for.

Chuck Anderson
University Place, Washington

A Since all your victim's physical needs are met, there would not likely be any physical problems. He could get pneumonia from the cold, damp air. He could suffer bone and muscle loss or develop a venous thrombosis in his legs from being inactive if incarcerated for many months.

But by far the most damaging effects would be psychological from what is called a sensory deprivation syndrome. When placed in an environment devoid of or limited in sensory input, the human mind fills in the blanks. The brain will create sensations, alter sensations, or both. It might produce these sensations from memories, which might be distorted, or create them from whole cloth. Anyone in such a situation is basically confined to living within his own mind, and the mind is capable of essentially any construct.

In the dark your character might see things such as colors, amorphous objects, floating images, faces, horrible creatures, and virtually anything else his mind can conjure. If it's quiet, he might hear voices (calling to him, talking about him, or even whispering or singing), bells ringing, scratching or scurrying sounds, growls, and anything else. He might feel cool or warm breezes, bugs crawling on his skin, snakes slithering over his feet and legs, and other sensations his mind might invent. Even the senses of taste and smell might play a role. He could smell a foul or sweet odor or perhaps an odor from the past, which could trigger memories, both real and imagined. Smell, the most primitive of our senses, often dredges up memories, frequently of a very visceral nature.

His sensory experiences would not all arise within his own mind. Ambient noises can serve as the seed, and his deprived mind could expand or alter these senses in any direction—good, bad, or just different. For example, he might hear the wind moving a tree branch against the outside wall and think someone or something is digging after him to save him, to kill him, or to eat him alive. He might hear voices or screams of others and believe they are howling demons coming to take him to hell or angels marching to save his soul. He might feel drips of water or real bugs and summon an army of horrible creatures bent on devouring him.

In the dark his sense of time and place would be severely distorted, and this would only add to his confusion and fuel his imagination further. Hypothermia (low body temperature) from prolonged exposure to the coldness of the room can alter his brain function and might increase his hallucinations.

How long would this take? It is widely variable. People

react differently to sensory deprivation. Some might be in trouble after only a few hours, while others might require weeks.

Once rescued, he might recover completely, be left totally insane, or anywhere in between. He can recover in an hour or two, a day or two, a month or two, or not at all. Any of these is possible.

This means that you literally have an unlimited array of possibilities. He can sense anything and everything. Whatever you can dream up, he can experience.

Spooky stuff.

HOW ARE DONORS AND RECIPIENTS OF TRANSPLANTED ORGANS MATCHED?

Q With a living donor kidney transplant, is matching blood type the only issue? I'd like to make finding a donor difficult for my character, requiring a search for her long-lost daughter.

Karen Sandler
Author of *Tankborn*, a young adult dystopian novel
Northern California
www.karensandler.net

A Transplant rejection is an immunologic problem. The body constructs antibodies to any foreign antigens. This is what keeps us alive. If a virus or a bacterium enters the body, it is recognized as foreign and the body builds antibodies against it. These antibodies attach to the antigen and then attract white blood cells that kill and devour it. In transplant rejection the same thing happens. A compatible donor is one that is not recognized as foreign, or if so, only slightly. In other words, the better the match between donor and recipient, the less likely there will be a rejection problem.

When people are analyzed for organ donation, the blood type and many other antigens are tested. There are many protein antigens in the blood and the body, and it is best if these match. A perfect match is rare, so the transplant surgeon will go for the best one possible.

ABO and Rh blood-typing are part of this matching

process. The ABO system tells you whether the blood is type A, B, AB, or O, while the Rh tells you whether it is positive or negative. Positive means that the Rh factor is present, and negative means that it is not. So A positive blood has type A blood and the Rh factor is present. The donor and the recipient should have the same blood type.

Of the many other blood antigens present in the body, the most important to the transplant surgeon is called the HLA group. HLA stands for human leukocyte antigen, and there are many types of them.

When someone is being evaluated as a donor, the surgeon will do blood-typing, HLA matching, and analyze the compatibility of several other antigens. The closer each of these matches, the more successful the transplant will be.

The doctor taking care of your character would perform these tests on any individual who is considered a possible donor and would then select the most compatible donor and go from there.

WAS LEPROSY A PROBLEM IN VICTORIAN ENGLAND?

Q For my story I need to know whether leprosy was an issue in England in the Victorian era, mid- to late 1800s. During my Internet research, I've found it mentioned in the 1700s and before but nothing after that. Was it a problem or am I on the wrong track?

Kim Lenox
Author of the award-winning Shadow Guards series

A Leprosy has been around for many centuries. By 1900 it was on the decline in most Western countries, but it was not absent. For example, in the final years of the nineteenth century, as much as 1% of the population of Norway had leprosy. And in England there were continual outbreaks largely due to immigrants from areas such as India, where leprosy was still a major health problem. Also, English soldiers, business people, and visitors to India would occasionally return with the disease and spread it.

So even though there were no major leprosy epidemics in Victorian England, there were occasional sporadic outbreaks. This scenario should fit your needs. Of course, there was no effective treatment for leprosy, and none appeared until the middle of the twentieth century.

COULD SOMEONE EXECUTED BY LETHAL INJECTION BE AN ORGAN DONOR?

Q I am working on a short story in which my protagonist will receive an organ donated by a serial killer. If a person is executed with lethal injection, can his organs be donated? Is there any danger of the chemicals used in the execution becoming residual in an organ, specifically the heart?

Vaughn C. Hardacker
Caribou, Maine

A None of the three drugs used during lethal injection would in and of themselves harm the organs, and yes, they could theoretically be used for donation. The major problem would be the logistics.

The types of individuals from which organs would be taken include someone in a hospital who has suffered severe brain damage to the point that she will be taken off life support or someone who is brought into the emergency room with such a severe head injury that survival is impossible. There are many other scenarios where individual organs are donated, but in these circumstances essentially every organ could be donated, and I assume that's what you're talking about.

Lethal injections are performed in a prison environment and not in a hospital, which makes removing and transporting the organs extremely difficult. In your story a team of surgeons would need to set up an operating room in the prison, remove the organs immediately after death, place them on ice, and transport them to a facility where they can be used. But this wouldn't work for all organs. Many organs can be removed from a corpse and will live for a long time outside the body if cooled and kept moist. Things like corneas and bones would do well in this scenario. But the heart and lungs must be used very quickly, usually within six hours.

Alternatively, the lethal injection could be done in a hospital operating room where they would be prepared for organ donation. Though I've never heard of this happening, it is at least theoretically possible.

The real problem is that in such donations the organs are taken before the donor is removed from life support. That is, the kidneys and liver and some other organs are taken while the donor is alive, then lastly the heart and lungs are taken as soon as the life support is removed. In a lethal injection it might take fifteen to twenty minutes for the doctor to pronounce the person dead. Though the heart, lungs, and other organs might still be useful, this is not the ideal situation. But it will work for your story.

WHAT SYMPTOMS AND PROBLEMS WOULD MY YOUNG LEUKEMIA PATIENT HAVE WHILE ON A RV ROAD TRIP?

Q In my movie script, a thirteen-year-old boy has leukemia and only three months to live. He and his family take a three-month RV trip to spend time together before he dies. What struggles would he face? Would he suffer fatigue or have to use a wheelchair? Could he pass out as a side effect of leukemia?

SC
Geneseo, New York

A Leukemias come in many varieties and many degrees of severity. Your young man would be well down the road and likely have exhausted all treatments such as the various chemotherapy protocols. I should point out this is unusual since most childhood leukemias are now curable. Not all are, however, so your young man could be in his last three months.

Leukemia is a disease in which the bone marrow produces large amounts of abnormal white blood cells (WBCs) that are not effective in combating infections. He would be prone to secondary infections such as pneumonia and urinary tract infections, which are often the immediate cause of death in leukemia patients.

Also, this overgrowth of WBCs takes over the bone marrow, suppressing the production of other cell types like red blood cells (RBCs) and platelets. A low level of RBCs is called anemia and results in fatigue, weakness, shortness of breath, dizziness, intolerance to cold, and a pale appearance among other things. Platelets are the first cells involved in blood clotting. If these decline to very low levels, as they often do in untreated or terminal leukemia, the victim is prone to bleeding. This is manifested by bleeding from the gums or the nose and with any injury. Victims tend to bruise easily. So your young man could have problems with nosebleeds, gum bleeding, and black and blue spots appearing on his body with minor trauma such as bumping into a table.

In terminal leukemia the victim would be extremely weak, pale, and suffer from the bruising and bleeding as described above. He would have an intolerance to cold, would be short of breath with almost any activity, could require a wheelchair for mobility, would sleep a great deal, and could indeed fall asleep easily when physically taxed or just worn out from a long day. In the end, he would likely get pneumonia or a urinary tract infection (UTI), both of which could lead to deadly septicemia, which is an infection of the bloodstream. He would develop a cough, shortness of breath, and fever if he had pneumonia and weakness, fever, chills, and back pain if a UTI started. Once he contracted sepsis he would slip into a coma and die. He could also suffer bleeding into the brain from his low platelet count and die from this. Here he would most likely become severely fatigued, disoriented, and finally fall asleep, lapse into a coma, stop breathing, and die.

HOW WAS LUPUS TREATED IN 1939?

Q My story is set in 1939. My antagonist suffers from lupus, and I need to know how it was treated then. Specifically, I want my detective to discover that the antagonist takes a certain medication and from this determines that he is being treated for lupus. Is this possible?

James Thorpe
Burbank, California

A In 1894 J. F. Payne presented his paper on the treatment of systemic lupus erythematosus with quinine, and four years later other investigations showed that adding salicylates (aspirin is one of these) to quinine had added benefits. This combination remained the standard treatment until the mid-1900s when corticosteroids came along. Though in 1939 these drugs were used for many illnesses, a testament to how little we knew then, this combination would suggest that the person was taking them for lupus if the person also had the lupus rash. The classic rash of lupus is pink or red and is found across the bridge of the nose and the upper cheeks. It is called a butterfly rash because of its shape. It might be very prominent or almost unnoticeable. It can also come and go. It can be present for days or weeks or months and then be gone for weeks or months. It can be covered with makeup.

If your detective saw such a rash and also learned that the person was taking quinine and salicylates, he could conclude that he suffered from lupus.

WHAT INJURIES MIGHT MY CHARACTER SUFFER IF KNOCKED OFF HIS MOTORCYCLE BY A NUCLEAR EXPLOSION?

Q My scenario: A person is riding a motorcycle when a missile hits the city. He is far enough from the epicenter that he isn't killed outright, but the aftershocks knock him off his bike and he hits the ground. What injuries would he sustain, and how serious would they be? Would he survive if he got medical care in time? If he survives, how long would it be before he's back on his feet?

AS
Tuscaloosa, Alabama

A If a nuclear warhead exploded in the city, many bad things would happen very quickly and over a broad area. The problem with your scenario is that if the shock wave was powerful enough to knock him off his motorcycle, the radiation exposure would be huge. This is because the shock wave carries the radiation with it. I'm not talking about fallout that can occur over the hours and days after the explosion in a downwind pattern but the radiation that is immediately expelled with the explosion. If he was far enough away to avoid this contamination, he would be too far away for the shock blast to take him down. At least directly. If he was exposed to radiation in this manner, any injuries he suffered would be the least of his problems. Depending upon the amount of radiation exposure, he could die within hours, days, or weeks, but he would die. There is no treatment for this.

But all is not lost. There is another way for your scenario to work. When the device goes off, he could be several miles away and feel very little of the impact, mostly a shaking of the ground rather than a blast wave. Also, the intense light of the explosion would be shocking and could blind him for a few minutes. Either the shaking ground or the sudden light could result in him losing control of his motorcycle.

In the subsequent wreck, he could suffer anything from minor scrapes and bruises to lethal brain and chest injuries. I'm assuming from your questions that you want him to survive without any aggressive medical care. Remember, after such an event the medical systems would be stretched to the limit and treatment would be less than ideal. It might be hours or even days before anyone could treat him because chaos would reign supreme. It would take a day or two for extra medical help to come to the area or for injured individuals to be transported to hospitals out of the area. Transportation and medical systems would be overwhelmed.

If he simply suffered scrapes, bruises, and strained muscles, he would heal without any treatment other than simply cleaning and covering the wounds.

If he also had fractured a leg or arm, he or someone else could splint his injured extremity. This would serve him well for a few days until he could reach medical care or until medical care had time to deal with him. Then his fractured extremity could be casted for four to six weeks, depending upon the nature of the fracture. After that he would have the usual post-fracture problems of stiffness and loss of strength in the extremity for a few weeks. He would recover from this completely and be back to normal in a couple of months.

If he suffered more serious injuries to his chest such as a collapsed lung or to his abdomen such as a ruptured spleen or damaged liver or kidney, he would require fairly immediate surgery or his life would be in jeopardy. He might be able to survive for several hours while reaching medical care, but if it was delayed much beyond this he could easily die. The type of surgery needed would depend upon the nature of his injuries. A spleen would be removed, and a liver or a kidney would be repaired. A lung injury might require more extensive surgery. Recovery from these injuries would be much longer. He might be in the hospital for a week or two, and full recovery could take three or four months.

There are many other possible injuries, but these should give you some choices.

HOW LONG DO HARVESTED ORGANS REMAIN USEFUL FOR TRANSPLANT?

Q I have a couple of questions about organ donation. If an organ is harvested and preserved properly, how long can it remain usable? If unexpected organs were delivered to a hospital and the source and donor were unknown, might those organs be used for transplants?

A An organ left on the hospital porch would not be used. It could be infected with HIV or hepatitis or the person could have had some type of cancer. There would be no time for testing the organ for these problems. It would be risky and foolish to use an organ that appeared in this manner.

The viability of organs removed from a donor depends upon the organ and the circumstances.

In general, organ preservation times between procurement and transplantation are:

Lung	2 to 4 hours
Heart	4 to 6 hours
Liver	12 to 18 hours
Pancreas	12 to 18 hours
Kidney	24 to 48 hours

COULD A FLIGHT ATTENDANT KILL AN ALLERGIC PASSENGER WITH PEANUTS?

Q A flight attendant wants to kill a passenger who she knows has a peanut allergy. If she opened a bag of peanuts, rubbed her hands with them, and then touched the sandwich, cheese, and ice that she gave the passenger, would he have a fatal reaction? And if so, what would the reaction be?

Lee Goldberg
Author of *The Walk* and *Mr. Monk on the Road*
Los Angeles, California
www.leegoldberg.com

A If he was severely allergic to peanuts, this could happen. It takes just a small amount of the peanut oil to trigger an anaphylactic reaction. The only question is whether this would place enough peanut oil on the sandwich. Probably. Or she could bring a syringe of peanut oil on board and place a couple of drops on his sandwich.

The reaction would begin in a few minutes. He would become short of breath, his lips would swell, and he would develop a diffuse rash that is typically red splotches and bullae (water-filled, blister-like lesions). His throat and airways would constrict, and he would have an acute attack of asthma with wheezing, gasping for breath, and clutching at his chest or throat. His blood pressure would fall, and as he slipped into shock he would become dizzy, lose consciousness, lapse into a coma, and die. This entire process could take two or three minutes or up to thirty, depending on the dose and his particular reaction to it.

CAN MY FEMALE CHARACTER SUFFER FROM POLYDACTYLISM?

Q Early this morning I woke up in a major panic, thinking I might have made a mistake. Central to my novel is a male character who fathers a male child with one woman and a female child with another. Both the offspring are polydactyl. My panic was spurred by my weak understanding regarding the gene for polydactylism. Is it unique to the Y chromosome and can it not be passed to a female offspring, or can females have polydactylism?

Marjorie
Rochester Hills, Michigan

A Don't panic. There are many types of polydactyly, but the one you are most likely dealing with in your story is inherited in an autosomal dominant fashion. What does this mean? Inherited genes can be considered of two major types: sex linked (the X and Y chromosomes) and autosomal (the other twenty-two pairs of chromosomes). Dominant means that the gene is dominant to its paired gene, and the disease will be expressed even if the person has only one abnormal gene (the other of the pair being normal). In recessive genetic disorders the person must have both pairs of the genes for the disease to be expressed in its fullest form. Both males and females can carry the autosomal polydactyl gene.

Your polydactylic father could have one abnormal gene

and one normal gene, so half of his sperm would get the abnormal gene and half the normal gene. Statistically, half of his children would have polydactyly and half would not. Since this is an autosomal dominant trait and not a sex-linked one, the sex of the child makes no difference. So you're okay with your story as it is.

Now you can go back to sleep.

HOW WOULD MY CHARACTER BE TREATED IF SHE WAS JABBED BY A BONE FRAGMENT AT A CRIME SCENE?

Q I have a scene where my heroine, a crime scene cleanup person, is jabbed with a bone fragment at a relatively fresh scene (shotgun death). What kind of treatment would she receive once she arrived at the hospital? Besides stitching the wound, would it be cleaned a specific way? If the victim was suspected to be HIV positive, would my heroine immediately begin a cocktail of drugs, and if so, could you name the drugs? Would there be a delay in beginning meds while they waited for the coroner to determine if the victim was indeed HIV positive? If so, how long would it take to get confirmation?

WR
Surrey, British Columbia, Canada

A The initial treatment in the emergency room would be fairly standard for any puncture wound by a foreign body. They would clean the wound and give her a tetanus shot if she had not had one in the past five to ten years. There would be no suturing since puncture wounds are best left open to heal inside out as this lessens the chance of a wound infection. They might or might not place her on antibiotics for the next five to seven days. That would depend upon the exact nature of the injury and the decision of the treating physician in the ER.

Because she was stabbed by a biological product, in this case a bone fragment, she would likely receive hepatitis B immunization since this can be a dangerous disease and is transmitted by blood. Chances are great that this would be done.

As far as treating her for HIV, this is controversial in a circumstance where the puncturing object might or might not be infected. Some docs would; others would wait for the gunshot victim's blood to be tested. But this could be done fairly quickly. Hours to a day at the most. A puncture of this type is of course very concerning, but it does not absolutely mean that she will get HIV.

If the test was positive, she would be treated for HIV exposure with one or more of the protease inhibitor drugs. There are several of them, and there are many treatment protocols that are constantly changing as our knowledge about HIV treatment evolves, so I can't give you an answer as to exactly what drugs would be used. If the test was negative, they would still perform an HIV test on her in the ER, repeat it in three months, and repeat it again in six months just to be safe. If all of those are negative, then she did not contract the disease at the time of her injury. If any one of these tests is positive, she would be treated as any other HIV patient.

WHAT INJURIES COULD BE CAUSED BY A BLOW FROM A SHOVEL?

 In the book I'm working on, my protagonist, a woman of medium frame and in her early twenties, is hit on the arm with a shovel by a strong man. Could it crack her arm but not break the bone all the way through? How would a doctor describe her injury? Secondly, the same man hits her on the head. She falls to the ground, stunned, striking her head on the pavement. What are the likely consequences of this? How long would she need to be in the hospital?

Charlaine Harris
New York Times best-selling author of *Dead Reckoning*
www.charlaineharris.com

In either case the possible injuries are many and depend upon the exact nature of the blow, the victim, and luck.

The arm could simply be bruised, or it could bleed within the muscle and form a hematoma (mass of blood), crack the bone (a hairline fracture), or fracture the bone in two (called a simple fracture) or into many pieces (called a comminuted fracture). If the shovel struck with its edge, it could sever an artery and lead to massive bleeding. It sounds as though a hairline fracture would work best for you.

Blunt force trauma to the head can be deadly or as simple as a bruise. The scalp is highly vascular, meaning that it's loaded with blood vessels. It would bleed profusely if the blow caused a laceration, and if not, the blood could collect beneath the scalp and form a hematoma (goose egg).

Any blow to the head can cause a concussion (head trauma without real brain damage) or a cerebral contusion (brain bruise), with the latter being a more serious injury. Both can result in loss of consciousness, but in a concussion this is typically very brief—a few minutes at most. With a contusion, unconsciousness could be brief or last for days. Such a blow could also cause bleeding into or around the brain if delivered with sufficient force. This can be deadly, and death can arrive instantly, over minutes, hours, days, or not at all.

Any of these injuries can occur whether the skull is fractured or not.

A bleed within the skull is generically called an intra-cranial bleed (bleeding within the cranium or skull). If the bleed is within the brain itself, it is called an intracerebral bleed. If it occurs within the space between the brain and the skull, it is termed either a subdural or epidural bleed, depending upon exactly where the bleed occurs.

Any bleed within the head causes pressure to rise. This effectively compresses the brain and forces it downward through the hole at the base of the skull through which the spinal cord exits and extends down the back to supply nerves to the body. This opening is called the foramen magnum, and the upper part of the spinal cord—the transition area between the brain and the cord—is called the brain stem. The process of squeezing the brain down through the fora-men magnum is called herniation of the brain stem. Since the brain stem controls respiration, this compression will shut down brain stem function and thus breathing, and the victim can die from asphyxia very quickly. For this reason intracranial bleeds are true medical emergencies and often require emergent surgery.

Your victim could suffer a simple contusion (scalp bruise), a concussion (loss of consciousness for a few minutes), a cerebral contusion with a variable period of unconsciousness, a scalp laceration with a great deal of bleeding, no external bleeding but the formation of a scalp hematoma, or bleeding into or around the brain. Any and all of these are possible.

Her treatment, recovery time, and long-term problems would depend upon the exact nature of her injury. Contusions, concussions, and scalp lacerations require little treatment (except suturing the laceration), and she would spend a day or two in the hospital and then be okay. With the other injuries, she would likely need surgery, and her recovery would be longer and more complicated.

HOW WAS SICKLE-CELL DISEASE DIAGNOSED
THIRTY YEARS AGO?

Q I have a question about sickle-cell disease. What would the test results twenty-five to thirty years ago for the trait form look like? Specifically, what would the test report likely be called? How would the test/disease be described on the report? How would a positive result for the trait be indicated?

Twist Phelan
Winner, Thriller Award
www.twistphelan.com

A Sickle-cell disease is a genetic disorder that results in the production of abnormal hemoglobin, the oxygen-carrying molecule in red blood cells (RBCs). Normal hemoglobin is called hemoglobin A, while that found in sickle-cell anemia (SCA) and sickle-cell trait is termed hemoglobin S. Victims of SCA have two hemoglobin S genes, and those with trait have one S gene and one normal gene. SCA is more severe than trait.

Thirty years ago there was no test for hemoglobin S as there is today. The diagnosis was made by the person's symptoms and by the morphology of the RBCs as seen under the microscope. Sickled RBCs look like little sickles or crescent moons.

The test would be a complete blood count with differential (called a CBC with diff). The differential is the counting of the various types of white blood cells (WBCs), so the percentage of each WBC type in the blood is known. A description of the RBCs is also part of the test, and this is where the diagnosis of SCA and trait comes in.

The test requires that the MD take a blood sample, smear a drop of it on a glass slide, stain it with hematoxylin and eosin (H&E), and view it under a microscope. Both SCA and trait would show sickled cells but much more so with SCA. The diagnosis would then be made.

The report would be a CBC with differential report, and it would state that numerous sickled RBCs were seen.

WHAT HAPPENS DURING SMOKE INHALATION AND HOW IS IT TREATED?

Q In my story, a police officer suffers smoke inhalation while extinguishing a barn fire. What injuries might hospitalize him for a few hours to a day but not result in enough long-term damage to end his career as an active police officer?

Coleen Steele
Two-time Arthur Ellis nominee
Bowmanville, Ontario, Canada

A The major effect of inhaling smoke and soot is irritation in the eyes, the throat, and the bronchial tubes in the lungs, causing redness, swelling, and the seeping of fluids in each of these areas. The eyes would water, redden, and burn. The throat and bronchial tubes would become irritated and inflamed and would weep fluids. This would lead to chest burning, shortness of breath, and painful breathing and coughing, with the production of small amounts of thin and watery sputum that could be tinged with flecks of soot and blood. These symptoms might last only a few hours or a day or two since the lungs rapidly heal themselves. Unless a secondary bacterial infection took hold, which would change simple bronchial irritation into an acute bronchitis. Damaged airways, as in this situation, are prone to secondary bacterial infections.

Your cop would be taken to the emergency room where he would have a chest X-ray and a check of the oxygen content in his blood with a pulse oximeter. This is a gadget that clips on a finger and continually measures the blood oxygen level. His treatment would include a couple of days of steroids to lessen the inflammation and a week of antibiotics to prevent a secondary infection. If his blood oxygen saturation and chest X-ray were normal, he would likely be sent home within several hours and seen a few days later as an outpatient. If either his oxygen level or his chest X-ray was abnormal or if his chest pain was considerable, he might be held in the hospital overnight or longer, and when all was okay he would be discharged.

WHAT MIGHT KILL MY CHARACTER WHO IS LOCKED IN A SMOKEHOUSE?

Q In my novel, a victim is either knocked or drugged unconscious (possibly partially strangled) and put into a smokehouse at a place where they make beef jerky. Would he then die from smoke inhalation, or are these commercial smokehouses ventilated too well? My research suggests that these smokers are held at around 130 to 145 degrees and are ventilated to some degree.

Kaye George
Agatha-nominated author of *A Patchwork of Stories*
and *Choke*, an Imogene Duckworthy Mystery
Taylor, Texas
www.KayeGeorge.com

A I'm unclear whether you intend for the person to be unconscious just long enough to lock him in the smoker or for the entire time it takes him to die. It makes a difference in what method you use to subdue and control the victim.

When someone is knocked unconscious, he wakes up after a minute or so. Think of every boxing match you've ever seen. The loser is knocked out and thirty seconds later is complaining that it was a lucky punch. If unconsciousness lasts more than five or ten minutes, then a serious brain injury has likely occurred. The same can be said for strangulation. A person who is strangled into unconsciousness will wake up in twenty to sixty seconds after the hands or the ligature is removed. Like a blow to the head, if the person is out longer than that, a significant brain injury would have had to occur. Either of these could help subdue your victim long enough to lock the door but not keep him unconscious longer than a brief time.

If you want him out for an extended period, drugs would work. Narcotics such as heroin or morphine, sedatives such as Xanax or Valium, barbiturates such as phenobarbital, and many other sedative-type medications, particularly if they are consumed along with alcohol, could render the victim stuporous or completely unconscious for hours.

Your victim would probably succumb to hyperthermia and not smoke inhalation. Exposure to a temperature of around 130 degrees for a few hours would lead to heatstroke. The victim would become dehydrated, his core body temperature would rise, his blood pressure would fall, and he would slip into shock and die. This could take as little as two hours.

HOW LONG COULD MY CHARACTER SURVIVE IN AN AIRTIGHT FREEZER?

Q How long could an average-sized adult male expect to survive locked inside an unplugged floor freezer with the approximate dimensions of six feet long by three feet wide by three feet high? What would be the outer time limits of believability for survival in this scenario? Also, how much difference would it make if he was rendered unconscious first?

Allan Leverone
Author of *Final Vector*
Londonderry, New Hampshire
www.allanleverone.com

A The exact time is impossible to predict since there are many factors involved, including the size and weight of the person and whether he panicked or not. If he remained calm or if he was sedated, he would consume the oxygen (O_2) within the freezer more slowly and survive longer than if he panicked or banged on the door and screamed.

Still, this is a very small area, and he would not only consume the oxygen in the air fairly quickly but also produce carbon dioxide (CO_2) with each breath, so the O_2 content would fall while the CO_2 level would rise. Since he is sedated he would not feel the symptoms that would occur under these circumstances: shortness of breath, dizziness, sleepiness, confusion, and finally loss of consciousness and death.

Survival in a situation like this would be measured in minutes and not hours. I would suggest a minimum of fifteen and a maximum of sixty minutes. The average would probably be around thirty minutes. This is pure guesswork because it would vary greatly from situation to situation, but if you stay within these broad parameters, you should be okay.

WHAT WOULD HAPPEN IF MY CHARACTER IS STABBED IN THE FEMORAL ARTERY?

Q My heroine, Wollie, is in a rural, mountainous area when the villain stabs her in the femoral artery with a meat thermometer. Where exactly would the point of entry be? Could she stop the bleeding by applying pressure over the wound? Would the blood loss make her light-headed yet still be conscious and lucid? Would this injury cause her leg to actually stop working, or would she be able to stand up and walk? How long before she absolutely must have medical attention, and what would that be?

Harley Jane Kozak
www.harleyjanekozak.com

A A stab wound to the femoral artery is a serious and potentially deadly injury. An artery that size will spurt a fountain of blood and lead to severe blood loss and shock. This could take anywhere from three to fifteen minutes, depending upon the severity of the injury and rapidity of the bleeding.

The femoral artery is in the groin. If you press your fingers there, you can easily feel its pulse. Pressure over the area is the best way—and really the only way—she could control the bleeding in the rural setting you outlined. Since the wound is in the groin there is no way to apply a tourniquet above it.

Blood loss leads to hypovolemia (low blood volume),

which in turn leads to low blood pressure and finally to shock and death. A victim of blood loss will go through a series of symptoms more or less in this order: weakness, fatigue, cold feeling, dizziness, thirst and dry mouth, numbness of hands and feet, sleepiness, disorientation, and maybe hallucinations, then coma and death. So Wollie could be dizzy yet awake and aware.

There would be pain at the injury site, but unless the femoral nerve was also damaged, she would be able to move it and even stand and walk as long as she controlled the bleeding. She would not be able to run or swim or do anything really strenuous and at the same time keep the bleeding under control. Better to sit and wait for help or stumble back to civilization.

The sooner she got help the better, but if she established good control of the bleeding she could wait hours. It's the blood loss, not the wound itself, that's harmful. But this type of bleeding is difficult to control for very long. It takes a significant amount of pressure, and hand and arm fatigue would set in fairly quickly. Unless she rigged up a type of device to apply the pressure. Maybe her jacket or shirt wadded up and a large rock placed on it would make her job easier. The rock would apply some of the pressure and require less from her. Or maybe she could tie her belt around the wadded clothing. Still, she would have to maintain careful control of any device she used. Any loss of pressure directly to the wound could lead to sudden and severe spurting of blood.

She would need surgery to repair the artery and could

be in the hospital anywhere from five to ten days if all went well. She would be treated with a blood transfusion to replace the loss and antibiotics and pain meds. She would stay in the ICU about forty-eight hours and would be limited in activity for three or four more days. She would then begin to walk and start physical therapy. Complete recovery would take about six weeks.

COULD MY VILLAIN INFECT HIS VICTIM WITH POLIO IN 1932?

Q Would it be possible in 1932 to infect a victim with acute anterior poliomyelitis? If so, how could the infection be induced? Could it be introduced through food? Assuming the victim is a young, healthy male of twenty-four, how long would it take for the disease to manifest itself? My story concerns a young intelligence operative put to death in this manner by the opposition, so the death appears to be from natural causes.

A Yes, your scenario could work. In 1932 there was of course no treatment and no vaccine for polio. Jonas Salk did not first test the vaccine until 1952, and it was not available for use until 1955. Prior to that polio was a common and devastating disease.

It is caused by a virus, and its most common mode of transmission is through contaminated food and water. It simply would require taking some saliva or blood or even fecal material from someone who had acute polio and contaminating the victim's food or drink with it. He might or might not contract the disease since exposure to the virus does not always lead to infection. It's unpredictable. But your bad guy could infect the victim's food, and he could come down with polio shortly thereafter. It would be even more likely if there were multiple exposures, but a single exposure could work.

The incubation period for polio is one to five weeks

with the shortest being three days and the longest slightly over a month. The initial symptoms tend to be fever, lethargy, headaches, and generalized muscular soreness and weakness, very similar to the flu. In many victims that's the end of it. They have no further problems, and the virus is ultimately killed by the body, leaving the victim immune to polio. But that's not always the case.

Polio can lead to various types of paralysis. This is called paralytic polio, and it comes in two basic varieties: spinal polio and bulbar polio. Spinal polio is when the virus attacks certain areas of the spinal column and the muscles of the body become weak. The legs and arms no longer move, the muscles of the diaphragm can be paralyzed, and breathing becomes impossible. This is where the old iron lungs came into use. The paralyzed muscles begin to wither and shrink.

About 2% of cases are the bulbar variety. Here the virus attacks the brain stem, which is the lower portion of the brain and the upper part of the spinal cord. In bulbar polio certain of the cranial nerves, which are nerves that come directly from the brain and not the spinal cord, become involved and can cause difficulty with breathing, swallowing, and speech, inability to use the face muscles, blurred and double vision, and other neurologic abnormalities. Both spinal and bulbar polio can exist together, and this tends to happen in approximately 20% of patients. This is called bulbospinal polio.

When someone develops paralytic polio, their muscles will cease to function, the muscles will atrophy, breathing will become difficult, and they will be placed in an iron lung. This was the standard treatment in 1932. The major complications that lead to death early on in this disease process are pneumonia and urinary tract infection. Penicillin was discovered in 1928, but it was not until 1934 that any real studies were done on it, and purification and its use as a true antibiotic did not occur until the 1940s. So in 1932 there would have been no method for treating these pneumonias and kidney infections, and they can be deadly, particularly in someone who is immobilized.

So your victim could be infected by presenting him with contaminated food or drink, and he could develop the paralytic variety and end up dying from either an infection or a slow wasting away. There would be no way medically or forensically to determine that the infection was intentionally directed at him and not something he contracted through normal person-to-person contact, which was how most cases occurred.

WERE MORPHINE DRIPS FOR PAIN MANAGEMENT USED IN 1965?

Q My MFA thesis novel is set in 1965. For a woman with cancer, probably ovarian that has spread to bones, would there have been a treatment other than pain medication used in 1965? I assume morphine drips were used then, but I'm not sure.

Carol Frischmann
Portland, Oregon
www.carolfrischmann.com

A There is little treatment for metastatic ovarian cancer today, and there was essentially none in 1965. None that worked anyway. Morphine sulfate (MS) was indeed used in this extremely painful circumstance, but it was not given by continuous IV drip. The simple reason was that in 1965 there were no reliable devices to ensure a slow and controlled infusion as we have now. Most IVs back then were simply set at a particular flow rate by a clip and wheel device on the IV tubing. This device pinched the tube to control the flow. Neither very accurate nor reliable. To administer a potentially lethal drug like MS this way would be dangerous and foolhardy. So instead it was given by intermittent injections. Early in the course of this disease, 5 to 15 mgs given IV or IM every two to four hours would work, but as the treatment continued over many weeks or months, the victim would become accustomed to the morphine, much as addicts do, and an ever-increasing dose would be needed to control the pain. It is conceivable that 30 to 50 mgs every three to four hours would be needed after a couple of months. Since addiction in this circumstance is of little concern, the doctor would use whatever dose was needed for the patient's comfort.

WHAT INJURY COULD MY TENTH-CENTURY DUKE SUFFER THAT MIGHT TAKE HIS LIFE A DECADE LATER?

Q I am writing a biographical historical novel about Queen Mechthild of Germany who lived in the tenth century. All the characters in my story are real. Her son, Heinrich, Duke of Bavaria, suffered an injury in battle but survived. According to historians, this same injury killed him approximately ten years later. This is all that is known about the injury. What injury could the duke have sustained during battle, survived, and then died from complications years later?

Mirella Patzer
Historical fiction author
http://mirellapatzer.com
http://historyandwomen.com

A The most likely battle injury he might suffer would be a stab wound from a sword, arrow, or lance. He would bleed but could easily survive the injury. Let's say the wound was to the upper or lower leg and deep enough to reach the bone. A wound infection, a common occurrence and cause of death at that time, could follow such an injury. People survived these infections, even though physicians then had no idea what an infection was or how to treat it. They did things such as bleeding the patient, which did no good and was actually harmful, but they also often opened an infected wound to release the pus, which was helpful. Exactly what we do today. Interestingly, physicians at that time thought the appearance of pus in a wound was a good thing and meant that the wound was healing properly. The truth is the exact opposite since the presence of pus suggests a bacterial infection. Still, people survived this in the tenth century. Never underestimate the power of luck.

So your victim suffers a stab wound that reached the bone, and an infection occurred. The infection could then settle into the bone and its surrounding tissue called the periosteum. We call this osteomyelitis. It can become a chronic infection that is difficult to treat even today. It smolders along for weeks and months and years. This could be the case with your young duke.

He would suffer chronic pain and swelling in the area. There would be times that this was mild and other times that it was more severe. When he had a flare-up of the infection, his physicians could open the wound to relieve the pus, and it could improve the infection for weeks or months only to have it recur. This cycle could continue for many years. Finally, he could succumb to a very severe infection that did not respond to what little treatment was available.

Actually this is what happened with King Henry VIII. He suffered a wound to his leg during a jousting match. It never healed properly and dogged him to his deathbed.

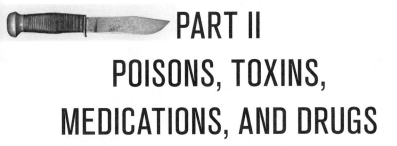

PART II
POISONS, TOXINS, MEDICATIONS, AND DRUGS

Q In today's age of high-tech forensics, do poisons still work for fictional murders?

GB

A Yes, people often get away with poisoning because it is not thought of. If an eighty-five-year-old demented person with heart and lung disease dies in his sleep in a nursing home, his private MD might sign the death certificate as a natural cardiac death, and the ME would accept it. Likely no autopsy would be done and no expensive toxicological exams would be undertaken, so an overdose of morphine or digitalis or whatever could go un-detected. But if a five-million-dollar inheritance was in play and if the insurance company didn't have to pay for a victim of murder or if one family member suspected another, the ME might be asked to open a file and investigate.

The first step in getting away with a poisoning murder is to make it look like something else. Keep the ME completely out of the picture or at least give him an easy answer for the cause of death. If no murder is suspected, he'll take the path of least resistance, which is also the cheapest route. The ME must live with and justify his ever-declining budget. If he is wasteful, he'll be looking for a job. So give him a cheap and easy out.

The second step is to use a poison that is not readily detectable and will slip through most drug screens. Drug screens on both the living and the dead typically test for alcohol, narcotics, sedatives, marijuana, cocaine, amphet-amines, and aspirin. Some screen for a few other classes. Once a member of a class is identified, further testing to determine exactly which member of the class is present and in what amount will follow. These tests are more expensive and time consuming, but if the screen shows something it will be pursued. If not, to save money the death is attributed to something else and life goes on. Remember that a common cause of death in middle-aged folks is a cardiac arrhyth-mia without a heart attack. There are no autopsy findings in such deaths. A heart attack can be seen but not an arrhythmia since it is purely electrical.

That said, if a poison is suspected and if the funds and

interest to pursue it are present, virtually anything can be found in an intact corpse. Using gas chromatography in conjunction with either mass spectrometry (GS/MS) or infrared spectroscopy (GC/IR) will give a chemical fingerprint for any molecule. Because each molecule has its own structure and thus its own fingerprint, every compound can be distinguished from every other one.

For these reasons, poisons are still rich tools for the writer of crime fiction.

WHAT DRUG MIGHT WORSEN MY CHARACTER'S APHASIA?

Q I have a character who is slowly poisoning her mother. The mother is a stroke victim with Broca's aphasia. I would like the symptoms to be progressive and not make anyone suspicious. Is there anything I can use?

HO
Author of *The Accidental Sleuth,* an Emma Winberry Mystery
Homer Glen, Illinois
www.helenosterman.com

A Aphasia is a fascinating and complex neurologic disorder. It can be divided into two basic types: receptive and expressive. Receptive aphasia is an inability to comprehend visual or auditory information while expressive aphasia is an inability to communicate words or thoughts. Broca's aphasia is an expressive type. Both expressive and receptive aphasia come in many varieties.

In a receptive aphasia, the person might not be able to comprehend spoken words, written words, pictures, or objects. For example, if someone wrote down the word *watch,* the victim might not understand the word or be able to say it, yet he might be able to point to a watch or a picture of a watch. Or the person might say the word *watch,* and the victim might be able to point to it but not be able to write it or spell it. Or the person might point to a watch, and the victim might be able to write it down but be unable to say the word.

An expressive aphasia is the inability to say what the person wants to say. He usually knows the word in his head but is unable to speak it. This is very frustrating in that the words seem to be trapped within the victim's head but he can't get them out.

Not infrequently expressive and receptive aphasias occur together. In its severest form this is called global aphasia. As you would imagine, people with this disorder have a great deal of trouble communicating.

Aphasias have multiple causes, including strokes, trauma, infections, alcohol or drug abuse, psychiatric disorders such as schizophrenia, and Alzheimer's or any of the other types of dementia. The aphasia can be mild or severe, temporary or permanent.

Broca's aphasia is of the expressive variety. This is extremely frustrating for the persons suffering from it because they know what they want to say, but they just can't get it out. This leads to several unusual situations. Sometimes they repeat a word or phrase regardless of the question asked or the circumstances. I once had a patient who repeatedly used the phrase "that's good." It didn't matter what question I asked; this was her answer to everything. Though she knew exactly what she wanted to say, this was all she could get out.

Others develop words known as neologisms. Basically made-up words. Again, I once had a patient who could only say something that sounded like "loop-nert."

There are no drugs that would specifically cause or worsen true aphasia. There are, however, many types of drugs that interfere with overall brain function and by doing so could make your character's aphasia seem worse. These would primarily be medications that cause some degree of lethargy, confusion, or a reduction in mental processes. Small doses of narcotics such as codeine or morphine, tranquilizers such as diazepam or alprazolam, barbiturates such as phenobarbital, or any of the common SSRI drugs such as fluoxetine or paroxetine could cause a progressive alteration of mental function as each of these tends to interfere with cognitive abilities. The same can be said for many of the sleeping medications such as zolpidem or temazepam.

Continued use of these medications over many weeks or months can cause them to build up in the body and lead to altered brain function, particularly in the elderly and in someone who already has neurologic problems.

Your character could give her mother any one of these medications on a regular basis for several weeks and months, and there would be a gradual decline in her brain function, mainly in regards to her alertness, memory, and cognitive abilities. Each of these would in turn make her aphasia appear much worse. Since older people have a gradual decline in mental function anyway and it would be especially true in someone who had a disorder that caused aphasia, this decline would seem to be a normal process, and no one would be the wiser that the daughter was chemically making things worse.

CAN INJECTED ALCOHOL KILL AN ALREADY INTOXICATED PERSON?

Q In my screenplay, the main character attempts to kill an already intoxicated man by injecting alcohol into his vein. He is passed out so she has easy access. If she used something like Everclear with a very high alcohol content, would this be enough to cause alcohol poisoning and death? How likely would a coroner be to find an injection mark, especially if she injected discreetly in the foot or ankle?

Alison R. Mauldin
Author of *Missy,* a feature film
Charlotte, North Carolina
www.missymovie.com

A Yes. The level of intoxication and the lethal dose are determined by the blood alcohol level or concentration (BAC). Everclear, or grain alcohol, is 100% (200 proof) alcohol. Injecting it would rapidly attain lethal levels. It would take very little in someone who already had a high BAC from drinking. How much? Highly variable and would depend upon the size, weight, and general health of the victim as well as whether he was a chronic user or not. So just give him some alcohol and let him die, and the reader will assume whatever amount was given was enough.

A BAC of 0.08 is the legal intoxication limit, a level of 0.20 or above is serious intoxication, and a level over 0.40 is lethal. This varies from person to person, but these are the general levels.

A careful ME would easily find the puncture mark if he looked for it. He should but that isn't always the case. MEs are busy or sloppy or tired or underfunded or incompetent or corrupt, so there are many reasons why this could be overlooked. He might simply write off the death as an alcohol overdose and never search further.

CAN ALCOHOL AND NARCOTICS BE FOUND IN A CORPSE TWO DAYS AFTER DEATH?

Q If a body is found two days after drowning (cool but not cold water), would the autopsy show that the person had been drinking before death? If the drowned person had ingested a small amount of OxyContin before death, would traces of that show up too?

Judy Copek

A Yes, both alcohol and OxyContin would be found in the body.

At death, the heart stops, the blood no longer flows, and all metabolic processes cease. Therefore, the destruction of the alcohol and the narcotic by the liver would also cease. These drugs would remain mostly unchanged in the blood, urine, and tissues until the decay process destroyed them. Under the circumstances you describe, after only forty-eight hours the decay process in the corpse would not be very far along. This means that chemically the tissues would be unaltered.

OxyContin is a narcotic and would be found in all the tissues but primarily the blood and the liver. The level of this drug at the time of death could be determined since it would remain unaltered in these areas postmortem.

The alcohol can be a little trickier because it can be produced during the decay process in some corpses. It would not be likely in the scenario you describe since there would not be enough decay for this to take place. But even if it did, the medical examiner has a way around it. He can extract the vitreous fluid from the eye. This is the jellylike liquid inside the eyeball. The alcohol level in this fluid tends to lag approximately two hours behind the blood level. This means that at any given time the level of alcohol in the vitreous fluid reflects what the blood alcohol level was two hours earlier. The vitreous is not affected by the decay process early on and would definitely be intact after forty-eight hours in the cool water you describe.

So your medical examiner would have no problems determining the levels of OxyContin and alcohol in the blood at the time of death. Now, what would he do with these levels? Could he say the victim died from the drugs versus drowning? Could he say the victim had been murdered versus drowning accidentally?

Alcohol and OxyContin are a very dangerous combination. Their effects are additive in depressing the brain's respiratory center and leading to death from asphyxia. Often the level of either if present alone is not enough to cause death, but a moderate level of the two together could lead to death. Or at least contribute to it. The person could've been so intoxicated that he fell into the water and drowned.

Whether this death was an accident, a suicide, or a homicide, it would look the same to the ME, and he might have much difficulty distinguishing one manner of death from the other. All he would see is a victim with high levels of alcohol and OxyContin who drowned. If he found bruises on the arms or legs or on other parts of the body that suggested the victim had been struck or had been restrained in some way, this might point more toward a homicide.

If the levels of the two drugs were sufficient to cause death, then that is likely what happened. These levels will not continue to rise after death (except possibly alcohol if the decay process is far enough along), so if they are high enough to definitely cause death, then the individual was likely dead before he entered the water. On the other hand, if they are not quite that high but enough to intoxicate the individual, all bets are off. Again, a homicide, a suicide, and an accidental overdose and drowning would look identical at autopsy.

One of the most difficult things the ME must determine is whether someone died from drowning. It is often impossible. The simple fact that the lungs are full of water is of no help. A body left in the water for forty-eight hours would be expected to have its lungs fill with water. This is simply a passive process where the air seeps out and water seeps in.

What would the medical examiner look for to conclude that drowning occurred rather than a drug overdose? Victims who drown struggle for air and in the process inhale anything and everything—water, dirt and debris in the water, microscopic animal and plant materials. The finding of these deep within the lungs would not happen by a passive process, and therefore would indicate that the victim had been alive when he went in the water. In addition, the medical examiner would search for evidence that the victim struggled to get air. As the victim inhaled deeply and with great force and as water and debris were brought into the lungs and the coughing convulsions that always follow occurred, the tissues of the throat and airways would be damaged, and there would be evidence of trauma and bleeding within the lining of the nose, throat, airways, and lungs.

So you can see that just finding the drugs inside the victim does not tell the medical examiner the cause and manner of death. He must look at other things. The levels of the drugs inside the body would help him decide whether they were enough to be lethal or merely contributors to the death. Bruises and other elements of body trauma might lead him toward homicide since these would be less likely in accidents and suicides. Water-filled lungs would not be diagnostic for drowning, but the finding of all the other things I discussed would highly suggest that a drowning occurred. But it would not distinguish among an accident, a suicide, or a homicide. As I said, these appear identical at autopsy. Determining what actually happened often requires good police work.

CAN THE COMBINATION OF AMMONIA WITH CHLORINE BLEACH BE DEADLY?

Q I know the combination of bleach and ammonia has a detrimental effect on the lungs. If a bathtub was laced with ammonia, how long would it remain reactive to bleach? Once it dried would it still react? If someone was trapped in a small room with no windows and a closed door and bleach and ammonia were mixed, would it kill them? Would the corpse have any identifiable indications of the cause of death? How long would the smell linger?

Jacqueline Vick
Santa Clarita, California
www.jacquelinevick.com

A The chemical reaction that occurs when ammonia and bleach are combined releases chlorine gas. The amount released depends upon the amount and concentration of the ammonia and the bleach used. This is difficult to calculate without going through some sophisticated chemical equations, and for your story I would simply gloss over the amount. Either there is enough to cause trouble or there's not, and you can construct your plot to fit your needs.

Chlorine is a highly corrosive gas that reacts rapidly with tissues such as the skin, the eyes, the mouth and throat, and the lungs. It can cause a minor irritation, blistering and peeling of these tissues, or severe tissue destruction. It all depends on the concentration of the chlorine and the length of the exposure.

The major danger is damage to the airways and lungs, which creates a massive outpouring of fluids from the injured tissues. The lungs can literally fill with water, and the victim can essentially drown. How long this takes depends upon the size and general health of the individual, the concentration of the chlorine in the air, whether there is a fresh air source such as an open window, and the duration of the exposure. This is extremely variable, so write the scene for the result you want and the reader will go along. If you want the victim to die, let him die. If you want him to survive but suffer severe and permanent lung injury, that's also a possibility. If you want him to simply have skin, eye, and lung irritation that aggravates him for a few days but otherwise he is unharmed, that'll work too.

In your scenario the victim dies, which means the concentration and the duration of exposure were significant enough to cause severe lung damage that resulted in death. The body could have blistering of the skin and fluids collected in the mouth and throat. At autopsy the medical examiner would see that the lungs and the airways were severely inflamed and filled with water, which would most likely be frothy in nature and tinged slightly pinkish due to bleeding from the injured airways. He would have no trouble determining the victim had died from inhalation of some noxious gas. He might be able to test the chlorine level in these lung fluids and decide the gas was chlorine. Or not. It could go either way.

These two chemicals mix much more rapidly and violently when both are liquid. However, it is entirely possible that enough dried ammonia could be left in the bottom of the tub to cause a significant reaction, and this would be particularly true in a small closed room.

WHAT INJECTABLE SEDATIVE COULD MY SPECIAL FORCES TROOPS USE TO SUBDUE AN ENEMY?

Q I want my special forces group to use a knockout drug that would be injected into the arm of an individual through his clothing. This drug would act like Ultiva in that it quickly makes the person unconscious. The special forces are arresting a drug lord in a foreign country. Is there a drug that can do this, or should I create a fictitious one?

NF
Sterling, Virginia

A Ultiva (Remifentanil) would work but so would many injectable sedatives, narcotics, and anesthetics such as lorazepam, fentanyl, ketamine, morphine, and heroin. Any of these can work within a few seconds to a few minutes, depending upon the dose and the victim. The victim would become lethargic, sleepy, weak, off balance, and finally lose consciousness. These types of drugs all cause a depression of the respiratory center of the brain, so if too much is given the victim could stop breathing and die from asphyxia.

Another possibility is a fentanyl spray. It works instantly. This is what the Russians used to stop the Chechen terrorists who took over a theater full of people several years ago. The terrorists had wired themselves with bombs, but the drug worked so fast they weren't able to detonate them. That was the good news. The bad news was the drug was so powerful that many of the hostages died from asphyxia before medical help could get to them.

The treatment for such overdoses is to breathe for the victim until the drug wears off or until a narcotic antagonist such as Narcan (naloxone) can be injected. Narcan immediately reverses the effects of narcotics such as fentanyl, morphine, and heroin but not the other sedatives mentioned above.

WILL SNAKE VENOM INJECTED INTO FRUIT CAUSE DEATH?

Q I am writing a mystery set in ancient Egypt. Could snake venom injected into a piece of fruit such as a date or a fig cause death when the fruit is eaten? Would the venom be toxic enough to kill?

Claudia R. Dillaire
Author of *Egyptian Prosperity Magic*
Mesa, Arizona
http://claudiardillaire.blogspot.com

A This is very unlikely to happen. The toxins in snake venom are of two types. One is a group of enzymes that destroy tissues and do damage in the area of the bite. The second is a neurotoxin that travels through the bloodstream and causes neurological problems.

But both of these toxins are proteins, and proteins are rapidly destroyed by the acids in the stomach. This means that the toxins will be deactivated or destroyed long before they can be absorbed. These toxins only work when injected, usually by the snake's fangs.

If the amount of venom in the fruit was very high and if the victim had an open sore in his mouth or maybe a fresh tooth extraction, then it is possible, not likely but possible, that enough of the venom could enter the bloodstream through that defect to cause death.

Poisons found in ancient Egypt were arsenic, copper, antimony, lead, henbane, mandrake, hemlock, belladonna, strychnine, cyanide, and opium among a few others. Any of these could work if ingested.

COULD MY KILLER USE INGESTED VENOM AS A METHOD FOR MURDER, AND WOULD IT BE DIFFICULT TO DETECT?

Q My murderer collects venoms and uses them to kill sexual predators. He's a psychiatrist and prescribes medications for his victims. One victim is taking Antabuse. If the patient ingests enough venom to die, would the Antabuse alter the results of the postmortem lab tests? I'm hoping to delay the discovery of the actual cause of death because the lab tests are inconclusive.

KK

A Antabuse (disulfiram) is a form of aversion therapy and is used in the treatment of alcohol abuse. It blocks the oxidation (breakdown) of alcohol and some other compounds. A by-product is the production of acetaldehyde, which causes a host of very unpleasant and potentially deadly symptoms. These include headache, sweating, nausea, vomiting, shortness of breath, chest pain, dizziness, syncope (loss of consciousness), cardiac arrhythmias, seizures, and death. The symptoms can occur in any combination and in any severity. Pretty good aversion therapy.

At autopsy and with lab testing done by the toxicologist, the ME would find that the victim's blood was quite acidic and contained a high level of acetaldehyde. He would then find the Antabuse in the victim's blood and tissues. If he found these at autopsy, he might conclude that the victim drank alcohol and died from that. End of story. No further testing would be done.

The presence of Antabuse would have no effect on the toxicological testing for the venom. But why would the ME look for a venom? The answer is that he wouldn't unless he had a compelling reason. Toxicological testing is expensive, and he must live with what is typically a less than adequate budget.

So he would not even consider or look for a venom. Until your sleuth discovered more about the perp and pointed him in the right direction. This gives you as much time as you need to delay the discovery of the true cause of death. Then the blood and tissues obtained at the autopsy could be subjected to more extensive testing, and perhaps the toxin could be found. Maybe not but most likely it would be.

As for venom choice, snake venoms wouldn't work because they are proteins and are broken down by stomach acids. This means they must be injected, not ingested. But venoms from things like the puffer fish (tetrodotoxin) or certain species of shellfish (saxitoxin) would work quite well. Since your killer is a venom connoisseur, so to speak, he could have access to all sorts of exotic toxins.

IF MY KILLER USES ANTIFREEZE FOR MURDER, HOW MUCH WOULD HE NEED TO GIVE THE VICTIM?

Q How much antifreeze would someone have to drink before it would be likely to kill him? Would the ME be able to differentiate between brands of antifreeze, maybe in traces left in the victim's stomach, so the perpetrator could be tracked down?

Cat Waldron

Sarasota, Florida

A *Antifreeze* is a general term for many different types of engine coolants. The most common ingredient in these products is ethylene glycol, a toxic substance.

In toxicology, LD50 stands for lethal dose 50% or the dose that will kill 50% of people who take it. Most of the studies on ethylene glycol have been done in animals so the true LD50 in humans is not known. It is estimated to be 110 grams, roughly four ounces. This varies greatly from person to person, and alcoholics are notorious for being able to tolerate the consumption of antifreeze without killing themselves. Drunks are hard to kill. Ask any emergency room physician. So about four ounces could be lethal in your story.

If the coroner tested the stomach contents and found residual antifreeze, it is possible that he could send it to a specialized lab, perhaps the FBI lab or a sophisticated state lab, and have it tested for the other ingredients that are added to ethylene glycol to make antifreeze. Most antifreeze products contain at least 90% ethylene glycol, so it is the other 10% that would be of interest. Since different companies use various solvents, alcohols, coloring agents, and other chemicals in their products, it is conceivable that the manufacturer could be determined. This might be helpful in tracking down the killer.

DOES ETHYLENE GLYCOL MAKE AN EFFECTIVE POISON, AND WILL ALCOHOL NEGATE ITS EFFECTS?

Q I'm working on a story in which a group of people at a party are poisoned. I need a poison that has an antidote and its presence is masked by alcohol. My research shows that ethylene glycol has the characteristics I'm looking for, but I'm confused about the role alcohol plays. I understand that traces of the poison would be masked since ethanol lessens its effects. Is this true? Is it possible to lace someone's drink with this and still have it work, or would the ethanol in the beverages make it impossible to actually poison someone?

A Ethylene glycol is a colorless, odorless liquid with a slightly sweet taste and is a favorite of alcoholics. It is also a treacherous poison and more than one alcoholic has done himself in by drinking it.

It is found in antifreeze, hydraulic brake fluid, and automotive cooling systems. When ingested it is rapidly absorbed from the GI tract into the bloodstream. It reaches peak levels in the blood in one to four hours. About 100 cc's, or less than half a cup, is lethal in adults.

Ethylene glycol itself is not toxic, but in the body it is converted by alcohol dehydrogenase, the same enzyme that breaks down ethanol (drinking alcohol), into glycol-aldehyde and then into glycolate, glyoxylate, and oxylate. These breakdown products (also called metabolites) are the toxic compounds. They cause acidosis (an accumulation of acid in the body), and the oxalates bind with calcium in the bloodstream to produce compounds that damage the kidneys, liver, brain, and blood vessels.

In the first twelve hours the victim will appear intoxicated and develop nausea, vomiting, poor balance, a staggering gait, involuntary muscle jerks (called myoclonus), and then seizures and coma. The next twelve to twenty-four hours are marked by elevated blood pressure and heart rate, heart failure, pulmonary edema (lungs filled with water), and kidney failure. Death follows in short order.

The treatment of ethylene glycol poisoning is to empty the stomach by inducing vomiting or lavage (passing a tube into the stomach and washing the stomach with water). This stops further absorption of the poison.

Ethanol is sometimes given by intravenous drip. What is the rational for giving alcohol in this circumstance? Both the ethanol and the ethylene glycol are metabolized by the same enzyme, alcohol dehydrogenase. Since the toxic effects of ethylene glycol depend upon it being metabolized into its breakdown products, anything that slows this transformation is helpful. Ethanol will compete with the ethylene glycol for the enzyme. That is, if the enzyme is "tied up" with breaking down the ethanol, there is less available for breaking down the ethylene glycol into its toxic metabolites.

The seizures, heart failure, and pulmonary edema are treated by the usual medical techniques, and kidney failure often requires dialysis.

WAS ARSENIC TRACEABLE IN 1950s ENGLAND?

Q I'm writing a story set in England in the 1950s, and I'm using arsenic poisoning as a means of murder. Was arsenic traceable then? If so, what other poison would be untraceable in that era?

BS

A The detection of arsenic dates back to 1787 when Johann Daniel Metzger developed the arsenic mirror. He found that arsenous oxide when heated with charcoal would deposit a black mirrorlike substance on a cold plate. Then in 1806 Valentine Rose used nitric acid, potassium carbonate, and lime to detect arsenic in human tissues. In 1911 Dr. William Willcox developed a method to quantify the amount of arsenic within a corpse. He did this at the request of Scotland Yard to help solve the murder of Eliza Mary Barrow by Frederick Henry Seddon. Seddon poisoned Barrow to steal her money. Willcox's procedure was later refined to the point that arsenic could be found down to parts per million, making it a very sensitive test. So, yes, arsenic was detectable in the 1950s.

In the nineteenth century methods were developed to analyze opium, strychnine, morphine, quinine, atropine, caffeine, and many alkaloids.

Arsenic is rarely thought of as the cause of death. Why? Because the symptoms of arsenic poisoning are easily confused with gastrointestinal (GI) disease. This is true today and was even truer in the 1950s. The victim develops nausea, vomiting, weakness, abdominal pain, diarrhea (perhaps bloody), possibly seizures, coma, and death. The early symptoms could be from ulcer disease or diseases of the colon such as the various types of colitis. Even at autopsy, the changes seen in the GI tract might be confused with "real" disease, so the possibility of arsenic poisoning would not likely be considered unless there was a suspicious circumstance surrounding the death. This is why it has worked for many poisoners through many centuries. Also, toxicological testing was expensive and not widely available in the 1950s.

Even though arsenic could be found, it probably wouldn't be looked for, and you can use that fact. Your victim's death could easily be attributed to some GI disorder.

COULD ARSENIC BE USED BY MY VILLAIN TO SLOWLY POISON SOMEONE?

Q My story is set in 1815 England. A fifty-eight-year-old lady doesn't know that her nightly glass of milk contains a poison. I'm thinking about using arsenic, but will the taste or color be disguised by the milk, or will the milk neutralize the poison? Can arsenic be liquid, so it can pass as a tonic to the unsuspecting maid who prepares the lady's milk? The victim's niece is an herbalist, so something from her stores could be pilfered if that would work better. What daily dose could she survive for three months, or should I plan a shorter time frame? After three months the potential killer is discovered, but will my lady live and recover fully?

Diane M. Downer
Shallotte, North Carolina

A Arsenic will work well for your scenario. I should also point out that even though arsenic was first found in a human corpse in 1806 and recovered from stomach contents and urine in 1821, it wasn't until 1836 that a reliable test for it in a living person appeared. So in 1815 there was no test for arsenic in a living human, and therefore no one would be able to prove that your lady had been poisoned, at least not scientifically.

Arsenic poisoning can be acute and quickly deadly if a large dose is given and more slowly and prolonged if intermittent doses are given over weeks or months as in your lady. If your victim received frequent small doses, she would develop loss of appetite, weight loss, nausea, diarrhea, and perhaps mild numbness and tingling in her extremities. This could go on for many months, and her symptoms could wax and wane as the dose and administration frequency changed. Her symptoms would be written off as some gastrointestinal ailment as these were very common in 1815.

If the doses were a little larger or if she was more sensitive to it, then as the arsenic was given day by day and accumulated in her body, she would have all the above symptoms but they would tend to be worse. She might have severe nausea, vomiting, and diarrhea. The numbness and tingling in her extremities would progress to loss of strength and coordination. She could become slightly confused. She could die anytime.

In either case, if the arsenic was stopped, her symptoms would begin to resolve and she would gradually improve. It might take three weeks or so for her to return to normal.

If the doses were larger still, she could develop all the above symptoms to a much worse degree and they would come on more quickly. Maybe in five to ten days rather than three or four weeks. Her vomiting and diarrhea would be more severe and could be bloody and associated with severe abdominal cramping. She could become extremely disoriented and have such profound weakness in her extremities that she could not stand or walk. In this case, it could take two or three months for her to recover once the arsenic was stopped.

In these latter two scenarios, her doctors might think it

was an acute case of colitis or some other GI problem. They would not think of arsenic until your sleuth uncovered the damning evidence.

So you have many possible scenarios to choose from. She could become only mildly ill or deathly ill or anywhere in between. Her symptoms could be mild or severe and appear in a few days or several weeks. She could die in a few days, a few weeks, a few months, or not at all.

I wouldn't worry about the arsenic dose since it varies widely between people and the person giving her the toxin would be guessing how much to give anyway.

COULD MY SLEUTH SUSPECT THAT SOMEONE WAS PLANNING A POISONING SIMPLY BY SEEING WHAT HE PURCHASED IN A GROCERY STORE?

Q In my next *Monk* book, Monk is working as a cashier at a grocery store. He is ringing someone up and realizes the customer is planning to poison someone. Monk deduces this from the customer's seemingly innocuous purchases. I was thinking perhaps arsenic poisoning. What could Monk see that might raise his suspicions? Later medical tests of the intended victim would, in fact, show a buildup of arsenic in her system, indicating chronic poisoning. Perhaps the customer is buying ingredients for making a cake or cookies but also buys some item that contains arsenic? Or maybe antifreeze?

Lee Goldberg
Author of *The Walk* and *Mr. Monk on the Road*
Los Angeles, California
www.leegoldberg.com

A You could use either arsenic or ethylene glycol (antifreeze). Maybe he gathered the ingredients for making cupcakes with a buttercream frosting. Either premixed packages or the individual ingredients such as flour, sugar, butter, chocolate, and things like that. He might also purchase a jug of antifreeze or a box of rat poison. The beauty of ethylene glycol is that it is sweet to the taste, and if it was used to make the frosting, the victim would not know that it had been tampered with. Also, the frosting is not cooked, and therefore, the ethylene glycol would retain all of its potency.

If simply seeing this list of items isn't enough to arouse Monk's suspicions, he might ask the guy about the cupcakes he intends to make. Maybe say he really likes cupcakes. The guy could say they're for his wife who has been sick, and he's hoping she'll be able to eat them. Monk could then ask what's wrong with her. The guy's answer could give Monk the clue he needs.

Once Monk notified the police and they did their investigation, testing the victim for either ethylene glycol or arsenic would uncover the murder plot.

CAN LARGE DOSES OF ASPIRIN MAKE MY CHARACTER'S TINNITUS WORSE?

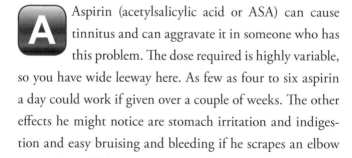

Q I have a character who suffers from tinnitus. My villain finds out and replaces the victim's nutritional supplements with megadoses of aspirin to aggravate the tinnitus to the point that the victim's work suffers and his colleagues note his distress. He begins to think he's losing his mind. His doctor is at a loss to explain his worsening symptoms, writes it off as stress, and prescribes Xanax. The sufferer is later thought to be the shooter in a suspected murder/suicide (which was in fact orchestrated by the bad guy).

Possible? How much aspirin would be needed, and would he suffer any other ill effects from it?

Dianne Emley
Best-selling author of the Detective Nan Vining thrillers
The Deepest Cut and *Love Kills*
Los Angeles, California
www.DianneEmley.com

A Aspirin (acetylsalicylic acid or ASA) can cause tinnitus and can aggravate it in someone who has this problem. The dose required is highly variable, so you have wide leeway here. As few as four to six aspirin a day could work if given over a couple of weeks. The other effects he might notice are stomach irritation and indigestion and easy bruising and bleeding if he scrapes an elbow or cuts himself shaving.

His doctor could dismiss the worsening of his symptoms

as stress but only after doing a neurological examination with a CT brain scan to rule out an acoustic (ear) nerve tumor and perhaps obtaining an ENT evaluation with an audiology exam. The CT would be normal, and the hearing test might show that he had some degree of hearing loss, which ASA can also cause. This is not an uncommon problem, and the doctor might diagnosis him with Ménière's disease. It causes hearing loss, tinnitus, and often vertigo, a feeling of being off balance or the room spinning at times.

If the victim told the MD that he did not take ASA, then the doctor would not suspect that ASA was the cause and would treat him for Ménière's with Dramamine or meclizine. The continued tinnitus could interfere with sleep, make him irritable, reduce his work performance, and definitely cause him stress. He could indeed become so frazzled that he might think he was going crazy.

CAN DEATH FROM CONSUMING BELLADONNA BERRIES BE CONFUSED WITH A HEART ATTACK?

Q My character doesn't realize a belladonna berry is among the variety of fruit on a dessert and eats two slices. How long will it take for him to die? Could it appear to be a heart attack or other unexplained death when his body is found, and would a routine autopsy reveal the reason?

Pat Remick
Award-winning mystery short story and nonfiction writer
Portsmouth, New Hampshire
www.PatRemick.com

A The alkaloid belladonna is found in a variety of plants, the most common being deadly night-shade. All parts of this plant are poisonous. What happens to your victim after ingesting the berries depends on the amount of the alkaloid in the berries, which varies from plant to plant, and the victim's individual response to the toxin. A smaller dose might make him ill, a larger one might kill him, and a still larger one might kill him quickly.

Your victim could become sick immediately and die within a few minutes, or he could have only mild symptoms, finish the meal, and be none the worse for wear. And anywhere in between. This wide variability gives you many options for constructing your plot. Since you want your character to die, simply have him consume the berries and die. There is no need to get any more technical than that.

The symptoms of belladonna poison are: dilated (widely open) pupils, blurred vision, dry mouth and eyes, skin flushing and redness, palpitations from an increased heart rate, shortness of breath, disorientation, hallucinations, seizures, coma, and death.

As we were taught in medical school, the signs of belladonna toxicity are:

> Dry as a bone
> Red as a beet
> Blind as a bat
> Mad as a hatter

The degree and rapidity with which these symptoms appear depend on the dose and the individual victim's response. The symptoms can come on in any combination and at almost any rate you want. The entire process from onset of symptoms to death could take five to fifteen minutes if a large dose was given and forty-five to sixty minutes if a smaller dose was given.

If your victim was simply found dead or if a witness said that he developed palpitations and shortness of breath and then collapsed and died, this would look very much like a heart attack. If his doctor agreed and signed the death certificate stating as much, that could be the end of it. The coroner would likely accept that and declare it a natural death.

However, if witnesses told the police and the coroner that the victim also exhibited dilated pupils, redness and flushing to his skin, and disorientation before collapsing, then the coroner would search for toxins, and belladonna would be near the top of the list because of the symptoms displayed by the victim. The coroner always uses police reports and witness statements to help guide him in his search for the cause and manner of death. This would be a situation where this was critical. Here toxicological testing would reveal the belladonna alkaloid in the victim's blood, tissues, and stomach contents, and the coroner would know that the victim had been poisoned.

WHAT CARDIAC MEDICATIONS CAN CAUSE DIZZINESS AND FAINTING?

Q I'm writing a crime story in which the killer wants the victim's death to be seen as natural or at least accidental, a result of taking too much of his pre-scribed medication and getting in an accident because of that.

Are there heart drugs (for blood pressure or some other condition) that have few or mild side effects when taken at normal dosage but cause dizziness and/or fainting when taken in quantity? What dosage would someone have to take to feel faint or dizzy, not to the point of actually passing out but just very wobbly or disoriented? Also, could the extra amount of these drugs be traced during autopsy?

A Your scenario is realistic and happens all too often even with no foul play involved. People, particu-larly the elderly, become confused regarding their medication and take too much, forget to take it, or take multiple medications together on an empty stomach, which causes a more rapid absorption and more powerful effect. Severe side effects can occur in each of these situations.

High blood pressure (HBP) medications would fit your needs perfectly. These meds are designed to lower the blood pressure. The type and amount required varies greatly from person to person.

The cardiovascular (CV) system (the heart and blood vessels) is a closed system. HBP is simply elevated pressure within this system. The best analogy is to consider a car tire. The simplest way to raise or lower the pressure within the tire is to add air or "bleed off" excess air. In HBP this "bleeding off" is accomplished with diuretics, which are meds that force salt and water from the body through the kidneys. Less salt and water, less pressure.

Another way to lower the pressure within the tire is to make the tire bigger. Of course, this is not possible, but if the tire expanded so that its internal volume was larger yet no more air was added, the pressure inside would drop. In HBP, this is accomplished by meds that dilate (open up) the arteries. This in effect increases the internal volume of the closed CV system, while the amount of blood remains the same, and thus the pressure falls.

There are several classes or groups of HBP meds available. For your scenario, the two classes that would work best are calcium channel blockers and beta-blockers. The calcium channel blockers primarily dilate the arteries, while beta-blockers lower the heart rate and lessen the strength of contraction of the heart. The net effect is that the right amount of these meds will bring HBP down to healthier levels, but too much can drop the pressure to dangerously low levels. This could lead to dizziness or syncope (loss of consciousness) or death if the dose is larger.

Common calcium channel blockers include nifedipine (typical doses would be 30, 60, or 90 mgs taken once a day) and verapamil hydrochloride (180 or 240 mgs once a day). Common beta-blockers include propranolol (10 to 80 mgs twice a day), atenolol (50 to 100 mgs twice a day), and metoprolol (50 to 200 mgs once a day).

Your killer could give the victim four or five times his usual dose, which would likely drop the victim's BP severely, cause dizziness or loss of consciousness, and result in an automobile accident. The onset of the drop in BP varies from med to med and from person to person. If you need an hour or two between administration of the med and the accident, give whole pills after a meal. If you need only ten to thirty minutes, crush the pills or empty the capsules and give with a small meal or drink. The absorption of the drug would be much faster, so the effects would appear more quickly and be more dramatic.

Would the ME find elevated levels of the med at autopsy? Yes, but only if he looked. Blood levels of HBP meds are not used to gauge treatment as are blood levels of some meds. The effectiveness of the treatment is determined by measuring the blood pressure. Since your victim is dead, no blood pressure could be evaluated (in dead folks it's 0 over 0), so no one would know that he had a very low blood pressure just before the accident. The ME might write off the death as a simple auto accident.

However, if the death was in any way suspicious, the ME might be more diligent in his search and might determine blood levels for the various meds the victim was taking. Why would he be suspicious? Maybe a witness saw the accident and said the victim was out of it or even unconscious right before the accident. Then the ME would consider a heart attack, stroke, cardiac arrhythmia, or low blood pressure. If the autopsy found no heart attack or stroke but revealed very high levels of the victim's prescribed HBP meds, his first thought still would not be homicide. He would think that the victim probably wasn't taking his meds correctly or took too many, and this caused his blood pressure to drop, which led to the accident.

COULD MY FIFTY-YEAR-OLD WOMAN WITH SEVERE CONGESTIVE HEART FAILURE BE MURDERED WITH HER PRESCRIBED MEDICATIONS?

 My character in her mid to late fifties is dying from severe congestive heart failure. Can she get up and walk? Would she be in a wheelchair? Could she also have angina? What medication would she take? Could either an overdose or a lack of digitalis or another of her meds cause her to die overnight? I want her death to pass as natural. If a medication could cause her death, could it be in the hot chocolate she takes at bedtime?

Carolyn Hart

If your victim had severe congestive heart failure (CHF), she would be compromised in her ability to perform activities. The level of this compromise is widely variable and can be almost anything you want it to be. Some people with severe CHF walk several miles every day, while others get short of breath walking to the bathroom. Some sleep comfortably at night, while others can't lie down without becoming severely short of breath and must sleep sitting in a lounge chair or propped up on several pillows. She could or could not have angina, depending upon what caused her CHF. If she had coronary artery disease (CAD) as the underlying cause, then she could easily have angina. If the cause was long-standing hypertension or what is called a cardiomyopathy, then she likely would not have angina.

Her medications would be numerous and could include digitalis, furosemide (a diuretic), potassium chloride, lisinopril (an ACE inhibitor), carvedilol (an alpha and beta-blocker), and others. Digitalis is particularly dangerous and can lead to toxicity and death either from a slightly increased dose each day over several weeks or a large single dose. Excess of this drug can cause deadly changes in the heart's rhythm. When given in excess over several days, furosemide can wash potassium out of the system and lead to deadly cardiac arrhythmias. In either of these situations, the victim would simply collapse and die. This would be especially true if the potassium that the person was supposed to be taking was withheld. Both lisinopril and carvedilol given in large doses would cause an immediate and severe drop in blood pressure and result in shock and death.

Any of these medications could easily be hidden in hot chocolate, soup, solid food, or almost anything else taken orally.

Since people with severe CHF are prone to such sudden deaths, the death of your character could be considered a natural event or accidental in someone who took their meds inappropriately.

IS THERE A DRUG THAT WILL QUICKLY INDUCE LABOR?

 Is there a drug that my character could slip into the OJ of a pregnant woman who is due to go into labor within a day or so? I need it to precipitate labor within a few hours.

Hallie Ephron
Award-winning author of *Never Tell a Lie* and *Come and Find Me*

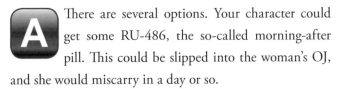 There are several options. Your character could get some RU-486, the so-called morning-after pill. This could be slipped into the woman's OJ, and she would miscarry in a day or so.

There are also several herbal alternatives. I'd suggest tansy (*Tanacetum vulgare*), also called bachelor's buttons. It's a fernlike plant with yellow flowers that grows throughout Europe and in the eastern and Pacific Northwest regions of the US. The leaves, flowers, stems, and seeds contain the toxic oil tenacetin, which is the active ingredient.

Tansy has been used as an herbal medicine for centuries and was apparently used in certain "witchcraft rituals" in the Middle Ages. Physicians and herbalists recommended it for the treatment of intestinal worms, gout, skin rashes, arthritis, sprains, and wounds; as a bitter stimulant and tonic; to relieve intestinal spasms and gas; and as an emmenagogue (to promote the onset of menses). It is this latter effect that made it an abortive and useful for the induction of labor.

Traditionally, tansy has been prepared as a powder by grinding the leaves, as an oil by pressing the leaves and collecting the extract, or as a tea by steeping the leaves in hot water. The roots were often mixed with sugar or honey for the treatment of gout.

The toxic symptoms of tansy ingestion begin an hour or more after intake. They include salivation, nausea, vomiting, dilated pupils, rapid pulse, abdominal cramping, vaginal bleeding, seizures, and death. These can occur in any degree and in any combination, depending upon the dose and the particular person's response to the drug.

Your character could drink some of the tea, or some of it could be added to the OJ, and an hour or two later develop nausea and abdominal cramping, with or without vomiting. She would then experience abdominal cramps as labor started. This would likely take two to three hours to appear, but the range is quite broad, so you can make it anywhere from two to eight hours as needed for your plot.

A similar tea can be made from pennyroyal (*Hedeoma pulegioides*), evening primrose (*Oenothera hookeri*), cotton root bark (*Gossypium hirsutum*), and angelica (*Angelica atropurpurea*).

COULD CAMPHOR CAUSE A MISCARRIAGE?

Q I'm writing a book that takes place in Iran during the 1979 revolution. One of the things I learned was that in the jails they would add camphor to the women's tea, so they would not get their periods. Saved money on sanitary napkins. Here's my question: If a woman was pregnant but drank that tea for a month or so, could the camphor cause a miscarriage?

Libby Fischer Hellmann
Author of *Set the Night on Fire* and *Doubleback*

A Yes, it could. Ingested camphor has been known to cause miscarriage for many centuries, and it could easily happen in the scenario you describe.

I don't see why it was used to prevent periods since in most cases it actually causes bleeding. I know they use it to treat bubonic plague, which is endemic there, but I've never heard of it preventing periods. It doesn't mean they didn't do it, though. Many of these herbal remedies are used for all sorts of things, often with no scientific basis. Camphor is frequently taken for headaches, the flu, cough, GI upset, and the list goes on.

COULD MY KIDNAPPER USE CHLOROFORM TO RENDER AND KEEP SOMEONE UNCONSCIOUS?

Q What are the immediate and residual effects of chloroform or ether if used to knock a person out during a kidnapping? How long would it take for each to work if applied with a saturated cloth or towel? How long would the person be out? Can he be kept unconscious indefinitely if he needed to be transported? How long would it take to rouse the person?

T. McCortney
Ohio

A Both chloroform and ether are inhaled anesthetics that are absorbed through the lungs. These types of agents have a very quick onset of action but also tend to dissipate quickly. With either, sleepiness and unconsciousness occurs after a minute or so. The victim will begin to arouse several minutes after the inhalation is stopped. If the soaked cloth is removed, the inhalation of anesthetic ceases, the body destroys what is within the bloodstream, and the victim starts to awaken. This may take ten to thirty minutes, depending upon initial concentration of the agent and duration of the exposure.

To keep someone out indefinitely, the cloth must be replaced each time the victim begins to arouse. This will take him back "down" again.

For your story a little of either on a cloth clamped over

the victim's face would produce loss of consciousness in about a minute. More could be added and the cloth could be removed and replaced as needed to keep the victim out, and when the cloth was finally removed, the victim would start to awaken after ten to twenty minutes and would be fully awake after about thirty minutes. Maybe a little groggy and with a mild headache and an unpleasant medicinal taste in his mouth but otherwise okay.

Two caveats. If the anesthetic is applied in too large a concentration and/or for too long, the victim can stop breathing and die. Also, the person applying the cloth will be breathing the fumes too and can become confused, sleepy, and even fall unconscious.

CAN MY KILLER USE CARBON MONOXIDE AS A MURDER WEAPON?

Q I am writing a short mystery story where a reporter believes that a student found in a car did not take his own life but was murdered by carbon monoxide inhalation. How would this work? How would the coroner distinguish between a suicide and a murder?

Julie Sparkuhl
San Juan Capistrano, California

A Carbon monoxide (CO) is extremely dangerous. Its treachery lies in its great affinity for hemoglobin, the O_2-carrying molecule within our red blood cells (RBCs). When inhaled, CO binds to hemoglobin producing carboxyhemoglobin. It does so three hundred times more readily than oxygen and thus displaces oxygen. In other words, if the hemoglobin is presented with both O_2 and CO, it is three hundred times more likely to combine with the CO. The result is the blood that leaves the lungs and heads toward the body is rich in CO (carboxyhemoglobin) and poor in O_2 (oxyhemoglobin), and this leads to death from asphyxia in short order.

This strong affinity of hemoglobin for CO means that very high blood levels of carboxyhemoglobin can occur by breathing air that contains only small amounts of CO. For example, breathing air with a CO level as low as 0.2% can lead to carboxyhemoglobin saturations greater than 60%

after thirty to forty-five minutes. So a faulty heater or smoldering fire that produces a small amount of CO becomes increasingly deadly with each passing minute.

This powerful attraction for hemoglobin explains how certain individuals succumb to CO poisoning in open areas. Most people believe that CO is only toxic if it is in an enclosed area, but this is simply not true. There have been cases of individuals dying while working on their car in a driveway. Typically the victim is found lying near the car's exhaust. Similarly, swimmers and water-skiers who loiter near a dive platform on the back of a powerboat whose engine is at idle can die from CO poisoning.

The degree of exposure to CO is typically measured by determining the percent of the hemoglobin that is carboxy-hemoglobin. The signs and symptoms of CO toxicity correlate with these levels. The normal level is 1 to 3% but may be as high as 7 to 10% in smokers. At levels of 10 to 20%, headaches and a poor ability to concentrate on complex tasks occur. Between 30 and 40%, headaches become severe and throbbing, and nausea, vomiting, faintness, and lethargy appear. Pulse and breathing rates will increase noticeably. Between 40 and 60%, the victim will become disoriented, weak, and will display extremely poor coordination. Above 60%, coma and death are likely. These are general ranges since the actual effect of rising CO levels varies from person to person.

Deaths from CO poisoning are usually suicidal or accidental. It is an unusual method for homicide, but it has been reported.

A running car engine in an enclosed garage is a common

means for suicide, but it could also be used for homicide. If the killer subdues the victim by force or intoxication, he could place the victim in his car and let the CO actually do him in. When determining the manner of death, the ME will look for evidence of trauma to the victim as well as perform a toxicology screen. Finding trauma such as evidence of a blow to the head might change the manner of death from suicide to homicide, but finding drugs might not. Some people use multiple suicide methods to ensure success, and a drug overdose combined with CO inhalation is not rare.

Carboxyhemoglobin is bright red in color and imparts this hue to the blood. When the ME performs an autopsy and sees bright cherry-red blood, he will suspect CO poisoning as the cause of death, though cyanide can cause a similar coloration. At autopsy the internal organs in victims of CO intoxication are also bright red. Interestingly, this color does not fade with embalming or when samples taken by the ME are fixed in formaldehyde as part of the preparation of microscopic slides. At times the presence of CO can be found in the blood as long as six months after death.

If the ME discovered elevated carboxyhemoglobin levels, he would know the victim was alive and breathing at the time of the CO exposure, but if he found a very low level he would conclude that the victim was dead before the exposure. If your villain killed the victim and then placed him in the car and attempted to make it look like a suicide, the ME would easily determine that wasn't the case. But if he sedated him and let the CO do the killing, the ME would have a more difficult time establishing the actual manner of death.

HOW COULD MY KILLER ENSURE A DEATH FROM CARBON MONOXIDE IN ANCIENT ROME?

Q My novel is set in ancient Rome, and I have a couple of questions concerning carbon monoxide asphyxia. I believe that a charcoal brazier produces carbon monoxide, which in an enclosed space could cause accidental asphyxia. It is reported that the emperor Julian nearly died of accidental asphyxiation from this while sleeping. Presumably most people didn't die, although charcoal braziers were commonly used in winter, so how could a murderer ensure that his victim died from carbon monoxide asphyxia? Is there some way to intensify the amount of carbon monoxide given off? What are the symptoms or physical signs of carbon monoxide poisoning?

Bruce Macbain
Author of *Roman Games*
www.brucemacbain.com

A The most common causes of carbon monoxide (CO) deaths in homes are smoldering fireplaces and faulty heaters where the wood or the gas is not completely converted to carbon dioxide (CO_2) but rather a considerable amount is converted to CO.

Your scenario is already fraught with danger because charcoal braziers are continuously emitting CO. The key for your killer is to lessen ventilation, so the CO more readily accumulates. Simply closing or covering windows and doors could ensure this.

How long would it take? There is no way to accurately determine that since it would depend on the amount of CO produced, the size of the room, the degree of residual ventilation, and the size, weight, and overall health of the victim. Anywhere from a couple of hours to overnight would be the ballpark, and of course this is a very broad range, which should give you great leeway in how you structure the plot.

The symptoms of CO poisoning are drowsiness and perhaps a headache. The victim will then go to sleep, lapse into a coma, and die from asphyxia.

CAN MY MURDEROUS GARDENER USE AUTUMN CROCUS TO KILL HIS VICTIMS?

Q I've read that the autumn crocus bulb can be deadly. Is this true? I want my victims killed by a badly maltreated gardener, but I want one to survive. If not, is there a plant poison that kills quickly in relatively small doses yet can be survived with treatment? What dosages would he have to use?

JL

A Autumn crocus (*Colchicum autumnale*) will work well for you. The toxin in this plant is the alkaloid colchicine. All parts of the plant are toxic, and the symptoms usually appear three to six hours after ingestion. The symptoms are nausea, vomiting, bloody diarrhea, abdominal pain, shortness of breath, low body temperature, shock, and death.

As far as dosing goes, it's impossible to say since each plant contains a different concentration of the colchicine and each person reacts differently. Besides, your villain wouldn't know how much to give, so he'd just add some to food or drink and see what happened.

Why would one person survive and another not? Luck is part of it. Also, one person might get a smaller dose of the toxin or might react less violently to it or might take it on a full stomach (as opposed to empty), which would slow the absorption and make it less toxic.

Treatment of the survivor would include an emetic to induce vomiting if he was awake and responsive and a large gastric tube to lavage (pump) the stomach if he was less responsive. Large amounts of IV fluids would be given to flush what was in the bloodstream through the kidneys. He would be kept warm, and drugs (vasopressors) to support the blood pressure (BP) would be given if his BP dropped to low levels. Common vasopressors would be epinephrine, dopamine, and dobutamine.

COULD MY KILLER MAKE HIS OWN CURARE AND THEN USE IT FOR MURDER?

Q In my story, the perpetrator injects his victims with curare and takes their picture as they die. I've been told this would take about twenty minutes. Correct? Where would a layperson find this poison, or could he make it himself?

Cynthia Hickey
Author of *Candy-Coated Secrets* and
Chocolate-Covered Crime
www.cynthiahickey.com

A Curare is a neuromuscular paralytic, which means that it paralyzes all the muscles of the body, including those used in breathing. The victim cannot move, blink, speak, or breathe and will die from asphyxia. The degree of paralysis and the speed of action depend upon the dose, the size of the person, any diseases the victim might have, and a few other factors. In general, the paralysis is complete and it occurs very quickly.

Curare is typically given by IV injection, and if so, it works in about thirty seconds. If given intramuscularly (IM), it would take a little longer—maybe three to five minutes. If your bad guy gives it IM, the victim would be active for a few minutes, then would gradually slip into complete paralysis, stop breathing, and die two to four minutes after that. This is a general timeline, so you can fudge it a bit either way. The victim would be awake and aware until he lapsed into a coma just prior to death.

Curare is available by prescription only or could be stolen from a hospital OR or ER or pharmacy or from a pharmaceutical supply house.

The plant can be ordered from some homeopathic medical suppliers. It could then be steeped in boiling or very hot water to make a curare tea, which could be evaporated to a thicker liquid, so only a very small amount would be needed. It could then be injected. Not pure, clean, or pharmaceutical but effective.

COULD MY ANCIENT EGYPTIAN MURDERER ADD CYANIDE TO THE VICTIM'S MAKEUP AND CAUSE DEATH?

Q I'm writing a murder mystery set in ancient Egypt during the reign of Thutmose III and the eighteenth dynasty. The victim is poisoned. I've read that the Egyptians could extract cyanide from peach stones and bay leaves. Could this be added to their kohl and cause death? I also found that antimony was sometimes used in their kohl. Is that right? What symptoms were they aware of that might indicate poisoning? Would they have been able to detect either of these?

A Egyptian kohl was the makeup many of them wore at that time. I found no reference to antimony being added, but it easily could have been. To make various colors they added several other potentially toxic substances: lead, iron, zinc, copper, and magnesium. If the makeup contained a significant amount and if the makeup was used frequently, these substances could lead to chronic poisoning. But this would take time and would be very unpredictable. It might or might not work for your killer.

Yes, they could extract cyanide, and this would definitely work if applied to the skin.

Cyanide is a metabolic poison that shuts down the ability of the body's cells to use oxygen. This process is immediate and profound and leads to death in a few minutes if a sufficient amount is used. If the dose is smaller, the victim could become ill but survive.

The symptoms of cyanide toxicity are shortness of breath, dizziness, flushing, nausea, vomiting, loss of consciousness, maybe seizure activity, and ultimately death. This can happen quickly, so the victim would develop sudden, severe shortness of breath, a flushed face, perhaps clutch at his chest, collapse to the floor, and die, with or without having a seizure in the process.

Antimony poisoning is similar to arsenic or lead poisoning. The major symptoms are nausea, vomiting, diarrhea (which can be bloody), abdominal pain, confusion, muscular weakness and loss of coordination, numbness and tingling of the arms and legs, seizures, coma, shock, and death.

Since cyanide and antimony worked the same way in ancient Egypt as they do today, the symptoms would be the same as described above. Your Egyptian killer, as well as the local physicians and priests, might be aware that these symptoms were due to a poisoning. Or not. They might think the victim was visited by a vengeful god or had a spell cast on him, both common explanations for disease at that time.

They had no method for finding any of these toxins in either the living or the dead. That wouldn't come for nearly three thousand five hundred years.

WILL A SEDATIVE ADDED TO COFFEE RENDER A GOOD-SIZED MAN UNCONSCIOUS?

Q I have a character who takes a prescription med to prevent panic attacks. I was thinking of either Ativan or Xanax. If she ground some up with coffee beans, brewed a pot, and fed it to a good-sized guy, could he become stuporous and then unconscious for six hours or more? About how many tablets would she have to use? I don't want him to require medical treatment or die.

Hallie Ephron

Award-winning author of *Never Tell a Lie* and *Come and Find Me*

A This could definitely work. Almost any sedative would do, but Ativan (lorazepam) is powerful in small doses. It comes as both an injectable liquid and in pill form. The pills are 0.5, 1.0, and 2.0 mg sizes. Since you simply want your character to have a very sound sleep for six hours, he would not need a large dose. I suggest 4 to 8 mgs. The actual dose needed is impossible to calculate since each person reacts differently, but this is a good ballpark range.

She could dissolve the crushed pills into the coffee or add them to the ground coffee before brewing it. He would begin to become sleepy around fifteen to thirty minutes after ingestion and then fall asleep. Very sound sleep. He might be arousable but would be somewhat confused and would easily go back to sleep. This dose could keep him out for the six hours you need.

WHAT INJECTABLE DRUG COULD MY WWII DOCTOR GIVE TO CAUSE A FAIRLY QUICK DEATH?

Q I am writing a story set in World War II France. A Nazi officer goes to a French doctor to be treated for syphilis, something he has been treated for before. Instead of giving him a shot of penicillin, I would like the doctor to inject him with something lethal that would give the doctor time to leave the scene before anyone, including the Nazi officer, becomes suspicious. Anywhere from a few minutes to a few hours would work so long as it is a sufficient amount of time for a second doctor to arrive, attempt to treat the Nazi officer, and have a conversation with the officer before he dies.

What would the first doctor inject, and what would the resulting symptoms be? The second doctor wouldn't suspect that his colleague had given the officer a lethal injection, so what sorts of diagnostic tests and treatments would he reasonably attempt? Finally, how much time would there be between the injection and the appearance of the symptoms and between the appearance of the symptoms and death?

Elaine Hargrove

Minneapolis, Minnesota

A The first point to make is that poisons don't have timers and can't be turned on and off at will. However, your brief timeline makes this essentially a moot point. There are three chemicals that were available during WWII that could work for you: opium, morphine, and cocaine. The first two are narcotics and would behave in a similar fashion. If any of these were injected intramuscularly (IM) rather than intravenously (IV), there would be a delay of several minutes prior to the onset of symptoms.

With either opium or morphine the victim would feel nothing for two or three minutes before becoming giddy, intoxicated, disoriented, and then he would experience shortness of breath and slip into a coma and die. The time required for this would depend upon the dose and reaction of the particular individual to the drug. This is highly variable, but I suggest that you have the onset of symptoms in approximately two minutes, have the symptoms progress over the next four or five minutes, and then have the individual stop breathing and die.

With cocaine the symptoms would again begin at approximately two minutes. Cocaine has amphetamine-like effects such as a warm flushed feeling, euphoria, palpitations, headache, chest pain, shortness of breath, perhaps seizures, then coma and death. These symptoms would follow a similar timeline to what is described above.

An overdose of any of these drugs would look like a heart attack or some other cardiac problem to the doctor. At that time there was no treatment for a heart attack or an overdose of cocaine or narcotics. In short, there is nothing he could do except watch. The victim would be able to talk for several minutes until he lapsed into a coma or suffered a cardiac arrest.

So you can inject any of these drugs intramuscularly, have the onset of symptoms in two or three minutes, have the progression of the symptoms over the next five minutes or so, and then have the person die.

WHAT DRUGS MIGHT MY BAD GUY USE TO WORSEN ANOTHER PERSON'S ALZHEIMER'S DISEASE?

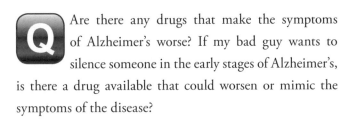 Are there any drugs that make the symptoms of Alzheimer's worse? If my bad guy wants to silence someone in the early stages of Alzheimer's, is there a drug available that could worsen or mimic the symptoms of the disease?

Harry Hunsicker

Former Executive Vice President of the Mystery Writers of America

Dallas, Texas

There are many drugs that can do this. Any narcotic (codeine, morphine, heroin), any sedative/tranquilizer (diazepam or alprazolam), any barbiturate (phenobarbital or secobarbital), or any sleeping pill (zolpidem or chloral hydrate) could alter his mental state in such a way that it would appear to be a worsening of his dementia. In larger doses, the victim would appear drunk or sleepy or uncoordinated, and these symptoms would be fairly obvious and might raise an eyebrow. But if smaller daily doses were given, he would become more forgetful and confused, and this would appear like a worsening of the disease process.

The same could be said for many of the psychotropic SSRIs (selective serotonin reuptake inhibitors) such as paroxetine or fluoxetine. They can alter the person's mental functions, so he becomes slower, lethargic, and disoriented. This is particularly true in someone who already has dementia.

Lastly, small doses of any of the so-called date rape drugs (ecstasy, GHB, Rohypnol, and ketamine) could confuse him too.

Each of these classes of drugs has psychotropic effects, and when given in small doses the symptoms can mimic progressive dementia.

WHAT DRUGS COULD BE SURREPTITIOUSLY GIVEN TO A DEPRESSED INDIVIDUAL THAT MIGHT LEAD TO HIS SUICIDE?

Q In my novel, a Wyoming game warden commits suicide with his service weapon. Although the death is no doubt a suicide, my protagonist cop suspects that someone encouraged the situation by secretly slipping the deceased certain drugs.

What kind of drug could be given without the victim realizing he was being drugged that would enhance his feelings of helplessness or depression and push him over the edge? It doesn't matter if the drug is readily available or not since one of the perpetrators is in the medical community. The drug needs to work in increments over a long period of time and not have obvious side effects that would tip off the victim that he was being targeted. If there is such a drug, would it be readily apparent to a forensic examiner as a catalyst for the suicide, or could it be realistically explained away?

C.J. Box
Edgar Award–winning author of *Cold Wind* and *Back of Beyond*
Cheyenne, Wyoming

A Great scenario. There are several possibilities. First, let's look at suicide and depression. Many depressed persons commit suicide every day, so it is a common occurrence. Those who are severely depressed often simply lack the energy to go through with a suicide.

After all there is much to plan. When, where, with what? Who will find the body? Are the person's affairs in order? All of this takes time, thought, and energy. Severely depressed people often just don't get around to it. But hand these same people a drug that gives them energy, and suddenly they can do the job. Sad but true.

Your perp could go with either uppers or downers to achieve his ends.

Sedatives and tranquilizers such as benzodiazepines (diazepam or alprazolam) and barbiturates (phenobarbital and secobarbital) are notorious for causing and worsening depression. A small amount of any of these added to the victim's food or drink once or twice or three times a day would cause him to feel sleepy and fatigued—both symptoms of depression. The dose could be adjusted according to how the victim reacted. Day by day the victim would become increasingly depressed. So these drugs not only mimic and worsen depression; they actually cause it.

Or your perpetrator could use uppers such as amphetamines or diet pills. These might create a sense of panic or restlessness or anxiety in your depressed victim. Again, these feelings are common in depression since anxiety is often part of the depression syndrome. With repeated use over several weeks, the user will become fatigued, lethargic, and depressed. And as I said above, these drugs could give him the energy needed to plan and complete the act.

The ME would find the uppers or downers at autopsy because they are part of almost any routine drug screen. He might or might not do the screen since the suicide was from a gunshot and the victim was known to be depressed. He should, however, since a thorough postmortem exam should include toxicology studies. Your ME could be thorough or lazy or corrupt as you need for your plot.

Even if he does find the drugs, depressed persons often use them with or without the knowledge of their family, friends, and physician. Finding them in his blood, urine, and stomach would not be alarming but rather almost expected. One of the problems with diagnosing depression is determining if it is caused or complicated by legal and illegal drugs. This must always be considered.

So your ME might or might not find the drugs, and he might or might not conclude that someone else gave them to the victim. Your hero cop will have to figure it out.

CAN ALCOHOL WITHDRAWAL BE DEADLY?

Q I've heard that alcoholics can die from alcohol withdrawal. Is this true? If so, what are some signs, and how would a person dying of alcohol withdrawal act? Could getting alcohol into his system save the person from the death caused by withdrawal?

Robin Connelly
Boise, Idaho
www.robinconnelly.com

A Yes, alcohol withdrawal syndrome can be deadly. This is usually called delirium tremens or DTs. The mortality can be as high as 30%. When someone enters a hospital with ongoing DTs, he is treated with sedatives such as chlorpromazine, haloperidol, or one of the other major tranquilizers. Chlorpromazine is usually injected, and haloperidol is either a pill or a liquid given by mouth. They both sedate the individual, so the signs and symptoms of the DTs are controlled. Sedation normally continues for several days, and then the tranquilizers are gradually withdrawn and the person wakes up and slowly becomes more coherent.

Alcohol by intravenous drip is often used to prevent DTs. Surgeons notoriously do this. If an individual needs an emergency surgical procedure such as an appendectomy, a gallbladder removal, or some surgery-related trauma and the person is a known alcoholic, the surgeon will look for signs of DTs approximately twenty-four to forty-eight hours after admission to the hospital, which is when alcohol withdrawal syndrome typically kicks in. If these signs appear, the surgeon will often institute an intravenous alcohol drip to prevent withdrawing until the surgical problem is healed. Then about a week after surgery the patient will be transferred to a medical ward, and the internist will wean him off the alcohol drip using the above tranquilizers as needed until the withdrawal process is completed.

The signs of alcohol withdrawal are agitation, aggression, confusion, and hallucinations such as pink elephants. The major complications of DTs include pneumonia, urinary tract infections, and seizures, any of which can be deadly. Seizures can also lead to vomiting with aspiration into the lungs, which would result in what we call aspiration pneumonia, another potentially deadly complication. Elevations in body temperature and blood pressure and changes in the cardiac rhythm all can be problematic during withdrawal.

WHAT LETHAL, SHORT-ACTING, HARD-TO-DETECT GAS COULD MY ANTAGONIST USE TO KILL A TRAIN CONDUCTOR?

Q In my story I need a lethal, short-acting, hard-to-detect gas. I discovered that the Russians used such a gas on some terrorists, but I couldn't find out what it was. Any idea? I need to rig it up to kill a train conductor when he engages the train's brake handle.

Barbara Seranella
Author of the Munch Mancini series
Sadly, my dear friend passed on January 21, 2007.
I miss you, Barb. —D.P. Lyle

A They used fentanyl and after a big stink finally admitted it. The scientific community did not know that there was either a gas or an aerosolized form of fentanyl, only a powder, a liquid for injection, and a transdermal analgesic patch. An aerosol is simply a liquid mixed with air or some other gas and sprayed. Fentanyl rapidly absorbs through the lining of the mouth and the lungs, so it acts immediately.

Your bad guy could employ a CO_2 cartridge like those that power everything from wine openers to pellet rifles. He could fill it with a little liquid fentanyl, pressurize it with the CO_2, and place it in a position by the brake handle, so when it was jammed forward a sharp projection would puncture the thin wall of the end. This would release an aerosol of fentanyl into the cabin. The engineer would almost immediately lose consciousness and die from asphyxia in two to four minutes. What happens to the train is up to you.

WHAT HALLUCINOGENIC DRUG COULD MY THIRTEENTH-CENTURY MURDERER USE TO CAUSE DEATH DUE TO CLUMSY OR RECKLESS BEHAVIOR?

Q My late thirteenth-century English murderer wants to give his victims a hallucinogen (preferably brought home from a crusade), which will not directly kill them but rather cause death by losing balance and/or hallucinating that one might be able to fly. The drug would preferably be drunk in wine, and if necessary, the flavor disguised by other spices. The effects should be felt an hour or more after ingestion, thus allowing the killer to be elsewhere. Opium and hashish were available at the time, but I couldn't find out if they had a long shelf life (survive many months of travel from Acre to England) or could be administered in the way described. Not even sure what these substances would look like if discovered by the sleuth. If these don't work, is there another drug of similar properties that would?

Priscilla Royal
Medieval mystery writer
www.priscillaroyal.com

A You are correct that both hashish and opium would work and they both have very long shelf lives. This is measured in years as long as they are kept in a dry place. They of course lose some of their potency over time, but after the few months that you describe it would be negligible. Hashish and opium were both transported around the world for centuries, and no one seemed to complain. So go with those if you want since they will absolutely work. The downside is that they have a distinctively bitter taste, but this could be at least partially masked with a spicy wine or food. They aren't true hallucinogenics but rather narcotics and as such could cause disorientation and poor balance, so a fall is a distinct possibility.

Other substances you might consider that were available in the thirteenth century would be henbane, belladonna, mandrake, psilocybin mushrooms, datura, and even rye bread or flour that had been infected with a fungus that produces one of the ergot alkaloids. This last scenario might have contributed to the famous Salem witch trials. This has never been proven, merely suggested. The rye fungus grows on the grain and makes ergot alkaloid that is a very powerful hallucinogen. Belladonna or the mushrooms might be your best bet as they each can cause powerful hallucinations. And someone under the influence of these drugs could do almost anything, including attempting to fly from the top of the castle.

WAS SOCRATES'S DEATH FROM HEMLOCK PEACEFUL OR PAINFUL?

 The death of Socrates seems awfully peaceful in the *Phaedo*. What are the real physical effects of drinking poisonous hemlock, and over what time frame do they occur?

NC

Hemlock (*Conium maculatum*) is known by many names, including deadly hemlock, poison parsley, and snake weed, while water hemlock (*Cicuta maculata*) is often called locoweed, cowbane, and beaver poison.

In either, the entire plant is toxic, and younger plants might be more so than those that are fully grown. Symptoms, which appear in twenty to sixty minutes, include stomach pain, nausea, vomiting, diarrhea, dilated pupils, frothing at the mouth, weak pulse, shortness of breath, muscular weakness, and convulsions. Paralysis of the muscles needed for respiration often occurs, and the victim usually dies from respiratory failure and asphyxia.

Death might not come for several hours, so this is neither a peaceful nor a pleasant way to die.

COULD SOMEONE DIE FROM INHALING
MERCURY-LACED CIGARETTES?

Q In the 1850s people used to try to steal gold amalgam (gold mixed with mercury) by hiding it in their cigarettes. They would smoke the cigarettes, flick the butts, which contained the amalgam, into the garbage, then collect the butts later from the trash. This scam ended when people died from mercury poisoning.

My questions are: How fast does someone die from inhaling mercury? What are the symptoms immediately before death? Are there any visible clues on the corpse that might indicate death from mercury poisoning?

Lee Goldberg
Author of *The Walk* and *Mr. Monk on the Road*
Los Angeles, California
www.leegoldberg.com

A Mercury is a heavy metal (not the rock band variety) and has similar effects to the other heavy metals lead, arsenic, and antimony. Mercury poisoning by indigestion or contact and indeed by inhalation, as in your scenario, can be an acute or chronic process. If your victim absorbed a large dose from the cigarettes, he could become ill in several hours or at least within a day or two. The symptoms would include nausea; abdominal pain; vomiting and diarrhea, which could be bloody; numbness, tingling, and weakness of the extremities; reddish rashes on the skin; and psychosis. There can also be excessive salivation, palpitations, and a pinkish flush to the cheeks, fingers, and toes. These symptoms can occur in any combination and in any degree of severity.

Inhaled mercury fumes more readily absorb into the blood than when it is ingested, so the symptoms would appear much more quickly. Perhaps within a couple of hours.

When inhaled, mercury can also cause what is known as metal fume fever. This is an inflammation of the lungs, much like pneumonia, that comes from the inhalation of the metal in the smoke. The symptoms are chest pain, shortness of breath, and cough, sometimes with the production of blood-streaked sputum. As a side note, these symptoms are also common with tuberculosis, which was prevalent in 1850.

If your victim repeatedly inhaled or handled smaller concentrations of mercury over weeks or months, the poisoning would be chronic rather than acute. Here the symptoms would come on much more slowly. He might initially experience nausea with vomiting and diarrhea, then a few days later develop skin rashes followed days or weeks later by neurological symptoms such as numbness and weakness in extremities, photophobia, headaches, confusion, and ultimately psychosis complete with delusions.

Would a physician—or at least a well-read person—in your story know the victim had been poisoned with mercury? Maybe, maybe not. The symptoms would suggest a poisoning, and mercury might be considered. Of course, they would not know how to prove that mercury poisoning was present since the first scientific studies of mercury poisoning were not undertaken until the 1920s. There was no treatment in 1850.

Another interesting fact is that the Mad Hatter in *Alice in Wonderland* is an example of mercury poisoning. In the eighteenth and nineteenth centuries, mercury poisoning among hat makers was common since mercury was used in the felting process. Mercury poisoning from hat making is still called mad hatter disease.

WHAT DRUG MIGHT KILL AN ELDERLY WOMAN SEVERAL HOURS AFTER ADMINISTRATION?

Q In my novel, six women have formed a friendship at a retirement village. One dies of natural causes, one goes with the suicide bit, and another OD's on her meds. I need to have two more expire before the reasons for all their deaths are discovered by the one remaining lady. Can a person without diabetes who is given a large dose of insulin die as quickly as if she did have diabetes? What drug could be administered in a hospital setting just before a patient is discharged that could then cause a cardiac death a few hours later?

Patricia Patterson
Atlanta, Georgia
www.patricia-patterson.com

A Insulin given IV in a large enough dose can kill anyone, diabetic or not. And it will do so very quickly. If your victim takes 100 units of insulin, she will lose consciousness in five to twenty seconds and could die in two to five minutes or at least suffer brain damage if she survived.

For your second scenario, the major problem is that drugs don't have timers. Some work quickly, some more slowly. Many drugs can cause cardiac arrhythmias and death, but they are unpredictable in this effect. Killers usually prefer predictability. Almost any drug will kill if enough is given, but very large doses typically work quickly, particularly if administered intravenously or intramuscularly. However, if given orally, several might work for your scenario.

Have your victim receive half a dozen to a dozen pills of quinidine, digitalis, or procainamide just prior to discharge. These cardiac meds would take a few hours to absorb into the bloodstream in sufficient amounts to be lethal, especially if taken just after a meal. The victim still might not die but easily could. As I said it is unpredictable.

One to four hours after ingestion of the pills, your victim might develop shortness of breath, palpitations, and dizziness followed by a sudden collapse and death. It would look like a heart attack but would actually be a cardiac arrhythmia generated by the drugs. The ME could find these if he looked for them, but he might not. He could simply write off the death as a cardiac event, as is common in the elderly, and be done with it. But since a death so soon after hospital discharge might appear at first to be a medical malpractice situation, the ME might do toxicological testing, and if so, he would find these drugs in the victim's blood and perhaps in the stomach contents.

HOW LONG WOULD KETAMINE BE DETECTABLE IN BLOOD OBTAINED AROUND THE TIME OF INTOXICATION?

Q I have a scenario for my next book where a character is attacked and injected with an unknown substance, probably ketamine. When she comes round, she finds herself next to a body but has no memory of what happened. I know from your book that ketamine hydrochloride produces sedation and amnesia, with possible hallucinogenic side effects, so what she thinks she remembers of the murder might or might not be real. How long would ketamine remain detectable in her system? Being medically minded, she took a sample of her own blood as soon as she woke, so would this still contain traces of the drug? If she placed the sample into a domestic fridge in a sealed glass jar, how long would it remain fresh enough to test? I want her to be able to prove after the event that she had been sedated and incapable of committing the crime for which she's being set up. I assume from reading *Forensics for Dummies* that the presence of ketamine could be confirmed by a combination of gas chromatography and mass spectroscopy.

Zoë Sharp
Author of the Charlotte "Charlie" Fox crime thriller series
Middle-of-Nowheresville, United Kingdom
www.ZoeSharp.com

Your scenario works quite well. The ketamine would remain in her system for at least a day if not longer. It could likely be found in the blood, urine, and other tissues such as the liver. Of course, liver and other tissues would require an autopsy, indicating that she didn't survive the event, which is not what you want. But ketamine should be obtainable from her blood and urine for at least twenty-four hours and perhaps longer. Remember, these blood levels aren't there one minute and gone the next. They gradually decline and the effects slowly wear off, so by the time she regained rationality and drew the blood, the drug would still be in her system.

For storage, she would simply have to place the blood or urine sample in the refrigerator, and it should remain usable for many days and perhaps even weeks or months. You are correct; the testing modality used would most likely be the combination of gas chromatography and mass spectroscopy (GC/MS).

It is also possible that for many weeks and even months later, the ketamine could be found in hair samples taken from her. But the blood obtained as she was coming out from the effects of the drug would be best.

WHAT PAINKILLER COULD BE USED FOR SURGERY ON BOARD A SHIP IN 1803?

Q What painkiller or anesthetic would be available to a midwife, the only nurse on board a ship in 1803, so she can stitch a very bad gash in the captain's arm? It happened during a storm, a tourniquet was applied, and she is the only person aboard with the skill to repair the wound. She doesn't want to hurt him (she's in love with him) but doesn't want to kill him with the anesthetic, either. Her teacher at the convent where she was trained has given her some laudanum for use only in the most dire cases. Could she use that and if not what?

Jackie Griffey
Cabot, Arkansas
www.jackiegriffey.com

A Surgery during that era was treacherous, not only because surgical techniques were extremely crude but because wound infection during this preantibiotic era was often deadly. At that time the major tool at the surgeon's disposal was speed. Fast surgeons were in huge demand since there was no general anesthetic available. Alcohol, opium, laudanum (which is tincture of opium), and restraints were about all that was available.

Your nurse could use alcohol or laudanum or a combination of the two to sedate the captain, and this would certainly help. The only real danger in using either of these or using them in combination is giving too much, which could lead to loss of consciousness and death from asphyxia. This is avoided by giving small, incremental doses until the desired level of sedation is achieved. Then she would need to work very fast. Regardless, he might still need to be held down during the procedure to prevent him from moving. He might also be given a stick or a piece of leather to bite down on.

She would likely use boiled or at least the freshest water she could find to clean the wound, then repair and dress it as best she could. It is interesting that some surgeons used salt or honey on the wounds because it was felt that they helped with healing, and indeed both have at least some antibacterial properties.

WHAT DEADLY DRUG MIGHT POINT TO A MEDICAL STUDENT AS THE POSSIBLE KILLER?

Q The victim in my story is a recovering heroin addict. She is having an affair with a premed student. When she becomes pregnant, he kills her and attempts to make it appear as if she accidentally overdosed. What could he use that would make the ME conclude not only that the death was no accident but that someone with ties to the medical profession killed her?

RW

A There are many possibilities, the best of which are general anesthetics and muscular paralytic agents. He could mix either with a dose of heroin, induce her to shoot up, and she would die in a few minutes. The initial drug screen would show the heroin, and after more complete drug testing was performed, the other drug might be found. Since these medications are not street drugs but rather hospital anesthetic agents used in surgery, the suspicion would fall on the premed boyfriend. The ME could also determine by DNA techniques that he was the unborn child's father and thus had a motive.

What drugs might he use?

Diprivan (propofol) is a general anesthetic agent, and like all such agents if given in large enough doses, particularly when combined with another sedative such as heroin, can lead to loss of consciousness, coma, cessation of breathing, and death from asphyxia. Mixed with heroin, a dose of 10 to 20 milligrams (mgs) would do the trick. Loss of consciousness would be immediate, and death would occur in a few minutes. This drug has been implicated in the death of Michael Jackson.

Norcuron (vecuronium bromide) is a muscular paralytic agent that almost immediately paralyzes all of the muscles, including those needed to breathe. Death follows from asphyxiation. A dose of 10 to 20 mgs could be added to the syringe with the heroin, and she would simply stop breathing and die. Identical effects would be seen with Anectine (succinyl choline). A dose of 20 to 40 mgs would be more than enough.

WHAT SUBSTANCE AVAILABLE IN 1579 COULD BE EMPLOYED FOR CHRONIC POISONING?

Q Part of my story takes place in 1579 in England. I need a slow-acting, chronic poison for one of my characters. The poisoner (a vampire) was born in the eleventh century, so I was hoping to find a poison from around that time. The victim is nineteen and a tad under-weight. I want the poisoner to give him a little each day (in food), probably increasing the dosage after a few days. I want the victim to get sick and near the end be bedridden, perhaps half-unconscious, and die a week or two later. The poisoner's brother (who has no idea that my character's being poisoned) brings a doctor to see the victim. I want the doctor to say he has some illness but not think of poison as the cause. I was going to use arsenic, but since that's rather cliché I want to try something that's beyond the usual poisons yet not too out there.

HD

A Any chronic, slow poisoning would work. A little each day and the victim would become ill, and when enough accumulated in the system, he would die. The initial symptoms would be mild, and they would progressively worsen as the poisoning continued. What symptoms the victim had would of course depend upon what poison was used. There were several commonly available at that time.

Arsenic was by far the most frequently used poison throughout the centuries. Chronic, slow poisoning causes nausea, vomiting, severe abdominal pain, bloody diarrhea, and numbness and tingling of the hands, feet, and face. Arsenic poisoning mimics other diseases, mainly gastrointestinal (GI) and neurological conditions. GI problems such as ulcers, colitis, gastritis, and any type of diarrheal disease can be confused with arsenic ingestion. Neurological problems such as strokes, dementia, and various neuropathies (diseases of the nerves that cause weakness, numbness, and tingling in the extremities) can also be confused with arsenic poisoning. A large dose of arsenic, which your villain could deliver at the time of the ultimate murder, would cause an acute poisoning that would have severe forms of all the above symptoms and ultimately would end with seizures, coma, and death. The timeline from ingestion of the final fatal dose until death could be four to twenty-four hours.

Deadly nightshade, also known as belladonna (*Atropa belladonna)*, could also do the job. All parts of the plant are toxic, but the leaves, berries, and roots are particularly so. Your villain could add both the berries and the leaves to a toxic salad.

Symptoms, which begin several hours after ingestion, include dilated (open) pupils, blurred vision, dry mouth and eyes, skin flushing and redness, palpitations from an increased heart rate, shortness of breath, disorientation, hallucinations, seizures, coma, and death. Small daily doses could be delivered in food by your villain, and this could cause shortness of breath, fatigue, and heart palpitations.

These symptoms could mimic a cardiac condition. Then a larger dose could be given at the end. All the above symptoms would occur and would be followed by death.

Lily of the valley (*Convallaria majalias*) is another option. All parts of the plant are toxic, especially the leaves. Water in which the cut flowers have been kept is toxic, but a tea made by boiling the leaves would certainly contain even more of the toxin and would be a more effective poison.

The toxin in lily of the valley is called convallatoxin. It is a glycoside in the same family as digitalis, which comes from the foxglove (*Digitalis purpurea* or *D. lanata*). Symptoms onset almost immediately and include nausea, vomiting, shortness of breath, palpitations, abdominal pain, flushing, hot flashes, dilated pupils, a red skin rash, excessive salivation, and finally coma and death. The glycosides can cause deadly alterations in cardiac rhythm, which can lead to sudden collapse and death. Your villain could give a little tea each day, and the victim would become progressively ill. His complaints of shortness of breath and palpitations could suggest a cardiac problem. When he died of the final arrhythmia, no one would be the wiser.

Cantharidin (*Cantharis vesicatoria*), also called Spanish fly, is a tasteless white powder that can be easily secreted in food or drink. Symptoms appear immediately after ingestion. Cantharsis irritates every tissue it contacts, and when it is filtered from the bloodstream by the kidneys, it causes irritation of the urinary tract and thus was felt to be an aphrodisiac. In larger doses it can cause acute burning and blistering of the gastrointestinal and urinary tracts and lead to abdominal pain, nausea, vomiting of blood, bloody diarrhea, painful and bloody urination, convulsions, a rapid pulse, a drop in blood pressure, shock, and death. Such a death could be confused with death from some GI illness.

WHAT POISON WAS AVAILABLE TO MY KILLER IN THE LATE NINETEENTH CENTURY?

Q I'm writing my first mystery. It's set in the late nineteenth century. Other than arsenic, what common household product could be used as a poison? What are its effects and could it be detected?

SC
Minneapolis, Minnesota

A Besides arsenic, there were several poisons available at the time, including opium, digitalis (foxglove), cocaine, deadly nightshade (belladonna), cyanide, and a few others. Many of these were readily available, particularly opium.

Opium was used for everything from headaches to anxiety and was a common ingredient in patent medicines. Opium would make the victim drowsy, confused, and then sleepy. The victim would fall asleep, lapse into a coma, stop breathing, and die from asphyxia.

Digitalis would give the individual heart palpitations, shortness of breath followed by a loss of consciousness and death from a cardiac arrhythmia.

Cocaine could cause the victim to become extremely agitated, sweaty, and lead to hallucinations, disorientation, headaches, shortness of breath, palpitations, and again the victim would collapse and die from a cardiac arrhythmia.

Deadly nightshade could cause dilated pupils, blurred

vision, headaches, loss of balance, palpitations, shortness of breath, confusion, hallucinations, and seizures. Here again the victim would ultimately collapse and die from a cardiac arrhythmia.

Cyanide works very quickly. The victim would immediately experience shortness of breath and chest pain and would collapse and die.

In the 1890s there was essentially no forensic toxicology available. The only test that was uniformly done was for arsenic, and you stated that you do not want to use it. Therefore, the only way to determine that a poison was likely involved in the victim's death would be from witness statements that revealed what symptoms the victim experienced prior to death. An astute physician might be able to determine the type of poison used if the victim displayed the symptoms described above. Otherwise it could remain a mystery, and the murder might never be solved.

CAN PROPRANOLOL BE USED AS A POISON?

Q I have two women who want to kill one of their husbands. They decide to grind up some propanalol, which one of them uses for stage fright, and mix it in Indian food to cover up the taste. How would the victim actually die? Does his heart stop? Is there any vomiting or anything like that? What would an autopsy and toxicological testing show? Could it look like a heart attack or some other natural death and avoid toxicological testing?

Laura Caldwell
Author of *Long Way Home* and *a Claim of Innocence*
Chicago, Illinois
www.lauracaldwell.com

A Propranolol is a beta-blocker, which means that it blocks the effects of adrenaline on the cardiovascular system. It lowers blood pressure (BP) and heart rate, which are desired effects when treating hypertension and certain cardiac arrhythmias. It is also used for stage fright and certain other anxiety syndromes. A large dose can cause the BP and heart rate to drop dramatically, and the victim can slip into shock and die. The first symptoms would be weakness, fatigue, shortness of breath, and dizziness followed by loss of consciousness and death.

The symptoms would start anywhere from twenty minutes to an hour after ingestion, depending on factors such as the exact dose, the size of the victim, how much food was consumed along with it, and the victim's general health. These symptoms would then progress to coma and death over the next thirty minutes to a couple of hours. This is highly variable, so have the symptoms begin and progress as you need as long as you stay within these broad parameters.

The death might indeed be declared a heart attack or a cardiac arrhythmia. An autopsy would show no heart attack, but a cardiac arrhythmia leaves behind no autopsy evidence. The ME would make a best guess. Propranolol would not appear on most routine toxicological screens, so the ME would have to look for it specifically. He would do that only if some evidence came forward that drugs might have been involved in the man's death. Otherwise it is too expensive to simply test for it and see what turns up.

WHAT ARE THE SYMPTOMS OF RICIN POISONING?

 What are the symptoms of ricin poisoning? Are they similar to heart attack or stroke? What would an autopsy reveal?

Susan S. Lara
Philippines

Ricin is a deadly toxin that is derived from the castor bean. It is a cellular toxin in that it blocks the ability of the body's cells to manufacture certain proteins, and this leads to cellular death.

It can enter the body through ingestion, inhalation, or injection. Symptoms begin in a few hours, and death can follow in twenty-four to seventy-two hours. The symptoms come on more quickly with inhalation and with injection (as soon as two to four hours) than they do with ingestion. A smaller dose might simply make the victim ill for many weeks or months, but a large enough dose is almost uniformly fatal.

The symptoms depend upon the route of entry. If ingested, it causes nausea, vomiting, abdominal pain, bloody diarrhea, shock, coma, and death. If inhaled, shortness of breath, cough, fever, chest pain, shock, coma, and death follow. The victim's lungs are damaged and fill with water, a condition called pulmonary edema. With injection the victim might suffer nausea, vomiting, fever, chills, seizures, shock, coma, and death.

Since a heart attack is often manifested by chest pain, shortness of breath, and pulmonary edema, ricin inhalation could be confused with this. Of course, evaluation in a hospital or at autopsy would reveal that the heart wasn't the culprit and that something else caused the symptoms and pulmonary edema. A search for toxins would then be undertaken, but ricin might or might not be uncovered. There is no simple test for ricin, and it might be difficult to find with toxicological testing.

There is no treatment for ricin exposure other than giving general supportive care such as intravenous fluids, oxygen, and the use of a ventilator if the victim's lung problems become severe.

IS THERE A DRUG THAT MIMICS SCHIZOPHRENIA?

Q I have a guy I need to murder a senator. He's thought to be a schizophrenic who went off his meds, and therefore, the murder was just one of those things. But further investigation will show that his schizophrenia was induced by medications given by the bad guys who are setting him up to kill the senator.

In my research I found that symptoms of hypothyroidism or hyperthyroidism can mimic schizophrenia. Could my guy have been given drugs to mess with his thyroid and cause symptoms of schizophrenia? Or is there a better cocktail of drugs that on an initial drug test would possibly be overlooked as innocuous as far as his current schizoid tendencies are concerned?

Robin Burcell
Award-winning author of *The Bone Chamber*
www.robinburcell.com

A Both hypothyroidism (low) and hyperthyroidism (high) can cause psychiatric problems, but these are rare and unpredictable. This means that even if your bad guy gave the victim thyroid or antithyroid meds, he couldn't be sure that the effect would be as he wanted. In fact, it probably wouldn't be. But phencyclidine (PCP or angel dust) could work for you. I'm sure in your career as a police officer you've seen these users. Dangerous and explosive. PCP was actually used to simulate acute paranoid schizophrenia in some very old studies. So this would have the desired effect and would make your guy very dangerous.

Your bad guys could slip him small doses over a few days or weeks. As the drug accumulated, he would begin to behave in a bizarre fashion and could easily be considered schizophrenic. This might also be accomplished by a single larger dose, depending on your plot needs.

He might then be told that the victim was out to get him or was going to kill him thus stoking his drug-induced paranoia. When he killed the senator, it would be self-defense. To him anyway.

PCP shows up in some routine drug screens but not in others. If not, it could be found later in stored blood samples taken from the killer at the time of his arrest after your hero figures out that things are not as they seem.

WHAT DRUG AVAILABLE IN 1977 COULD BE USED TO SEDATE A TEN-YEAR-OLD CHILD?

Q It's 1977. A doctor wants to drug his ten-year-old daughter, so she'll sleep through a not so pleasant experience and not recall it. What drug would he use, and how would a cop refer to it?

P.J. Parrish
Shamus, Thriller, Anthony award–winning author
and Edgar nominee
Fort Lauderdale, Florida, and Petoskey, Michigan

A There were two commonly used medications in the 1950s through the 1970s for sedating children: chloral hydrate and paregoric. Paregoric is tincture of opium, so it is a narcotic sedative. Chloral hydrate was mixed into alcoholic drinks for the original Mickey Finn or Mickey as it was called. Both are powerful sedatives and work very well in children. Both are liquids so are easily given, and the recommended dose used to be listed on the bottle according to the child's age.

A small amount of either could make your young lady sleepy and lethargic and interfere with or at least cloud her memory.

IN 1962 COULD THE CORONER DISTINGUISH DEATH FROM AN AUTO ACCIDENT FROM ONE CAUSED BY SUCCINYLCHOLINE?

Q If my victim is given a lethal dose of succinylcholine and his car is then pushed off a cliff or into a river, could the coroner determine the true cause of death? I assume any injuries to the body would clearly be recognized at the postmortem examination. Since succinylcholine would have been undetectable then, what would the coroner assume was the cause of death?

Lee Goldberg
Author of *The Walk* and *Mr. Monk on the Road*
Los Angeles, California
www.leegoldberg.com

A If the victim was dead before being pushed off the cliff, any injuries sustained would not bleed or bruise. Broken bones would show little if any bleeding along the fracture lines. The coroner would then know that the victim was dead at the time of the so-called accident. As you pointed out, there was no test for succinylcholine (Sux) at that time, and even today testing for it is controversial, so the coroner would not be able to determine that Sux was involved in the death.

If the victim was alive at the time of impact, his injuries would bleed, including any fractured bones. The body would be bruised. If the injuries were severe enough to have caused death, then the coroner might determine the death an accident.

But it's not quite that simple. Remember that the victim would live for several minutes after the Sux was given. Death only follows after the victim suffocates from being unable to breathe and the heart stops, and this can take several minutes. In the scenario you describe, the Sux could be given and the car could be immediately pushed off the cliff. The victim would be alive but paralyzed, and the impact injuries would be premortem since the heart would still be beating. The coroner would assume the injuries and the death were from the crash and never suspect that the victim had been paralyzed before the impact.

In a river a living and active victim might drown, and the coroner might be able to determine this as the cause of death. A dead body would not drown and neither would a live but paralyzed one. If the victim is not breathing due to death or paralysis of the breathing muscles, there would be no water deep in the lungs or any of the other signs of drowning. The coroner could likely conclude that the victim had not drowned and would consider all of the above mentioned factors in determining the likely cause of death.

WHAT HOUSEHOLD SUBSTANCES COULD A WOMAN INJECT AS A METHOD FOR SUICIDE?

 A female character injects herself with something deadly. Something found in the house. Her death is immediate. What substance could she have used? Ammonia? Antifreeze?

Matt Witten
Writer, producer
Los Angeles, California

If given intravenously (IV), ammonia could be lethal very quickly. It would burn severely as it traveled up the vein. Antifreeze might do the job, but it would be less deadly than ammonia. Chlorine bleach would work and would also be painful.

Another option is hydrogen peroxide, which would burn much less. It is found in most households. When given IV, it would foam within the bloodstream just as it does when you pour it on a wound. This would create a collection of gas in the right ventricle, and the heart would stop. Think vapor lock. At autopsy the ME would find the gas in the ventricle and know she was injected with either air or a gas-producing substance such as hydrogen peroxide. It could also be seen on a chest X-ray, which could be done as part of the autopsy. There would be a mass of air bubbles visible in the heart area.

Air could work too. Not a small bubble. That's a myth. Small bubbles are filtered by the lungs and are harmless. It takes about 200 cc's (about a cup) or more. If that amount is given, the air mass collects in the right ventricle and stops the heart.

Of course, morphine, heroin, or insulin would be immediately lethal if she had access to any of these.

HOW DO HALLUCINOGENIC DRUGS AFFECT A BLIND PERSON?

Q I have a story idea that involves a blind man imbibing hallucinogenic mushrooms. Is there any research available that would shed light on how a blind person would respond to a hallucinogenic substance?

Brian Roemer
North Carolina

A Mushrooms, LSD, PCP, and other hallucinogens affect the blind as they would anyone else. That is, the psychological and physiological effects would be the same. The difference might come in the person's perceptions, particularly visual distortions and hallucinations. Since the blind do not see, they would likely respond differently in this regard. I suspect it would be similar to how the blind dream because dreams are often visual in nature.

Blind individuals can be considered in two broad categories. Congenitally blind persons are sightless from birth, while adventitiously blind persons lose their sight at a later time. Children who are blinded before age five or so tend to have much in common with those who are congenitally blind. Since their blindness onsets at such an early age, they possess little memory of images and colors and thus are less able to "see" things as compared to those who became blind after age seven. This lack of imagery spills over into their dreams.

Many researchers in this area consider dreaming a

constructive cognitive process. That is, we base our dream worlds upon our sensory experiences. What we see, hear, feel, smell, and taste contribute to the building of our dreams.

Most congenitally blind people are able to see spatial relationships in their dreams, and some can even create visual forms, but they do not see the actual objects. What they see in their dreams tends to parallel what they see in their waking lives. Some are able to construct at least amorphous images better than others. Those who become blind later in life tend to have dream visualizations that parallel their waking visual experiences before they became blind.

The congenitally blind and those who become adventitiously blind before age five may have vivid and detailed dreams, but they do not see images of people or structures or objects. They tend to feel the same emotions and have similar reactions to nightmares, but their dreams are more amorphous.

Those who become blind between ages five and seven may or may not see images. It's individual.

Interestingly, many people who become blind after age seven may have visually detailed dreams forever, while others may do so for only twenty to thirty years. It is as if their memories of images fade, and thus the images also fade from their dreams.

Your character would not see images but could still have very emotional dreams and frightening nightmares. He would describe his dream experiences in terms of feelings and sounds and smells, which can be even more frightening than visions, but the images he would see would be vague and poorly defined. As with all of us, what he experiences will reflect the things that occur in his waking life. His problems, fears, wants, interests, conflicts, preoccupations, attitudes, and fantasies will play out in his dream world.

So depending upon the type and duration of your character's blindness, he could have concrete visual hallucinations or ones of a more amorphous nature. He may also have hallucinations richer in or exclusively auditory (sound), olfactory (smell), or sensory (feeling). He might hear sounds or music or voices. He might smell pleasant or foul odors or odors from his past. He might sense pleasant, painful, or annoying sensations—itchy, crawly, warm, cold, etc.

IN THE 1920S WOULD A PHYSICIAN GIVE STRYCHNINE TO TREAT POISONING FROM GREEN POTATO SKINS?

Q What would be the effect if someone was feeding my victim just enough green potato peel to give him gastrointestinal trouble (to keep him out of action), and the doctor prescribed nux vomica. Would it help? Would there be side effects from the combination? Might the doctor (1920s), unable to find any specific cause of the attacks, suspect arsenic poisoning, or would he be more likely to write it off as a delicate digestive system?

Carola Dunn
Author of *A Colourful Death*
http://CarolaDunn.weebly.com

A Potato skins turn green when stored improperly due to the accumulation of an alkaloid chemical called solanine, which is similar to the alkaloid found in deadly nightshade. Even small quantities can be toxic. When consumed, the predominant symptoms are gastrointestinal and neurological: nausea, vomiting, diarrhea, abdominal cramps, burning in the mouth and throat, headaches, dizziness, palpitations due to cardiac arrhythmias, weakness, numbness, paralysis, hypothermia, and dilated pupils. These symptoms can begin anywhere from thirty minutes to twelve hours after ingestion and can be mistaken for gastrointestinal disorders, particularly during the 1920s. Treatment at that time would be simply to avoid eating any more of the product and allowing the body time to get rid of the toxin.

These symptoms are also consistent with arsenic poisoning. Your physician would most likely assume that the victim had a gastrointestinal problem such as colitis or gastroenteritis and treat him accordingly, perhaps with tincture of opium to settle the abdominal cramps and control the diarrhea. If the patient did not improve, he would consider other possibilities, and one of these could indeed be chronic arsenic poisoning.

Nux vomica might also be used in the treatment program. It not only wouldn't help but would rather aggravate things. Nux vomica contains two other alkaloids: brucine and strychnine. Strychnine is deadly in very small doses, so using this in a situation where green potato skins had been consumed would only increase your poor victim's problems. Still, it was used, and your doctor could employ it as part of the treatment. I would not expect your patient to do well if he added this toxic alkaloid to the mix.

PART III
THE POLICE,
THE CRIME SCENE,
AND THE CRIME LAB

Q I have been trying to find information on the history of forensics for my story set in the West in the late 1800s but have come up empty. I have not been able to find any books that cover forensics or crime solving earlier than the 1930s or so. Were there any tools available in the late 1800s?

P. Williams

A The reason you've had trouble finding any forensic tools before the 1900s is that there were very few. Forensics is a modern science. There are a few exceptions, though.

Toxicology: Arsenic has been a common poison for centuries, but throughout most of its nefarious history there was no way to prove that it was the culprit in a suspicious death. In 1775 Swedish chemist Carl Wilhelm Scheele showed that chlorine water would convert arsenic to arsenous acid. If he then added metallic zinc and heated the acid mixture, arsine gas would be released. When this gas contacted a cold vessel, arsenic would collect on its surface. In 1821 Sevillas used this technique to find arsenic in the stomach and urine of poisoned individuals, and the field of forensic toxicology was born. It progressed slowly from there, however.

Fingerprints: Mark Twain understood the discriminatory power of fingerprints and used the technique in his books *Life on the Mississippi* and *The Tragedy of Pudd'nhead Wilson*. In *Life on the Mississippi*, a thumbprint is used to identify a murderer, and in *The Tragedy of Pudd'nhead Wilson*, a fingerprint pops up in a court trial. These predated the groundbreaking work on fingerprints by Sir Francis Galton, who received his knighthood due to his "discovery" of the value of fingerprints.

Juan Vucetich, a police official in La Plata, Argentina, became convinced that fingerprints could be used to identify criminals and devised a classification system. He finally published a book on the subject in 1904. His classification system is still in use in most of South America.

In 1892 Argentina became the first country to use

fingerprints to solve a crime. On June 18, 1892, the children of Francisca Rojas were murdered, and she accused a man named Velasquez. Alvarez, a police investigator who trained under Juan Vucetich, discovered that Rojas had a lover who had previously stated that he would marry her if she did not have children. A bloody fingerprint found at the scene matched Rojas's right thumb, and she confessed.

Ballistics (actually firearm examination): In a book authored by Harold Peterson, the rifling of firearms by Emperor Maximilian of Germany between 1493 and 1508 was discussed, making it one of the earliest references on this subject. The recognition that this rifling could be used to match a fired projectile to the firearm that fired it didn't occur until late in the nineteenth century. It wasn't until early in the twentieth century that Calvin Goddard perfected a system for comparing bullets under a comparison microscope to determine if they came from the same weapon. This technique remains in use today.

So you can see that it wasn't until the late 1900s that any real forensic science appeared and most techniques arose in the twentieth century. Since each of the above existed or could have existed in the time frame of your story, your sleuth could employ any or all of them.

WHAT BLOOD AND TOXICOLOGICAL TESTS WERE AVAILABLE IN ENGLAND IN 1924?

Q What blood analyses were available in a British laboratory in 1924? Could the police have found veronal (a common barbiturate) in a blood sample? And if so, could they have determined the difference between the various formulae for creating veronal?

Laurie R. King
Edgar Award–winning author of *God of the Hive*
and *Pirate King*
Freedom, California
www.LaurieRKing.com

A Karl Landsteiner discovered the ABO blood-typing system in 1901, and in the same year Paul Uhlenhuth developed a test for distinguishing human from animal blood. In 1915 Leone Lattes invented a method for determining the ABO type of dried blood-stains, a discovery critical to crime scene analysis. So by 1924 there were several blood testing procedures available.

Toxicology testing was a little more difficult. Before 1924 there were few drugs or toxins that could be analyzed in a laboratory setting. The first was arsenic. In 1775 Carl Scheele developed the first test for arsenic, and in 1806 Valentine Rose recovered it from a human body. Following this Sevillas learned to isolate arsenic from the human stomach and urine, and this launched the field of forensic toxicology. In 1836 Alfred Taylor developed the first test for arsenic in human tissues, and in the same year James Marsh developed a very sensitive test for arsenic that bears his name: the Marsh test.

The barbiturate class of drugs was discovered in 1864 by Adolf von Baeyer and was used in medicine in the early 1900s. In 1903 Fischer and von Mering created the first therapeutic barbiturate: diethyl barbituric acid also known as veronal. It became a popular sedative and sleep aid in Italy where it was discovered. Phenobarbital, a common barbiturate, was synthesized in 1912. In 1924 there was no way to test for any of these drugs in a human body, either living or dead. That didn't happen for another thirty years.

So at the time of your story there were tests for arsenic but none for barbiturates.

WHAT EVIDENCE MIGHT LINK MY KILLER TO THE RURAL SITE WHERE HE DUMPED THE CORPSE?

Q I am in the midst of my latest *Monk* novel. I'm looking for a way to tie a murderer to the location where he dumped a body: a hiking trail in the forest. He committed the murder at night, hid the body near the trail, then went back the next morning and placed the body on the trail so it would be discovered.

Lee Goldberg
Author of *The Walk* and *Mr. Monk on the Road*
Los Angeles, California
www.leegoldberg.com

A Why not employ a forensic botanist to make the connection? If the dump site was in an area where a certain type of plant or tree grew, the crime lab could find plant fragments, seeds, pollen, etc. on the victim and on the perpetrator's clothing. For example, he could have pine pollen in his clothing, which could match pollen found on the victim, the victim's clothing, and at the dump site. Pollen is tiny, easily overlooked, and settles into fabrics and remains for some time.

The botanist could not only analyze the pollens and say that they came from the same type of tree, but he could do a DNA profile on the pollen from the suspect, the victim, and the trees near where the body was found. If all three matched, that would link the killer not simply to a type of tree but to a particular tree, and such a match would connect him to the corpse and the dump site. Similar to humans, each plant has its own particular DNA.

CAN BEACH SAND BE USED TO CONNECT A KILLER TO HIS CRIME?

Q I am thinking of having a crime scene on sand at the beach. The body would be dumped elsewhere, so the original scene would not be discovered for some time. I am also thinking of the stabbing taking place right by the water's edge. Would the sand soak up the blood and then the tide wash it away? Does sand have any special properties in regards to blood and other trace evidence?

TC

A Sand is a silicate, which means it is basically glass. Each grain is crystal hard and will not absorb blood. Sand "absorbs" blood when it seeps between the grains and is held there. If the killing took place along the water's edge, it would be unlikely that investigators would find any blood as the action of the waves would wash it away. If farther up on the beach, then maybe so. The ME needs only a small amount to do DNA testing. The problem is that finding even a small amount would be difficult. Even if the ME knew the murder took place on a certain beach, it would be difficult to pinpoint the exact spot. The blood would not be visible because it would seep into the deeper parts of the sand.

But all is not lost.

The sand along beaches can vary in grain size, shape, color, refractive and reflective properties (how light bends or bounces off the grains), and chemical makeup (sand is a silicate, but there are many types of silicates). These differences can often be used to determine if a specific sample came from a specific site. If the ME found sand on the victim, he might be able to match it with sand from nearby beaches and determine which beach was the murder scene.

Also, tiny, even microscopic, plant and animal life vary from location to location, and a forensic botanist can often conclude where a specific sample came from. One area may have trees nearby while another has wildflowers. The leaves, needles, seeds, and pollens from these would be mixed with the nearby sand. Certain birds may nest in one area and not in another, and their feathers or nesting materials or droppings might be found in the sand of one place but not at another ten miles up the road.

These techniques can be helpful in locating where a body had been.

If you have the murder take place near a particular type of tree or shrub or sea oat and this type of plant grew in only one place, the ME might be able to further pinpoint where the corpse must have been. Even better, he may be able to match the plant DNA of a leaf or seed fragment or grain of pollen to the exact plant it came from. He could then say that the body was at some time near this specific plant. This is very powerful evidence for linking the body to the murder site.

HOW LONG DOES IT TAKE BLOOD TO DRY?

Q I'm working on my third John Jordan novel and have a couple of questions. How long does it take blood to dry when someone is stabbed to death and loses a lot of blood? What are the factors that affect drying time? In my scenario, an inmate is murdered in his Florida jail cell in October. The blood is on the cement cell floor and the victim's clothes.

Michael Lister
Florida Book Award–winning author of *Double Exposure*,
The Body and the Blood, and *The Big Goodbye*
Panama City, Florida

A Blood clots in approximately five to fifteen minutes after exiting the body and will initially be dark maroon, gelatin-like, and sticky to the touch. Over a couple of hours it will gradually separate into a dark maroon-blackish clot surrounded by a pale yellow serum. This is due to contraction of the clotted blood and a "squeezing out" of the serum, which is not involved in the clotting process.

We do this in the lab quite often since many blood tests are done on the serum, while others are done on whole blood. The blood is allowed to clot in a test tube, and the tube is placed into a centrifuge and rapidly spun for several minutes. This pushes the clotted blood into the bottom of the tube, and the serum will float on top. The serum is then removed and used for various tests.

The blood on the floor will dry to a crusty brownish state over a few hours to three or four days, depending upon the actual temperature, humidity level, and the degree of ventilation. Warmer, drier, and breezy conditions would dry it faster. Blood on clothing is likely to dry faster than that on the floor since the clothing serves as a wick and spreads the blood over a larger area. If the clothing is placed inside a container or is wadded, it will take much longer to dry than if the clothing is spread out on the floor or draped over a chair or other object.

In your scenario, I'd allow at least six hours for the drying process to occur if the clothes are spread over something and twenty-four or more hours if not. Since you said that there is a lot of blood, it would take twenty-four hours or longer to completely dry on the floor unless someone spread it out in a thin layer. If so, it could also dry in six or so hours.

CAN STORED BLOOD BE USED TO FAKE A DEATH?

Q If my character stockpiled her own blood to use in a disappearance scheme, would it be obvious that the blood was not all the same age? Would it be something that a rural sheriff's department might question or investigate?

LM

A There are two basic ways to store blood. In either, the blood would need refrigerating to prevent decay.

The first way is to let the blood clot before storage. Blood clots by producing protein strands that increase in number as the process continues. These strands give the clot strength, which makes the clot an effective barrier to further bleeding when you cut your finger. Blood takes about five to fifteen minutes to clot. Over the next several hours, the clot "organizes" as these strands contract, pulling the clot into a tighter and stronger bundle. Under a microscope the fibers appear more organized rather than random strands, so the age of the clot can be determined to some extent. Not very accurately but the difference between two hours and two months would not be difficult to identify. But clotted blood is hard to "spread around the scene." It would be like using a butter knife to spread Jell-O. Not an easy proposition.

The second method is to store the blood as a liquid. The problem is that the blood would have to contain an anticoagulant to prevent clotting. Usually this is something like EDTA or heparin. These would be easily found during testing. The key at the crime scene would be that the blood would still be liquid and not clotted as would be seen if the blood had actually been bled at the scene. Once blood has been anticoagulated it will not clot on command.

One other point is that the pattern of the blood at the scene is a problem in staging. Forensics experts use the blood spatter pattern to determine how the blood was spilled, where the victim was at the time, perhaps where the assailant was, and what weapon and type of blow caused the particular pattern. Such crime scene analysis is a complex process, but it is often crucial to solving a crime and proving or disproving a suspect's or witness's version of the events. Pouring or slinging blood around the area will look exactly like it was poured or slung.

You can see that using stored blood to stage a scene is fraught with problems. That's the bad news. However, the good news is that all of this is in an ideal world. In your story's rural location, the sheriff might not be very sophisticated, interested, honest, whatever. He might not know the difference between clotted blood and unclotted blood or have any experience in crime scene analysis, so he would see a lot of blood and simply assume someone must have died.

Your scenario might not be feasible in a big city, but it could be if your town is small and rural and your sheriff is unsophisticated, lazy, or corrupt.

WHAT SUBSTANCE AVAILABLE IN 1924 WOULD PREVENT BLOOD CLOTTING?

Q What in 1924 would be used to keep blood liquid and free of spoilage for several days? If it makes any difference, this is chicken blood, which the encyclopedia informs me does not clot if the sample is taken with care. It would, however, no doubt spoil and perhaps clot after some days.

Laurie R. King
Edgar Award–winning author of *The God of the Hive* and *Pirate King*
Freedom, California
www.LaurieRKing.com

A In 1924 as today, blood would have to be refrigerated to prevent decay. The blood sample in your story would have to be placed in an icebox or stored in a bucket with ice.

The common anticoagulant heparin was not discovered until 1935, so it would not be useful in your story. In 1924 the only true anticoagulant available was sodium citrate. It is a white powder and when added to a blood specimen prevents clotting. This should keep the sample liquid for the several days you need.

It's true that the blood of chickens and some other birds is a bit odd. Not sure why but it is. Under certain circumstances it seems to be deficient in thrombokinase. So what the heck is that?

If blood didn't clot, every species on Earth would be in

trouble. Liquid blood clots through an elegant and complex series of chemical reactions we call the clotting cascade. It's too complex to explain in detail, but basically it is composed of two separate pathways—the intrinsic and the extrinsic. The intrinsic pathway takes place within the body when tissues are injured, and the extrinsic is activated after some trauma that results in blood loss. Both of these paths merge into the common pathway near the end of the process when factor X (X) is converted to activated factor X (Xa).

Thrombokinase is part of the intrinsic system and is the enzyme that converts X to Xa. Since chicken blood is deficient in this enzyme, intrinsic clotting is slower, but once the blood leaves the chicken's body, clotting would proceed more rapidly. In your scenario, the chicken blood would still need an added anticoagulant like sodium citrate to remain liquid.

WHAT CLUES WOULD AN MD SEE IN A GUNSHOT VICTIM THAT WOULD SUGGEST THE TIME OF THE MURDER?

Q My hero, who is a physician, hears gunshots, goes to a nearby home, and finds the occupants murdered. When he examines the wounds, he realizes they were shot at least half an hour earlier and not when he heard the shots just minutes before. (He later discovers a CD-R recording of several gunshots in the victims' high-end stereo system, which is also outfitted with outdoor speakers.) What physical signs might tip him off that the victim was actually killed thirty minutes before he heard the gunshots?

Lee Goldberg
Author of *The Walk* and *Mr. Monk on the Road*
Los Angeles, California
www.leegoldberg.com

A When someone is killed by gunshot, he will bleed for a few minutes as death occurs, and any blood that has exited the body will take five to fifteen minutes to clot. If your MD finds the body two minutes after the gunshots and if the blood on the floor is completely clotted, he could suspect that the person had been shot much earlier.

If the blood was still liquid, the shooting was very recent, only minutes. If the blood was freshly clotted, then ten minutes would be the best guess. If the blood was not only clotted but also had begun to separate into clot and surrounding yellowish serum, thirty minutes or longer would be a more likely time frame.

CAN BLOOD FOUND AT A CRIME SCENE BE MATCHED TO A MISSING PERSON?

Q Say a girl is missing. A bloody rock is found near her abandoned car. How could they tell if the blood is hers since they don't have her to compare it to? Could they take blood from her parents to help narrow it down?

April Henry
New York Times best-selling author
http://www.AprilHenryMysteries.com

A There are a couple of ways. Her DNA could be obtained from her hairbrush, toothbrush, a letter or stamp she had licked, or a cup she had drank from that hasn't yet been washed. If a match between this and the blood on the rock is made, it would be conclusive proof that the blood on the rock was hers.

Also, DNA from both parents could be submitted for paternity testing. This could prove that the blood came from their offspring and thus identify the blood as the missing girl's. DNA from only one parent could suggest paternity, but to be certain DNA from both parents would be needed.

CAN DNA ANALYSIS BE DONE ON A VERY SMALL BLOOD SMEAR?

Q My villain has kidnapped an eleven-year-old girl from her home. He's in full winter gear. She keeps a pair of scissors on her bedside table and manages to stab him in the arm, drawing blood. I assume the heavy coat would prevent any blood from leaking out, but the scissors drop to the bed and leave a very small smear on the sheets. The scissors are taken with the girl. What information can be obtained from testing that small smear? DNA or only blood-typing?

Kylie Brant
Award-winning author of *Deadly Sins*
www.kyliebrant.com

A Yes, the jacket might absorb any blood and prevent the attacker's blood from dripping on the bed or floor, but the smear on the sheet would do him in. They should be able to do both ABO blood-typing and DNA analysis on the blood smear. Using the PCR and STR techniques, it takes only a very small sample; theoretically a single cell will do. They could then obtain the victim's DNA and match it to the blood smear and know the blood wasn't hers and therefore was likely from the killer. They could enter it into the Combined DNA Index System (CODIS) to see if the killer is in the system. If they found a match, they would have their man, and if not, they would hold the DNA until a suspect was identified and then make the match.

Where would they get DNA from the missing girl? Her toothbrush, hairbrush, or letters or stamps she might have licked. DNA is found in saliva, hair follicles, and the cells collected by a toothbrush when brushing.

Also, the blood smear could be just an amorphous smear, or it could reveal the shape of the scissors. If closed, it might look like a knife shape, while if the scissors fell with the blades open, the ME would know that the scissors were the weapon used by the girl. The police would include this item in their search.

CAN THE ME DISTINGUISH WOUNDS FROM AN ATTACK FROM THOSE SUFFERED IN AN AUTOMOBILE ACCIDENT?

Q I'm nearing a deadline for a new Molly Blume novel and have a few questions. My killer uses a sharp object in a fit of panic and slams it into the victim's head, causing a fatal injury. Or he shoves the victim onto the edge of a table, killing him. Trying to cover up the killing, he places the body in a car, drives the car over an embankment, hoping the injuries from the crash will mimic the injuries he inflicted. Would the ME be able to reveal the cover-up?

Rochelle Krich
Author of "Squatters' Rights" in the anthology
Home Improvement: Undead Edition
www.rochellekrich.com

A The staging of a crime scene can be tricky. The ME would examine the victim and the car both directly and by the photos made at the scene. He would measure the length, width, and depth of the wounds and estimate the size and shape of the object that likely made them. For example, if a wound was tiny, round, and deep, he might suggest that an ice pick or similar object was the weapon. If it was an inch long, narrow in width, and six inches deep, he might say that a knife with at least a six-inch blade did the deed. If a wound was a pyramidal-shaped depression, he might decide that it was a cabinet or a table corner or a similarly shaped object. He would then look at the vehicle's interior, especially any objects or structures that had blood on them, to see if any fit the wounds. If not, he might conclude that some outside object had caused the injury.

Secondly, he would study the blood spatter patterns both on the victim and within the car. If the patterns didn't make sense, he would be suspicious. For instance, if the victim's shirt was soaked with blood but there was no significant blood on the car seat, he might say that the victim had been killed somewhere else and placed inside the car. The reason is that if the victim bled enough to soak his shirt there would have to be blood on the car seat and floorboard and other places.

He would evaluate the timing of the victim's injuries. If he determined that some of the injuries were postmortem, he might conclude that the accident was staged and that the victim was dead before the car went over the embankment. Postmortem wounds do not bleed. So if he found a lethal bloody wound on the victim's head and several cuts and scrapes on his arms and legs that had not bled, he might state the victim was killed by the blow to the head and the other wounds were postmortem. Since dead people don't drive, except in vampire and zombie movies, the scene must have been staged.

COULD MY CHARACTER QUICKLY RECOGNIZE THAT BLOOD ON A HALLOWEEN COSTUME WAS REAL AND NOT FAKE?

Q Here's the situation: It's Halloween. A guy shows up trick-or-treating at Monk's door. He's covered in blood and carrying a bloody knife. Monk knows instantly that this is no costume, that the man has just murdered someone and is trick-or-treating so he doesn't stand out but rather mixes in with the other bloody killers and monsters on the street. With just a glance, Monk knows the man is covered with real blood, the spatter pattern indicates it came from a struggle, and the murder happened within the last hour. From the candy in the bag, he can backtrack which house the murder occurred in, and from the perfume he can smell on the man, he knows the victim was a woman.

What might indicate the blood was real? What characteristics of the blood on the knife might suggest the time of death?

Lee Goldberg
Author of *The Walk* and *Mr. Monk on the Road*
Los Angeles, California
www.leegoldberg.com

A When people create a Halloween costume in which blood is involved, they invariably use some form of red paint. This is because blood is red, of course. However, when blood dries it changes color. Partly due to the simple loss of water but mostly due to a change in the chemistry of the blood itself. It has to do with the oxygen and hemoglobin and other proteins in the blood and is not really important to understand. Just know that the blood will turn mahogany, maroon, rusty brown, or purplish brown. So when Monk saw someone wearing a costume with this color blood instead of red, he would become suspicious.

It takes time for blood to dry, so the bloodstained clothing would still be damp, even tacky, to the touch. If a nearby light source reflected off the clothing, Monk might be able to see that the substance had not completely dried. This would tell him that the liquid material (blood or paint) got on the clothing within the last hour, which could help him with the timeline.

Blood also has a distinctive odor that is described as metallic or coppery. If Monk was close to the person, he might detect this distinctive odor just as he did the perfume. That would be so Monk-like.

The blood spatter pattern might also give him a few clues. When people paint fake blood on a costume, they tend to pour and smear and brush it around. The pattern of the stains would reflect that. In a stabbing, the blood doesn't follow the same pattern. It would reveal what are called impact spatters, which occur when the fist is slammed down onto a blood source. Very similar to slapping your fist into a tub of water. It spatters in all directions, creating a fan of droplets. As the victim was repeatedly stabbed, the spatter would increase.

Also, as the knife is raised and lowered, blood would fly off it in what are called cast-off blood spatter patterns. These are streaks of droplets similar to what would happen if you dipped your hand in paint and then flung it toward a surface. The liquid would be cast off in long streaks. This might be visible on the chest, abdomen, and shoulder areas of the killer's shirt and pants. In addition, there might be blood that passively fell from the bloody knife in the killer's hand as he walked away. Here there might be streaky droplets along the outside surface of the pant leg on the side where he was holding the knife and some circular drops of blood on his shoes. A costume maker would not likely do any of this.

CAN A CHANGE IN PLANTS REVEAL THE LOCATION OF A BURIED CORPSE?

Q I wonder if you can answer a few questions that have stalled my writing. I know where a body is buried affects the surrounding flora and fauna. I also know that the plants die down for a time and then because of the nitrogen have a growth spurt. My question is: What is the timeline when the nitrogen would rekindle the flora?

Terri Buzzelli
Edinburg, Ohio

A Your question is impossible to accurately answer since there are many variables involved, but you are correct that the presence of a corpse alters nearby plant life. Some of the chemicals produced by the decomposition process damage, stunt, and even kill certain plants. As the decay process continues, nitrogen (N) is deposited in the soil, and this can in turn act as a fertilizer, stimulating growth.

The timing depends on the rate of decay, and this depends on the conditions of the burial, most importantly the ambient temperature and the moisture in the soil. In a warm, moist area such as Florida in summer, significant decay could appear in a few days, while in a cooler, drier area such as the mountains of Colorado, it could take many weeks, even months. Regardless, after the decay begins, it takes weeks and more likely months before the local flora shows any visible effects. Again, just like adding fertilizer to your garden.

When searching suspected burial sites, investigators look for areas where the flora has changed, usually more lush as compared to the surrounding area. This is often more readily visible from the air, and aerial photography is often employed. Even satellite photography. New evidence suggests that these changes can still be seen many decades after the burial.

HOW LONG DO CRIME SCENES USUALLY REMAIN SEALED?

Q My victim is an apparent suicide by pills and gas. How long would the crime scene typically be sealed before the family could move back in? If further evidence escalates the crime to suspected homicide, would the scene be held longer or resealed if already released? What is a realistic range?

Craig Faustus Buck
Sherman Oaks, California
www.CraigFaustusBuck.com

A Police investigators and the coroner can hold the scene as long as they need to. This could be a few hours, days, or weeks. It's indefinite. Typically it is for hours or a day. Once they release it, they need another warrant to return, so they would need a very specific reason to do so.

In you scenario, if they found important evidence during the first search, they would simply hold the scene until all the necessary evidence collection and crime scene analysis were done. If they released the scene and then realized some of the evidence they had suggested another crime such as a homicide, then they would have to get a judge to sign off on a search warrant. They could then reseal the property as long as needed.

CAN MITOCHONDRIAL DNA HELP MY CHARACTER DISTINGUISH HER MOTHER FROM HER AUNT?

Q For plot purposes my character needs to distinguish her maternal aunt from her mother. I've read that mitochondrial DNA will not do this. Is that true? If so, how can she separate the two?

SZ
New York, New York

A Mitochondrial DNA (mtDNA) is inherited down the maternal line unchanged for many generations. This means that anyone (man or woman) would have the same mtDNA as their mother, maternal aunt, grandmother, great-grandmother, and so on. The difference is that a woman would also pass this mtDNA on to any offspring while a man would not. But each of these people would have different nuclear DNA, the DNA used for standard DNA fingerprinting.

Your character, her mother, and her maternal aunt would all have identical mtDNA but different nuclear DNA. So mtDNA will not distinguish her mother from her aunt. But if nuclear DNA from the real mother, the aunt, and her father were available, DNA paternity testing would reveal which of the women was the actual mother.

CAN PATERNAL DNA ALONE PROVE THAT TWO STEPSIBLINGS ARE RELATED?

Q I have stepsiblings, a male and a female, with the same father but different mothers. The father and the siblings are alive, both mothers dead, and DNA samples from the mothers are unavailable. Can the sibling relationship be positively proven or suggested with a high level of confidence by DNA analysis?

JT

A Both children would share a great deal of their DNA with their mutual father, but this would not be conclusive proof. If DNA from both mothers was available, then the children's DNA would reflect that both were the offspring of the two parents. The mothers' DNA could be obtained from hair in an old hairbrush, an old toothbrush, or perhaps a stamp or envelope sent to and kept by a family member.

But even without maternal DNA all is not lost. The brother would share the same Y chromosomal DNA as the father, and this would prove that they were indeed father and son. This would not work for the daughter since she has no Y chromosome.

Mitochondrial DNA (mtDNA) might help. This DNA is passed down through the maternal line only and remains unchanged for many generations, perhaps up to six thousand five hundred years. All members of the maternal line possess the same mtDNA. This means that each of the two children would have the same mtDNA as their particular mother, maternal grandmother, and any maternal aunts. So if the maternal grandmother or aunt of either child was known and available and if mtDNA obtained from either matched that of the sibling, it would prove they belonged to the same maternal line. This would be fairly strong evidence of who the mother was, but it would not be conclusive.

CAN DNA BE EXTRACTED FROM A FETUS?

Q In my story, a pregnant woman is murdered. Does the fetus have to be past a certain point before paternal DNA can be determined? If she's very early in her pregnancy at the time of her death, say five weeks or so, can paternal DNA be determined?

Linda Castillo

New York Times best-selling author of *Breaking Silence*
www.lindacastillo.com

A The DNA of the fetus is set at fertilization, never changes throughout life, and can be determined at any time from fertilization forward. But this will not give you the paternal DNA. That is, you can't take the fetal DNA and conclude what came from the mother and what came from the father. Paternity can only be proved if you have DNA from the mother, the father, and the fetus. Having two won't do it. You need all three.

Why? Because the DNA the child gets from each parent is not the same in each egg or sperm that person produces. If so, everyone would look like Adam and Eve. Each parent donates a different combination of their DNA to each egg or sperm produced. We have forty-six chromosomes and they are inherited independently of each other, which creates millions of possible combinations. That's why you don't look like your siblings unless you have an identical twin.

In your scenario, the fetal DNA will not reveal who the father is, but if DNA from the fetus, the mother, and a suspect father are compared, the results can verify whether he is the father or not.

DOES THE DNA IN A TRANSPLANTED ORGAN ADOPT THE DNA PATTERN OF THE RECIPIENT?

Q Does the DNA of a transplanted organ such as a kidney retain its unique signature in its new host, or is the organ's DNA somehow altered by the recipient's system?

BDM
Renton, Washington

A Each organ of the body is composed of cells, and inside each cell, with the exception of our red blood cells, is DNA. Every organ repairs itself by replacing old and damaged cells with new ones, with DNA that's exactly the same as the other cells in the organ. This means that any organ such as the kidney that is transplanted will retain the DNA it had before. It is not possible for the body to alter the DNA or to replace damaged kidney cells with cells of its own construction. If the DNA of the transplanted kidney was tested, it would be the DNA of the donor and not that of the recipient.

Bone marrow transplantation offers an unusual situation. In the treatment of persons with some forms of leukemia or a few other blood diseases, powerful drugs are given to completely wipe out the bone marrow. Not just the leukemic cells but all the cells in the marrow. Then donor bone marrow is infused intravenously, and this material migrates to the bone marrow where it produces each of the cell types found in blood—white blood cells, red blood cells, and platelets. Since the bone marrow will retain the DNA it had from the beginning (the donor's DNA), the blood produced by this bone marrow will also have the DNA of the donor and not that of the recipient. If this individual undergoes DNA testing, his blood will show the DNA of the donor and not his true DNA that is present in the remainder of his cells. What if he committed a rape and left his semen at the scene or perhaps some bits of his flesh beneath the victim's fingernails? If his blood was tested, it wouldn't match and he'd get off. How do you get around this? Use buccal cells obtained from scraping the inside of the cheek. They would contain the person's original DNA and not that of the donated marrow. This DNA would match the semen and the skin beneath the victim's nails.

CAN DNA BE OBTAINED FROM A SUBMERGED GUN?

Q I am a reference librarian in Los Angeles. A client, who is a novelist, needs to know if viable DNA can still be recovered from a weapon such as a gun, which has been submerged in salt water. No specific time period was given for the immersion, but he is wondering if enough DNA from blood or body oils would remain for DNA typing to occur.

SH
Los Angeles

A The answer is yes, no, and maybe. There is an adage in science that says whatever happens, happens. If the gun has blood on it within the barrel or cylinder, in the cracks, in the pattern on the handle, or virtually anywhere, these stains can be washed away with water or not. Even if most of it is washed away, small amounts might be found in the crevices and inside the barrel, a place where blow-back blood splatter occurs not infrequently in close range gunshots. The calmer the water, the less washing will occur. In an ocean or a rapidly moving river more blood would be washed away than if the gun was placed in a bucket of water or tossed in a calm pond or bay. Regardless, there might or might not be DNA, and it might or might not be found. Tell your writer it can go either way, so have the blood found or not found as he needs for his plot.

CAN DNA BE OBTAINED FROM A HALF-EATEN BAGEL?

 If a half-eaten bagel was found at a crime scene on the beach, would DNA be preserved from the biter's saliva? Would such testing be routinely done?

Elizabeth Zelvin
Two-time Agatha finalist
Author of *Death Will Help You Leave Him*
and *Death Will Get You Sober*
www.elizabethzelvin.com

DNA can often be found in saliva on cups, cigarettes, stamps, and even food products. There was a famous multiple murder case in which DNA was found on chicken bones tossed into the trash at a fast-food restaurant. DNA can sometimes be obtained from fingerprints. The oils of the fingers that make up the print also contain a few skin cells, and these can sometimes supply DNA for testing.

Though saliva and tears don't really have DNA, these liquids always pick up DNA-containing cells from the lining of the ducts (tear and salivary) they traverse, and in the case of saliva, the lining of the mouth. Modern DNA techniques employ PCR-STR analysis, which theoretically can use DNA from a single cell.

Such testing isn't routine, but an astute investigator might recognize the possibilities the bagel offers and request the testing.

CAN ANIMAL DNA DETERMINE THE TYPE OF ANIMAL INVOLVED IN A FATAL ATTACK?

Q In my novel, an eighteen-year-old Ojibwa woman, found dead in the bush in early October in northern Ontario, is the apparent victim of an animal attack. She has been partially eaten and is found one to two hours after being killed. No precipitation that night, temperature around 45 degrees Fahrenheit.

What DNA evidence might be found at the scene that could help determine what kind of animal killed her? Animal hairs? Would a delay of ten days and the corpse being found buried change things? Assuming investigators have immediate access to an appropriate lab, what is the fastest time frame to achieve results of such a test in this situation?

Douglas Smith
Aurora Award–winning author of *Chimerascope* and *Impossibilia*
Toronto, Ontario, Canada
www.smithwriter.com

A Simply examining the hair for its physical characteristics might reveal the animal involved since the hair of a wolf and a bear are very different. An expert zoologist should be able to identify the species or at least narrow down the choices based on the hair alone.

DNA could be taken from saliva left in and around the bite wounds as well as from any follicles found on the hair. Typically, follicles are attached to hair that is pulled out, though it is sometimes found on hair that is naturally shed.

If there was a struggle between the victim and the animal, the victim could have pulled out some hair, and follicles would be attached. DNA testing from either source would help determine the species of the animal involved.

The sooner saliva samples were obtained, the better. Once the body decays so will the saliva. A couple of hours would not be a problem, but ten days could be. Or not. If the corpse did not decay significantly, then even after a week or two, the saliva DNA could still be useful.

If the body had been washed, embalmed, and prepared for burial in the normal fashion, there would probably be no hair or saliva, but if it was simply buried in a hastily dug pit, it is likely that both hair and saliva would remain.

In high-profile and time-sensitive cases, DNA can be done very quickly if the lab has good samples. Twenty-four hours or less. The fact that this was an unusual situation would probably delay the DNA testing because the ME would likely send it to another lab for confirmation. This could take several days or even weeks.

CAN FIBERS FOUND AT A CRIME SCENE BE LINKED TO A PARTICULAR PAIR OF SHOE COVERS?

Q My detective finds fibers at a crime scene and sends them to the "hair and fiber" lab. Could the lab determine the fibers came from protective booties routinely used by crime scene investigators? Could they connect them to the actual bootie worn?

EE Giorgi, PhD
Author of the Chimeras thrillers
Los Alamos, New Mexico

A The lab would analyze the fibers physically, optically, and chemically and based on these results should be able to determine the type of fiber and what product it was used in. This would lead to the conclusion that protective shoe covers had been worn. They might even be able to narrow it down to the actual manufacturer since each company uses its own unique products and processes. If they found similar booties in a suspect's home, they could say that the fibers were consistent with that type of shoe cover and with that manufacturer. But that's about as far as they could go.

In order for the lab to determine that these were the actual booties worn during the crime, they would have to find some substance such as blood on the suspect's booties. This could then be matched to the victim's blood and if it matched would be strong evidence that these booties had been worn at the crime scene.

Or they might find fibers from the carpet at the crime scene or hair from the victim or dirt from the place where the murder took place, and each of these could also create a link between that particular shoe cover and the crime. They would not be as strong as DNA blood evidence, but they would add another connection.

DO GLOVES WORN DURING A CRIME LEAVE THEIR OWN FINGERPRINTS?

Q Do latex gloves leave fingerprints on objects the wearer touches? I've found articles describing how latent prints can be found from the inside of latex gloves, but I can't find anything about prints left on the object touched. I'd like to know if a print can be identified as having been left by a latex glove even if the print won't identify the person wearing the glove.

Joel Goldman
Edgar and Shamus–nominated author
www.joelgoldman.com

A You are correct that, though rare, prints have been obtained from inside latex gloves. And though it's possible that ridge detail could be passed through a thin latex surgical glove, it would be unlikely. So the gloves would prevent the perpetrator from leaving his fingerprints behind. But if the surface was soft such as a fresh, thick layer of paint, putty or clay, or maybe even a firm stick of butter, a plastic (three-dimensional) print with some ridge detail might be left at the scene. Not likely but possible.

The gloves themselves could also leave prints at the scene. Leather and fabric gloves have weave, crease, and defect patterns that are unique to that glove and would show that a leather or a cloth glove was used. These patterns might also be matched to a suspect glove and prove that particular glove, to the exclusion of all others, made the print.

Latex gloves are a bit trickier. They tend to be smoother than those mentioned above. Perhaps the finding of a clear print in the shape of a finger yet without ridge detail would suggest to the clever investigator that a latex glove must have been involved.

Also, the glove could have one or more manufacturing defects—a thicker area, a crease, a small ridge, almost anything. These defects, like fingerprints, would be unique to that glove. If a suspect glove was found, the crime scene glove print could be compared to the glove surface or lab-made control prints made from the glove. If they matched, it would be fairly strong proof that it was this particular glove that laid down the print and not just any latex glove. Perhaps not as clear or strong as fabric or leather patterns but still useful.

IS GUNSHOT RESIDUE UNIQUE TO A PARTICULAR WEAPON OR AMMUNITION, AND COULD IT BE FOUND ON A JACKET A WEEK LATER?

Q Let's say the police are investigating a homicide by gunshot and a week or so later execute a search warrant at a suspect's house. This suspect is actually innocent but recently went to a shooting range to learn about firearms protection and shoot a handgun. Could the cops see gunshot residue on a light-colored jacket hanging in a closet and then take it to the lab to test? Could this help build a false case against the suspect, or is gunshot residue so unique authorities would be able to tell it wasn't from the murder weapon?

Julie Kramer

Author of *Stalking Susan*, *Missing Mark*, and *Silencing Sam*
Winner of Minnesota Book Award,
RT Reviewers Choice Best First Mystery
Finalist for Anthony, Barry, Shamus, Mary Higgins Clark,
Daphne du Maurier Awards
White Bear Lake, Minnesota
http://www.juliekramerbooks.com

A Whenever a gun is fired, gunshot residue (GSR) is sprayed not only from the muzzle but from any opening in the gun such as the ejection port. Revolvers tend to spray more GSR because they are more loosely built than other handguns. Regardless, GSR often gets on the shooter's hands, and clothing and the sleeve of a jacket is a good place to look. If the jacket had not been cleaned, GSR would likely be found when the jacket was confiscated and tested. So they would know he had fired a weapon or at least that a recently fired weapon had come into contact with the jacket. The latter caveat is because GSR can be transferred from person to person and from object to object. If someone fires a gun and then shakes hands with another person or grabs his arm, GSR could be found on the other person's hand or arm. This type of transfer often causes problems.

GSR is not usually visible, so they would not see it on the jacket. They could swab several articles of clothing and take the samples back to the lab for testing, or they could take all his jackets and long-sleeved shirts. Perhaps someone saw him wearing a specific article of clothing on the day of the murder, and they could hone in on that.

In the lab GSR is often tested for with scanning electron microscopy (SEM) alone or in conjunction with energy dispersive X-ray spectroscopy. The combo is called SEM/EDX. Some labs use neutron activation analysis (NAA) or atomic absorption spectroscopy (AAS).

If they found GSR on his jacket, they could perform a chemical analysis to determine its makeup. Different manufacturers make slightly different powder, and this is reflected in the relative amount of things such as antimony, barium, and lead. If they found that the GSR on the jacket chemically matched that on the murder weapon, they would strongly suspect that he had indeed fired the gun. Not absolute proof just suggestive. It would simply mean that he had fired or come into contact with a weapon that had fired a chemically similar ammunition. If no match is made, his explanation that he had fired guns at the firing range could stand up.

If the lab found GSR on your character's jacket, he would likely become the primary suspect. They might even arrest him if other evidence also pointed his way. Later when the chemical testing was completed and no match to the murder weapon was found, he might drop lower on the list of suspects. This more sophisticated testing could take a week or two, so he would remain the prime suspect for at least that long.

WHAT IS THE DIFFERENCE BETWEEN MO AND A SIGNATURE?

I'm working on a serial killer story. What is the difference between MO and signature?

Signature is a term often used in profiling serial killers. Many serials commit their rapes, tortures, mutilations, and murders as part of some fantasy. These fantasies can be very elaborate and usually require many years to develop. A killer's signature reflects his psychological needs.

MO, or modus operandi, involve the things the killer must do to plan, perpetrate, and cover crime.

Examples of MO include the following.

How does the killer capture his victim? Does he employ some ruse as did Ted Bundy with his fake broken arm or John Wayne Gacy with his offers of employment, or does he use a blitz attack, where he quickly incapacitates the victim?

Does he use drugs, force, or threat of violence to control his victim?

What tools does he use? A crowbar to open a window, bolt cutters to snap a lock, gloves to prevent fingerprints, a mask to prevent later ID by any witnesses, tape or ropes to secure the victim, and anything else that allows him to commit and get away with the crime.

How does he transport the victim or corpse to the place where he kills her or dumps the body?

MO can change over time with serial predators. They

learn from past mistakes or discover better ways of doing their deeds. They often learn from information leaked to the press. For example, the killer might discover that the police know he is wearing a certain type of shoe or using a pirated cell phone or driving a particular type of car. He would change shoes or dump the phone or the vehicle. Maybe he encounters a combative victim who puts up a fight. He might then use different methods to subdue and control his victims.

Signature is something that he does for his own personal needs and has little to do with pulling off the crime. Serial killers often have highly developed and very specific fantasies. Their victims are not human to them but rather characters recruited into their fantasy play. These "plays" are often ritualistic. The positioning or posing of the body, the use of religious relics, certain mutilations of the victim, carvings and writing on or near the corpse, and almost any other thing can be part of the fantasy, and thus would be his signature. These do not often change as do portions of the MO. Why? Because his fantasy has been developed within his mind for many years and often decades. This fantasy is rigid and does not change easily. It is what excites him.

His fantasy drives his actions; his MO puts him in a position to make his fantasy come true. Even though he might change his MO, his signature usually remains unchanged.

HOW DO INVESTIGATORS ANALYZE THREATENING NOTES?

Q In my story, the killer leaves a threatening note on the victim's front door along with a bloody fingerprint. The note says that he's going to kill a young schoolteacher in the next few days and she will be next. The killer knows his fingerprints are not in the database and leaves it to taunt the authorities. How would the authorities handle this situation? Would they perform forensic tests on the note, or is that too costly and time consuming? Would they keep the note in the evidence room, even though no crime has been committed yet?

Cynthia Combs
San Diego, California

A What they do depends upon how seriously they took the threat and how competent they were. If they felt the threat was credible and not just a prank, they would do several things.

Any fingerprints on the door or the note would be run through Automated Fingerprint Identification System (AFIS), but since the perpetrator isn't in the system, there would be no hit. The prints would be retained as evidence and used when and if a suspect was identified.

From the blood they could determine if the person was male or female, and this would help narrow down the suspect list. If the blood was the murderer's, that is.

They would talk with the woman, her family, friends, coworkers, creditors, debtors, and anyone else who might help identify potential suspects. The killer would have a motive for threatening her, and motives are often uncovered by this type of police work. If a disgruntled student, coworker, or ex-lover is turned up, they would dig into this person's past and present to look for more evidence.

The note would be logged in as evidence and inspected by a forensic document examiner. These individuals are usually hired by larger labs or the FBI, so the materials might have to be sent to one of these labs for processing. Small city labs would be unlikely to have such a person on staff.

Forensic document examination is a complex and fascinating field and can't be covered in this short answer, but in general the examiner would analyze the physical nature and content of the writing and attempt to profile the type of person who wrote the note. Writing style and language usage can often point to the person's age, sex, educational level, ethnic background, occupation, and might offer clues to the motive. Also, the FBI maintains a threatening letter file, and the note could be compared with others already on file.

An analysis of the paper and ink might reveal their origin. Is the paper a common type, or is it a more specialized variety? The size, color, texture, raw materials, watermark, and chemical makeup can often tell who manufactured the paper and when. This might lead them to the store that sold it, and a list of customers for this type of paper would be cross-checked against people who knew the victim. Same is true for the ink, which would be analyzed for color and chemical makeup. Was it a fountain pen, ballpoint, typewriter, or computer ink-jet? Each of these might point to manufacturer.

The more unusual the ink and paper, the more easily its source could be traced. The more unusual and distinct the writing style, the more easily investigators could expose the note's author.

PRIOR TO DNA TESTING, HOW WAS SEMEN USED IN RAPE INVESTIGATIONS?

 I have a question about identification before DNA was widely used. In cases of rape, how was semen traced to the man? Or was identification impossible?

SV

They used the ABO blood type and a few other markers such as the enzyme group known as phosphoglucomutase (PGM). There are several of these, and the amounts and types vary from person to person. Using blood type and this group of enzymes could narrow down the suspect field. For example, if the semen showed type AB blood, it would eliminate 95 to 97% of men since the AB type is found in 3 to 5% of the population. If he had three or four PGM markers that were found in only a small percentage of people, the evidence would be stronger.

Let's say a semen sample was found that showed type AB blood and three PGM markers that were found in only 1% of the population each, and an identical profile was found in a suspect. The odds that anyone other than the suspect left the semen found at the crime scene would be:

Odds of type AB x odds of PGM1 x odds of PGM2 x odds of PGM3

The math:

.03 x .01 x .01 x .01 = 0.00000003

Or:

3/100 x 1/100 x 1/100 x 1/100 = 3/100,000,000

This means that only three out of every one hundred million men would have the same profile. That's very strong evidence that the suspect is the perpetrator, and to most juries it would be sufficient to convict. DNA works essentially the same way but with greater odds. Often in DNA analysis you get numbers like one in fifty billion.

If the suspect was a mismatch for ABO type or any of the PGM markers, then he is excluded as the donor of the sample. If he matched, he would remain in the pool of possible assailants. So ABO and PGM could be used to exonerate but could not point the finger with the certainty that DNA can.

PART IV

THE CORONER, THE BODY, AND THE AUTOPSY

CAN THE ME DISTINGUISH BETWEEN PREMORTEM AND POSTMORTEM ELECTROCUTION?

Q My villain is trying to confuse the ME as to the cause of death in his murder victim. The female victim is murdered by suffocation on a Friday night and then put in cold storage until Sunday night. He then gives her corpse a high-voltage shock with the point of entry above her left breast and exit point at her right shin. Her body is recovered Monday morning. I've read that it is difficult to determine if electrical burns were delivered premortem or postmortem. I'm counting on this fact to be true. Any light you can shed would be appreciated.

Barbara Seranella
Author of the Munch Mancini series
Sadly, my dear friend passed on January 21, 2007.
I miss you, Barb. –D.P. Lyle

A The ME might be able to determine that the true cause of death was suffocation since this often leaves behind clues such as petechial hemorrhages in the conjunctivae (the pinkish tissues around the eyeball). They are more prevalent in strangulation but can occur in suffocation. The mechanism is a rise in pressure in the veins as the victim struggles to breathe, which in turn raises the pressure in the capillaries and causes them to leak blood. This produces the petechiae, which appear as tiny red dots or streaks. These might or might not be present. Also, suffocation requires the forceful application of something over the victim's face. This can bruise the face and mouth and can cause abrasions inside the lips as the teeth are pressed against these tissues. If the ME saw these signs, he could conclude that the victim had been suffocated.

The problem with electrocution is timing. In an electrical current injury, the body responds with an inflammatory reaction, whereby white blood cells and mast cells rush into the injured area. If the electric shock stopped the victim's heart immediately, which of course can happen, this reaction is minimal, but if the victim survived for several minutes, the reaction would be more pronounced. It can be seen with microscopic examination of the tissue at the current's entry and exit points. In the case of someone who is already dead, there is no inflammatory reaction.

Also, changes in skin color at the entry and exit sites offer another clue. In a "live" electrocution, the skin is darkened and hemorrhagic, while in a corpse the skin takes on a yellowish tinge.

If your ME saw a yellowish discoloration to the skin and no inflammatory reaction, he might conclude that the electrocution was postmortem, while if he saw darkened skin with an inflammatory reaction, he would know the victim was alive at the time the electrical current was applied. In your scenario, with the current being applied forty-eight hours after death, he would see the former and not the latter and would know the current application occurred after death.

HOW WOULD THE ME DETERMINE CAUSE OF DEATH AND WHETHER A VICTIM HAD BEEN MOVED AFTER A FALL DOWN A FLIGHT OF STAIRS?

Q In the story I am working on, a woman is killed in a fall down some stairs. Her body is later moved and dumped in a lot. I'd like my hero to be able to deduce from looking at the body that it was moved and a probable cause of death. In *Murder and Mayhem*, you mention that someone can die from a fall shattering her femur, which causes internal bleeding. If the bone hasn't punched through the skin, are there other visible signs that would indicate internal bleeding as the cause of death? Or if she died from an intracranial bleed rather than a fractured femur, are there visible indications that my investigator could see?

Lee Goldberg
Author of *The Walk* and *Mr. Monk on the Road*
Los Angeles, California
www.leegoldberg.com

A The injuries sustained from a fall down the stairs can look like a fall off a building or a car accident or even blunt force trauma from an attack by a strong and aggressive killer. The medical examiner could look at the wounds and at least guess the type of weapon or object that made the injuries. He might see splinters or paint or varnish from the stairs or perhaps bits of plaster or stucco from the wall in the wounds, and if these materials are analyzed and determined to be household materials, then he might suspect that the wounds were not from a lead pipe or a baseball bat but from stairs and walls. This would require chemical and microscopic analysis of the materials found in the wounds.

If the victim sustained blows to the head during the fall that were powerful enough to cause bleeding into or around the brain, then she would likely have some bruising and perhaps hematoma formation in the scalp. Even a bloody laceration. This isn't always the case, but in a situation such as you describe it would be very likely. If the ME found significant brain trauma or bleeding at autopsy, he might conclude that blunt force head trauma was the cause of death. Then an analysis of the wound characteristics might allow him to determine that the injuries came from a fall down stairs as opposed to blunt trauma from an object.

As for determining whether the body has been moved or not, there are several things that might suggest this. She would likely suffer some form of scalp wound during a tumble down the stairs. Any large scalp wound would bleed profusely. There would be blood matted in her hair, but if no blood was found around the body, the ME would know that she had not been injured at the dump site.

The lividity pattern would also help. Lividity is the bluish-gray discoloration of a corpse in its dependent areas. If supine, the lividity would appear along the victim's back. Lividity shifts in the first two or three hours and is fixed by about eight hours. This is a process so it takes time. In between two and eight hours some of it will become fixed in the dependent area that the body first lay in, then more will become fixed in the dependent areas of the body's new position.

If the ME saw fixed lividity along the back of the body, yet the body is found facedown, he would know that the body was moved six to eight hours or more after death. If he found the discoloration along the back of the body and the body is lying on its back, he couldn't tell whether the body had been moved or not. Because this position is consistent with the pattern of lividity, it could be that the body was dumped where it was found immediately after death or more than eight hours after death. The pattern would be the same in either case.

If the body was facedown for three or four hours and then was moved and placed on its back, the medical examiner would see partial lividity on the front of the body as well as on the back. Since dead folks don't move themselves and the lividity pattern suggests that the body lay in two different positions during the first eight hours after death, the ME might conclude that someone moved the body somewhere between two and six hours after death.

So using the lividity pattern the ME might be able to determine whether the corpse had been moved or not and get a general idea as to the timing of the move.

A fracture of the femur that protrudes through the skin is called a compound fracture. If the skin is not broken, it is a simpler fracture yet still potentially deadly. Several quarts of blood can collect in the thigh with absolutely no external bleeding, and this can be enough to push the victim into shock and death. The external signs would be a massively enlarged thigh that would be much larger in diameter than the other one. Simple inspection or employing a tape measure would reveal this difference. The thigh could also show a blue-black discoloration from the blood collecting inside. If a massive amount of blood was found within the thigh at autopsy, the ME could conclude that the fracture and the bleeding were the cause of death.

CAN THE ME DETERMINE IF A FEMALE CORPSE HAS HAD A PREVIOUS ABORTION?

 I have a question about a story I'm going to pitch to the head writers tomorrow. Can an ME tell if someone has had an abortion?

Matt Witten
Writer, producer
Los Angeles, California

Maybe. It's a matter of timing and technique.

The major factor would be the time elapsed between the abortion and the death of the victim. If only days or weeks, the ME could easily make the determination. He would see trauma to and inflammation of the endometrium (the lining of the uterus) as well as the cervical canal (the passageway between the uterus and the vagina). This would be particularly true if the abortion was by dilatation and curettage (D&C). In this procedure a curette, a metallic instrument with a sharp-edged loop-like end, is passed through the cervical canal and used to scrape the fetus and placenta from the uterus. This causes trauma and scarring. The scars can be seen for weeks, months, even years in some cases.

If the abortion was performed by saline injection, there would be less trauma and after several weeks he might not be able to tell an abortion had occurred. In a saline injection, salty water is injected through the cervical canal into the uterus, killing the fetus. The fetus is then passed the next day or so. Here no scraping instrument is used so there would be less short-term trauma and long-term scarring.

So with D&C he could tell for many weeks and months and perhaps years. With saline injection, he could tell for a few weeks but after many months maybe not.

HOW WOULD THE CORONER DETERMINE THAT A SIXTEEN-YEAR-OLD MURDER VICTIM WAS PREGNANT AT AN AUTOPSY?

Q I am currently doing preproduction script revisions for a Canadian television mystery set in 1890. My murder victim is a sixteen-year-old girl who is discovered during the autopsy to have been ten weeks pregnant. Would the coroner have determined this by opening the uterine wall and seeing the tiny embryo, or would there be other signs that would reveal it?

JM

A Yes, the coroner would open the uterus and visually inspect the fetus. Would he know this ahead of time? Possibly. If she was thin, he might note minimal swelling in the lower abdomen, though this would be unlikely at only ten weeks. Once he opened the abdomen, he would see that the uterus was larger than normal and on palpation of the organ would probably notice that the wall was slightly thinner than normal. This would depend upon how the pregnancy was advancing (it varies from person to person) and the experience of the physician performing the postmortem exam. Regardless of his suspicions or lack thereof, he would open the uterus and see the fetus.

IS IT POSSIBLE TO DETERMINE THE AGE, SEX, AND CAUSE OF DEATH FROM ONLY ONE OR TWO FINGERS?

 Can you tell the age and sex of a victim from a single finger? Can you tell the cause of death from just one or two digits?

Taryn Blackthorne
Manitoba, Canada
www.tarynblackthorne.com

Sex could be determined from the DNA present in the tissues.

Age is trickier and would likely require a forensic anthropologist to examine the bones for anatomy and signs of degeneration. This is a complex subject, but some of the general principles might help you. Early in life, bone growth occurs in areas near each end of our long bones, including the fingers. These areas, known as epiphyses or growth plates, fuse (close by becoming hard like the rest of the bone) once puberty is completed, typically by age eighteen to twenty. Also, the size, length, and degree of ossification (the process of bone replacing cartilage) increase with age over the first ten or so years of life. It's highly variable, but a good guess can often be made.

With older people there might be arthritic changes in the finger joints and loss of calcium from the bones themselves. An anthropologist can usually determine the approximate age from infancy to about eighteen, give or take a year or two, and from about age forty-five to old age. In between, it is more difficult to pinpoint.

So the size, length, degree of ossification, epiphyses that are open or closed, and the presence of arthritis in the joints can be used to give a range of ages. For sure the bones of a five-year-old could be distinguished from an eighty-year-old. A fifty-year-old from a sixty-year-old is much harder, if not impossible.

It would be extremely unlikely that the cause of death would be revealed by a finger or two. Perhaps toxins such as arsenic or lead could be found in either the flesh of the fingers, if any remained with the bones, or the nails. Such a finding would suggest that the poison was involved in the death. Still not proof, however.

CAN A DECAYING CORPSE PRODUCE ALCOHOL?

 Is it possible or likely for blood alcohol levels to increase or decrease in a decomposing body, and if so, during what stages of decomposition?

SL

Alcohol is usually destroyed in the decay process, but it might indeed be produced by the bacteria that cause decay. This means that alcohol can only appear during active decay.

The onset and rate of decay depends on the ambient temperature more than anything else. The reason is that these bacteria thrive in warm, moist environments and become sluggish in colder and drier climes. Freezing will stop their activities completely.

Whether a particular corpse produces alcohol or not is unpredictable. If it does, the timing of this production depends on the conditions the corpse is exposed to. In an enclosed garage in Houston in August, this process will be very rapid, and the corpse will be severely decayed after forty-eight hours. If in a snowbank in Minnesota in February, it might not begin the decay process until April or May when the spring thaw occurs. And anything in between. The appearance of any alcohol would coincide with the time frame of the bacterial activity.

COULD THE EXHUMED BODY OF HOUDINI REVEAL WHETHER HE WAS POISONED OR NOT?

 I read that one of Houdini's descendants wants the magician's body exhumed and tested for poison, possibly arsenic. Houdini died eighty years ago. Would any arsenic last that long, and if so, where would they find it? Hair? Bones?

Pat Browning
Author of *Absinthe of Malice*
Yukon, Oklahoma
http://pbrowning.blogspot.com/

Whether it is found of course depends on whether or not he was poisoned with arsenic as well as the condition of the body. If he had enough arsenic in his system to kill or at least harm him, it might be found in the tissues (if any remained), the hair, and perhaps the bones (less likely). The hair would be the best bet since it is fairly hardy and could survive even if the corpse is completely skeletonized, which is probable after eighty years.

The hair might also reveal a timeline for his exposure. Hair is made of dead follicle cells. Only those cells that die and become incorporated into the growing hair while the arsenic level in the body is elevated would contain the arsenic. Those that did so while the levels were low would not. Hair grows about half an inch to one inch each month. Let's say he had been exposed to arsenic about six months before death and again during his final month. The hair near the root and the hair between about three and six inches from the root would contain arsenic, while the hair in between would not. The hair can be cut into sections and each section tested. If something like this was found, it would mean that whoever poisoned him had access to his food or drink during those time frames.

HOW WOULD THE CORONER'S REPORT DESCRIBE A DEATH FROM A BLOW TO THE HEAD?

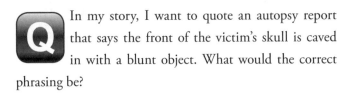 In my story, I want to quote an autopsy report that says the front of the victim's skull is caved in with a blunt object. What would the correct phrasing be?

Sandra Parshall

Agatha Award–winning author of the Rachel Goddard Mysteries,
including *Under the Dog Star*
www.sandraparshall.com

The coroner or medical examiner places at least these three things in his report: the time of death, the cause of death, and the manner of death. Your question relates to a description of the cause of death. In this case, he would probably state something like this:

Cause of death: Blunt force trauma to the head with fracture of the cranium, cerebral contusions and lacerations, with subdural and intracranial bleeding.

What this means in English is that the victim was struck with some blunt object, which resulted in a fracture of the skull and led to bruises and tears of the brain tissue and bleeding into and around the brain. He would also include the location of the injury: front (frontal), side (lateral or parietal), or back (occipital) area of the skull. He might add a description of the wound. He would measure its length and width and then perhaps estimate the size and type of instrument that might have delivered the blow.

The manner of death would most certainly be homicide since it is not natural and probably not accidental or suicidal.

WHAT WOULD AN EARLY TWENTIETH-CENTURY AUTOPSY ROOM LOOK LIKE?

Q I'm having trouble finding descriptions of early twentieth-century English mortuary/autopsy rooms. I know that prior to this time autopsies were often conducted in sheds and public houses. My research indicates that by the early twentieth century they were located in hospitals, but this is about as far as I have gotten.

By 1910 would the morgues have refrigeration facilities? Wooden or tiled floors and walls? What kind of ventilation? Drainage? Would the surgeons smoke to mask unpleasant odors?

Felicity Young
Author of *A Certain Malice*, *An Easeful Death*,
and *Harum Scarum*
Australia

A These rooms came in many types, and by today's standards were very primitive as were hospitals in general. The structure would depend upon the building, usually a hospital, that housed the autopsy rooms. They could be wooden, brick, plaster, almost anything. The floors might be painted wood or tile or brick or even covered with sheet metal. The dissection table would most likely be wooden, sturdy, and simple. Lighting could be from windows, candles, or electric bulbs, depending upon the sophistication and location of the hospital. Ventilation could be from open windows or fans or both. Drainage might be through floor drains, or the floor might simply be scrubbed with water, brooms, and mops at the end of each day. Odors could be masked by smoking or burning incense and other odiferous products.

In some major teaching hospitals, the room was sometimes like a theater where the table was on the floor and benches rose around it in a circle. Students and other physicians would sit on the benches and look down on the autopsy. Surgery was sometimes done in similar theaters, so doctors and students could watch and learn surgical techniques.

Refrigeration was in its infancy in 1910, so few if any hospitals would have a cold storage area for corpses. Most corpses were literally kept on ice; therefore, autopsies were done as soon after death as possible.

WHAT CAUSE OF DEATH IS DIFFICULT TO DETERMINE AT AUTOPSY?

 What condition—that might kill an apparently healthy young adult—might be difficult to detect through autopsy?

Charlaine Harris

New York Times best-selling author of *Dead Reckoning*
www.charlaineharris.com

Most illnesses and injuries are readily determined at autopsy, so these would not work. Poisons usually leave behind no physical signs and are not readily found with a routine autopsy.

For instance:

Cyanide and carbon monoxide: bright red color to the blood and tissues.

Arsenic: erosions of and bleeding from the stomach lining.

Cantharidin (Spanish fly): swelling and blistering of the urinary tract.

Strychnine: rapid rigor mortis from the muscle spasms this drug causes.

Any of these might tip the ME off to look for the toxin.

Most poisons require toxicological tests, and they can be expensive and time consuming. Often poisons are not pursued for this reason or because they aren't considered.

The coroner will sign off the death as something else, maybe a cardiac arrhythmia since it leaves behind no physical evidence. He's saved time and money, which he might not have in his limited budget, and no one is the wiser.

Toxicological testing is two-tiered: screening and confirmatory. Tox screens done as part of a routine autopsy typically test for alcohol, narcotics, sedatives, marijuana, cocaine, amphetamines, and aspirin. Some screen for a few other classes. If no toxins are found, that might be the end of the investigation. Again, time and money are saved.

If a member of a class is identified, confirmatory testing to determine exactly which member of the class is present and in what amount should be done. These tests are more expensive and time consuming. Using gas chromatography in conjunction with either mass spectrometry (GS/MS) or infrared spectroscopy (GC/IR) will give a chemical fingerprint for any molecule. Since each molecule has its own structure and thus its own fingerprint, every compound can be distinguished from every other one.

If your coroner is lazy, incompetent, corrupt, or limited by a sparse budget, toxicological testing might never be done, and a death from poisoning might be overlooked. Even if he does tox testing, it might consist of only the screening tests, and if they came back negative he would stop there.

What poisons might slip through the tox screening? Things like oleander, digitalis, deadly nightshade, selenium, thallium, sodium azide, Taxol, tetrodotoxin, and many others.

WHAT WOULD A CORPSE LOOK LIKE AFTER FIFTEEN YEARS BURIED IN A MINE, AND HOW WOULD IT BE IDENTIFIED?

Q My novel is a contemporary mystery set in a tiny coal mining community in south central Ohio. My murder victim is an adult male whose body was recently found in an abandoned underground drift (coal) mine fifteen years after he was stabbed to death with a pickax. A drift mine is relatively close to the ground as opposed to an underground shaft mine. He was wearing his work clothes and boots and hard hat at the time of the murder. My bad guy covered up the murder by detonating a small explosion, making it look like a natural rock slide had occurred, effectively entombing the body. Over the years subsidence created a little opening to the mine, and the body was discovered.

What condition would the body be in? Could identification be made other than through a metal tag/ID chain he had on his person as well as his lunch box and name-embroidered coveralls? If the pickax is found near the body, will it be obvious that it was the murder weapon? What wounds might remain fifteen years later on the skeleton, assuming it's relatively preserved? Is it likely that the medical examiner will declare the death a murder? An accident?

Anna Slade
Austin, TX

A After fifteen years they would most likely find only skeletal remains. All the tissues of the body would have long since decomposed. I should point out the skeleton would not be intact since the ligaments and tendons that hold the bones together would also have decayed. It would simply be a pile of bones.

Identification could be made using dental records if any were available, his wallet and the materials inside it, his lunch pail, his clothing, or any jewelry or leather products he wore. Any metal and perhaps any leather products would still be intact, but clothing might or might not be. The ME might also be able to extract DNA from the bones or the teeth, and this might provide the ID.

Since no tissues remain there would be no visible wounds. However, the ME still has the bones to work with. His best piece of evidence would be finding a puncture wound into an intact skull that exactly matched the dimensions of the ax blade. If so, he could state with fairly good confidence that this was the murder weapon. Of course, the skull might not be intact because it could have shattered during the explosion and cave-in. Also, he might see chips and scrapes and channels cut into other bones that he could then match to the ax blade. Not as good as the skull but still suggestive.

Even if these things are seen, he still might not be able to determine that the bony damage came from the pickax and not from the explosion and the falling rocks. Since falling rocks can produce chips and scrapes and cuts and fractures to bones, he would have to consider the possibility that the rocks caused the injuries rather than the ax. Again, finding a skull injury that exactly matched the dimensions of the ax blade or pick would be the most compelling evidence for murder.

The ME might also find dried blood on the ax, and if so, he might be able to obtain usable DNA. If this matched the victim's DNA, it would strongly suggest homicide.

WILL MY DEAD VICTIM BLEED IF THE KILLER SAWS OPEN HER CHEST?

Q My victim was killed by suffocation. Rigor mortis has come and gone, so she's flexible again. After death the victim lay prone until the rigor passed. Then the killer arranged her body on a bed, partially propped up on pillows in a sort of parody of a woman waiting for a lover. The killer then cut open the victim's chest from sternum to pubis and cracked open her rib cage, almost like open-heart surgery. Would there be a lot of blood or bodily fluids, or would they have settled? What sort of tool could be used to make such a cut? A saw or perhaps what might be used in a medical setting?

Kait Nolan
Author of *Forsaken By Shadow*, *Devil's Eye*, and *Red*
Starkville, Mississippi
http://kaitnolan.com

A In the scenario you describe, the body would have to be found a minimum of thirty-six hours after death for rigor to have come and completely gone. The general rule is 12-12-12. That is rigor comes on over twelve hours, stays approximately twelve hours, and then resolves over twelve hours. This obviously is under normal conditions, whatever they are, and is variable from case to case.

Since your victim lay facedown for this time period, the lividity would settle along the front of the body. The forehead, chest, and thighs just above the knee area would be islands of white skin as opposed to the blue-gray color of the lividity. The reason is that these would be the support areas of the body. The weight of the body would compress the capillaries in these areas and prevent the leakage of blood into the tissues, which is the cause of the lividity. The coroner would see this pattern and know that the body had been facedown for at least six to eight hours after death and was then moved to its current position. It takes approximately six to eight hours for the lividity to become fixed.

At death, the heart stops and the blood ceases to flow. This means that any wounds applied to the body after death will not bleed. In your scenario, the opening of the chest would result in no bleeding. The coroner would be able to determine that the wounds were made after death since there would be no bleeding either grossly or microscopically.

The instruments used in the operating room include scalpels, sternal (breastbone) saws, and a spreader device that has a crank that when turned separates the breastbone widely apart and opens the chest. For your purposes any type of knife and saw would work well. Shears might also be helpful if he used them to cut through the joints where the ribs join the breastbone on one side. If this approach was used, a saw would not be needed since dividing the breastbone would not be necessary.

AFTER A KNIFE WOUND DOES THE BLOOD CLOT OR DRY ON THE VICTIM'S SKIN?

Q Does blood coagulate after death or simply dry when it's on the surface of the skin? If a victim's throat is cut and she dies soon thereafter from blood loss, would the blood at the wound be coagulated or dried? How long does it take for blood to coagulate? In my story, the woman's body is found just minutes after death. The dirt around it is drenched in blood. Would the blood at her neck be coagulated? Would the blood in the earth still be sticky?

Catherine Mambretti
www.ccmambretti.com

A A major function of the body is to protect itself. One of the most elegant protective systems we have is blood clotting, a carefully orchestrated series of biochemical reactions involving blood proteins and other substances that we call the clotting cascade. Blood begins to clot immediately upon leaving the body and completes this process by about five to fifteen minutes.

Once clotted, the blood would appear like a shiny maroon blob or pancake of blood. Over the next few hours the blood would start to separate into a darker maroon clot surrounded by a straw-colored liquid, the blood's serum that is squeezed out as the clot contracts. After this, blood will either decay if in a warm environment or dry to a hard brown crust if in a warm and dry area. Often it will do some of each. This decay or drying depends entirely upon the ambient conditions (temperature and humidity) and can take anywhere from a day or two to a week.

In your scenario, the body is found only minutes later (I assume you mean within three to five minutes and not forty to fifty), so the blood would still be liquid and just beginning its clotting process. The part that soaked into the soil would make the soil a dark mud, which would feel pasty or even sticky to the touch. The blood on the victim might be liquid or could be more sticky in quality. Since this is variable, you can have the blood at the scene either fully liquid, somewhat tacky, or completely clotted, depending on whether the body is found five minutes, ten minutes, or fifteen minutes after the murder.

CAN THE HANDEDNESS OF AN ATTACKER BE DETERMINED BY THE NATURE OF A THROAT SLASH WOUND?

Q I'm working on my next Monk novel. This one takes place in 1855 and stars Artemis Monk, an ancestor of Adrian's. If someone's throat was slit from behind, could he tell from the wound whether the killer was left- or right-handed?

Lee Goldberg
Author of *The Walk* and *Mr. Monk on the Road*
Los Angeles, California
www.leegoldberg.com

A He may not be able to tell definitively, but there are certain clues that might suggest the handedness of the killer. The wound on the victim could be flat and horizontal but more typically begins high on one side, swoops down across the neck, and then finishes high on the other side. It tends to start slightly higher than it ends. A right-handed attacker would begin high on the left side of the victim's neck, maybe just beneath the ear, swoop down and across the throat, and then back up slightly on the right side of the neck. The wound would probably be higher on the left side than on the right side. In addition, the wound tends to begin shallow and then deepen as the knife is drawn across the throat. The opposite would be true for a left-handed attacker.

The reason for this pattern of injury is simple mechanics of the arm. Pretend you have a knife and try that move on an imaginary victim, and you will see that it is very difficult to make the knife travel completely horizontally or to end higher than it started. Possible but not likely since it is an uncomfortable motion.

WHAT CRIME SCENE EVIDENCE MIGHT EXONERATE THE DAUGHTER OF A MAN MURDERED BY THROAT SLASHING?

Q So here's my story: A mild-mannered scholar is murdered in his home office when a bad guy sneaks in, slits his throat, and then removes his head with some kind of knife. The assassin escapes clean by wrapping the head and perhaps his own shoes in plastic. The scholar's teenage daughter, asleep a few rooms away, is awakened by the click of the door closing, discovers her father's headless body, and calls the police.

Assuming the cops and the medical examiner arrive within thirty minutes, can they establish the time of death with any real accuracy? I want the cops to initially suspect the daughter until they realize that she has no blood on her, the apartment sinks have no blood in them, and the bloody clothes, murder weapon, and head are missing (and never found). Therefore, the girl couldn't have killed her father, cleaned herself up, disposed of the weapon outside the apartment, and returned in time to make the call.

Can you suggest a kind of knife that might remove someone's head? Would an autopsy tell the ME whether the head was removed by a left-handed or a right-handed killer? This also could exonerate the girl if my time of death excuse doesn't work.

Harley Jane Kozak
www.harleyjanekozak.com

A There are several issues here, so let's take them one at a time.

If your killer attacked the father from behind and severed the throat, he would not have a great deal of blood on him. The blood spray would be forward and away from him, so only his hands and forearms would realistically be contaminated with blood. If he wore gloves and a jacket or a long-sleeved shirt, he could simply remove these and stuff them into a bag with the head and walk away. Anyone who saw him would not see any blood on him. Nothing to really alarm anyone.

As for the weapon, almost any sharp knife with a blade of six inches or more would work. Cutting through the windpipe, muscles of the neck, and the blood vessels is easily accomplished with a very sharp blade by someone with normal strength. Severing the spinal cord is slightly more problematic and would take a couple of minutes. The killer would have to angle the blade so that it slid between two of the cervical vertebrae (neck bones) and slice through the spinal cord to completely remove the head.

It is possible that the medical examiner could determine whether the killer was right-handed or left-handed by the nature of the wound. When someone attacks from behind and sweeps the blade across the neck, he tends to start high on one side and finish slightly lower on the other. That is, a right-handed person would begin to cut on the left side of the victim's neck just below the ear and sweep down and across, ending at the middle or lower portion of the neck on the opposite side. The opposite would be true for a left-handed person. Your medical examiner could look at the path of the wound and make an educated guess as to the handedness of the attacker. If it didn't match the handedness of the daughter, he would know she didn't do it. People rarely use there nondominate hand for this type of attack.

Now for the time of death. Body temperature would help because under normal circumstances a corpse will lose temperature at approximately one and a half degrees per hour. Since the victim is found in thirty minutes, the body temperature would have dropped less than a degree from normal body temperature. This would alert the investigators that the murder had happened within the last hour anyway. Lividity and rigor mortis would be of no help here since it takes both at least a couple of hours to begin.

The medical examiner could also use stomach contents. The stomach tends to empty within two or three hours after a meal, but this process stops at death, so whatever stage the digestive process was in at the moment of death is frozen in time. Let's say someone ate dinner with the victim, ending the meal at 8 p.m., and the police are summoned at midnight. At autopsy if the ME found that the food in the stomach had been only slightly digested, he might conclude that the death occurred in the neighborhood of 10 p.m., some two hours prior to the police being called. On the other hand, if the food had been digested and had moved from the stomach into the small intestine, the murder must have taken place three hours or more after the meal. This would be consistent with the murder taking place around the time the police were summoned.

The use of body temperature, lividity, rigor mortis, and

stomach contents are not all that accurate and are merely suggestions. There is wide variation in the appearance and the timeline of each of these, so no hard and fast rules exist. The medical examiner would simply take everything into consideration and make his best guess.

There is one other trick that might work well in your scenario: the nature of the blood. When the daughter found the victim, it would be only a few minutes after the murder. She could tell the police she saw liquid blood in the wound and on the floor, and indeed there was still some blood oozing from the cut tissues. When the heart stops, bleeding will stop because there is no driving force behind the blood, but blood that has collected in and around the wound will drip under the dictates of gravity until the blood source is exhausted or the blood clots. Blood clotting takes five to fifteen minutes, so she could see liquid blood.

If the police arrived thirty minutes later, they would find that the blood was clotted but had not begun to separate. When a clot forms, the blood initially looks like a maroon gelatinous mass. As the blood clot matures, what we call organizes, the clot contracts and separates from the blood serum. It looks like reddish-brown slugs floating amid a yellowish, straw-colored liquid. This takes a few hours. So the police would immediately know that the murder had taken place at a minimum of fifteen minutes earlier but less than a couple of hours. This should also help them determine the time of death.

The daughter would remain a suspect for some time. They would not exclude her simply because she did not have blood on her and they could find no bloody clothes in the house. That would obviously help her case, but it would take time to search the entire property, the Dumpster down the street, the neighbors' trash cans in the alley, the attic and basement of the house, the property where things like this could be buried, and the dismantling of the plumbing to look for washed blood in any of the sinks or bathtubs. You get the picture. It would take several days for the police to make all these determinations, and only then would they feel more comfortable about eliminating her as a suspect.

HOW LONG WOULD A CORPSE REMAIN INTACT
IN A MICHIGAN LAKE?

Q A corpse is found in a northern Michigan lake or reservoir by a diver. The murder took place a few months earlier, and the time of this is very flexible, but the body is found when it is warm enough for someone to be diving. Is there any way a body could *not* decompose if left in this lake? Depending on the time of year, how long would there still be a body or at least more than just bones? Is there any weird factor that might forestall decomposition in this scenario and make it hard for cops?

P.J. Parrish
Shamus, Thriller, Anthony award–winning author and Edgar nominee
Fort Lauderdale, Florida, and Petoskey, Michigan

A In northern Michigan deep lakes and reservoirs stay fairly cold all year. If they warmed much at all, it would be briefly in July and August. Since deep bodies of water tend to hold their temp fairly stable throughout the year, even this wouldn't be much. I'd suspect that it would freeze over in the winter and thaw in about March or April.

The surface water temps in Lake Michigan are about 44 in March, 52 in June, and 71 in August. Deeper, the temperature is probably a good fifteen degrees cooler. This means that at one hundred or more feet down, the temps would be about 30, 37, and 56, respectively. Three-quarters of the year the temp would be below 40 and only above that for two or three months. In this type of environment it could take years before the corpse skeletonized. These numbers would probably hold for your smaller lake or reservoir too.

So if the body was dumped in the October to March range and not found until the May to August range, the corpse would be mostly intact. The diver could go in anytime from March on, I'd suspect. Overall, this gives you a very broad time frame to work with.

IN 1935 COULD A CORONER DETERMINE THE TIME AND CAUSE OF DEATH IN A VICTIM STRUCK ON THE HEAD AND TOSSED INTO A COLD MOUNTAIN LAKE?

Q I have the fully clothed body of a twenty-year-old male killed by a blunt object to the back of his skull. He is found ten to twelve hours later in a cold mountain lake in July 1935. Would the coroner be able to tell the time of death and that he was killed from this blow rather than drowning? What in the condition of the body would he base that on? Lividity? Rigor mortis? Would the victim's lungs be full of water if he died from the force of the blow an hour before being dumped in the water?

S.W. Dunn
Mystery/thriller writer
Reno, Nevada

A It is difficult to determine the time of death when the environmental conditions vary from normal, and a cold mountain lake would be such a variation. Very cold conditions such as in your scenario would hasten heat loss from the corpse and delay the onset of decay, rigor mortis, and lividity. Your coroner might or might not be able to guess the time of death.

In this situation there might be little or no rigor mortis and lividity, and after only ten to twelve hours there would be no decay. The body would simply appear pale, perhaps bluish or grayish, and dead. If he found some rigor in the hands and the jaw muscles, which would normally begin two to three hours after death, and if he was aware that the cold situation delayed rigor, he might say the death occurred eight to twelve hours earlier. That's about the best he could do.

As for the cause of death, he would definitely see the scalp injury and probably assume that was the cause of death. The lungs might or might not be filled with water. In 1935 the thinking was that if the lungs were filled with water, a drowning likely occurred. So if he saw this, he might state that the person was hit on the head, knocked unconscious, and died from drowning. We now know that's not the case. When someone is thrown into the water alive, he will inhale water as part of a drowning process, and his lungs will fill with water. However, if someone is dead when he is thrown into the water, his lungs will passively fill with water as air seeps out and water enters. This takes many hours, but twelve hours might be enough. Or not. Either is possible.

Your examiner will have his hands full in discovering exactly what happened in this case, which is good since it allows you to plot your story almost any way you want. He could find a small amount of rigor and determine the time of death was actually a lot longer because he was aware that cold conditions change that. He could find that the lungs were filled with water and assume that the victim drowned. He could discover that the lungs were free of water and that the victim died from a blow to the head. Any of these would be possible, so he could come to any of those conclusions.

WHAT WOULD A CORPSE LOOK LIKE AFTER TWELVE HOURS IN A BOILING HOT SPRING?

Q In the novel I'm working on, a handcuffed woman is pushed into a boiling hot spring (198 degrees). The body is discovered twelve hours later. Would fingerprint ridges still be intact? Would teeth loosen and fall out? Would rigor occur or would that happen later? How would one determine the time of death? Would death likely happen before the person had a chance to inhale water and drown?

Patricia Sexton
Portland, Oregon

A Your spring could be bubbling from gases released into the water, but at 198 degrees Fahrenheit it would not be boiling. The boiling temperature of water is 212 degrees Fahrenheit. Regardless, the water you describe would easily be hot enough to cook the victim. It would not kill her instantly, so she would likely inhale water, and the actual cause of death would probably be drowning. The coroner would be able to determine this by finding water in the lungs along with trauma to the bronchial tubes and the back of the throat. This trauma would be bleeding and petechial hemorrhages due to the forceful inhalation and exhalation of water during the drowning process.

The body would be swollen to some extent, and the digits would be pruned from the water. However, the tissues would not be grossly destroyed, and therefore, fingerprint ridges could be found. This might require removing the skin of the finger pads and spreading the skin between two glass slides for examination under a low-power microscope. In this time frame it is unlikely that the teeth would have loosened and fallen free.

Determining the time of death would be difficult and a best guess. Heat, as in this case, greatly increases the onset of rigor and decay. The normal sequence of rigor follows the 12-12-12 rule. It comes on over twelve hours, remains for approximately twelve hours, and resolves over twelve hours. This is broadly general and affected by many things including ambient temperature. This means that using rigor would be of marginal value in deciding the time of death. Body temperature is only useful until the body reaches the temperature of the surrounding medium, which in this case could happen within twelve hours. Or not. Here the corpse would gain heat rather than lose it. The coroner would of course measure the body temperature and should also measure the water temperature. From these he might be able to make a best guess as to the time of death, but it wouldn't be very accurate, and he would give a fairly broad range.

In your scenario, the body would be essentially intact, fingerprints would be obtainable, and the time of death would be very difficult to determine.

IS IT POSSIBLE TO DETERMINE THAT BONES ARE ONE HUNDRED OR MORE YEARS OLD AS OPPOSED TO BEING "FRESH" SIMPLY BY LOOKING AT THEM?

Q We are revising our latest book and might have a problem. We have our medical examiner looking at recently excavated bones and telling the cops that they are one hundred to one hundred and fifty years old. The bones came from plain dirt in the floor of an old barn. Is this even credible? We need for this to be possible. If we have to, we could give our ME a forensic anthropology background.

P.J. Parrish
Shamus, Thriller, Anthony award–winning author
and Edgar nominee
Fort Lauderdale, Florida, and Petoskey, Michigan

A Yes, this will work. As bones age they lose the proteins that make up the protein matrix, the framework that holds the calcium. With aging and the disappearance of the protein, the bones will become chalky, pale, dry, and more brittle. When someone presses a fingernail into a very old bone, it will easily give and crumble a bit, leaving behind an indentation or scratch. When one is broken, instead of splitting like a green stick as would happen in "fresher" bones, it will break in a straight line across the long axis of the bone, and the fracture line will crumble and powder a bit.

If your ME picked up a finger or an arm bone and

pressed a fingernail into it or snapped it, this is what would happen, and he would know the bones were very old. How old? Impossible to tell but unless the area is a dry desert, the bones would need to be at least fifty years old to be this brittle. So your ME could say that the bones were at least this old and probably older.

CAN DNA BE OBTAINED FROM ONE-HUNDRED-YEAR-OLD BONES, AND CAN FINGER BONE BE DISTINGUISHED FROM SKULL BONE?

Q In my story, the FBI has a small piece of bone (Bone A) from a skull that is over one hundred years old. They are sent another small piece of bone (Fragment B) to match the DNA against Bone A. Fragment B is from the same person's skull, but the sender is attempting a subterfuge. He wants the match to be affirmed, but for his purposes he has labeled Fragment B as coming from the person's hand. Would the lab analyst immediately know that Fragment B is actually from a skull and not from a hand, or would he simply accept the bone, extract the DNA from Fragment B, test it against the DNA from Bone A, and conclude it matches?

Joel Fox
Author of *Lincoln's Hand*
www.lincolnshand.com

A Whether he can determine the origin of Fragment B depends on the nature of the fragment. If it is only a splinter of bone probably not, but if it is a full-thickness piece, such as half a finger bone or a punched-out section of skull, he would easily distinguish skull bone from finger bone. The structure of these bones is very different. A finger has a round marrow cavity, while skull bones are trabeculated—like scaffolding—inside. If the piece was large enough to show these internal differences, then no problem. If he received only a splinter of bone with no internal structures present, then it would be much more difficult.

DNA might or might not be extractable in a one-hundred-year-old bone. It varies, so you can have it as you need for your story. If DNA is found, they would match since the bone fragments came from the same person.

WHAT CAN MY KILLER ADD TO THE BURIAL SITE THAT WOULD HASTEN CORPSE DECOMPOSITION?

Q My killer buries a body in a field. He wants to toss something on the body to aid decomposition. I remember something about throwing lime over the body to help destroy it. Is that right or should he use something else?

Simon Wood
Author of *Paying the Piper*
Bay Area, California
www.simonwood.net

A The putrefaction of a corpse is dependent upon bacterial growth. Anything that promotes bacterial growth will hasten destruction, and anything that kills off or slows the growth will slow it. Heat is the major factor. Warmth favors growth and coolness slows it. Just like refrigerating beef.

Acids and lye might destroy some tissues, but they can also kill bacteria, so they might actually work against your killer. His best bet would be to stash the body in a warm place and add bacteria. Fertilizer, the manure kind, not the chemical kind, would add a large amount of hungry bacteria to the corpse, and the decay process would take off.

HOW WOULD MY KILLER COMPLETELY DESTROY A CORPSE?

Q I've got a killer who burns bodies. What would he use? Is there any way for him to burn them completely? Are there methods that criminals try that don't work? I'd like for him to try a few different things before he succeeds.

Michael Lister
Florida Book Award–winning author of *Double Exposure*,
The Body and the Blood, and *The Big Goodbye*
Panama City, Florida

A It is very difficult to destroy a corpse with fire. Not impossible but difficult. A crematorium employs temperatures of around 1500 to 1800 degrees for two hours and yet bits of bone and teeth often survive. So a fire must be extremely hot and burn for a couple of hours. This means that some type of accelerant rather than just wood or setting a house on fire would likely be needed. Gasoline and kerosene are readily available, and if the corpse is put into a metal container and the fire is continually fed, then the body could be destroyed. Or not. So for your story you could have the corpse completely consumed or some or all of the teeth could survive, and this could be your sleuth's way of identifying the corpse. Whatever you need.

Lye has been used in this situation with mixed results. It could work but usually doesn't. If it does, it can take many weeks or months. Sometimes the lye simply damages the corpse on the surface and actually kills the bacteria that cause decay, which helps preserve the corpse. So lye is slow and unpredictable.

Another choice would be a strong acid such as concentrated hydrochloric acid, sulfuric acid, or chlorosulfonic acid. These will dissolve bones and teeth if enough is used and enough time is taken. Again, this requires many hours, even days, to complete.

However, there are a few problems with acids. They will eat up plumbing and metal tubs, and their vapors will peel off paint and wallpaper as well as damage the skin, eyes, and lungs of anyone nearby. And the neighbors would notice the fumes. So your killer would need to have an old bathtub in a remote outdoor area. He could then keep adding acid until the corpse was reduced to a mass of goop.

WHAT WOULD A CORPSE LOOK LIKE AFTER SIXTY YEARS IN A SUBMERGED FREEZER?

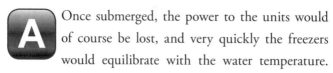 I am writing my first novel. It is set in north Georgia in the 1950s. My character kills his victims and places their bodies inside two freezers, which he locks and bolts to the floor of a house. The house is located in a zone that will be flooded by the building of a massive lake. The house will be exposed when the lake is drained sixty years later.

What would be left of these bodies after sixty years? Would there be DNA? How about any papers, wallets, or pictures left on the bodies?

CJ Burk
Buford, Georgia

Once submerged, the power to the units would of course be lost, and very quickly the freezers would equilibrate with the water temperature. After sixty years the corpses would almost certainly be skeletonized. The bacteria that cause decay come from the GI tract and not the environment, and most of these are anaerobes, meaning they don't need or use oxygen. So the corpses would simply be piles of bones. A wallet or a plastic-encased license might survive intact, but papers would likely disintegrate. Or not. It could go either way. If they survived, the ink would have faded, but a document examiner might be able to bring out any text by drying the sheets and using laser,

UV, infrared, or another alternative light source. Leather belts and shoes, jewelry, and any other firm objects could be intact, and these can often be used to make an ID.

DNA might be obtained from the bones or by drilling into the pulp of the teeth. Or the DNA could be so damaged by the decay process that none is found. Again, this can go either way.

CAN MY CHARACTER FAKE HIS OWN DEATH BY SUBSTITUTING ANOTHER CORPSE?

 My question is whether I could effectively conceal the identity of a body by dumping it in the ocean close to the coast (New England) in late summer. My killer is trying to make it look like he's been murdered himself and has found someone of about the same age, build, and general good health and killed him by shooting him in the face and cutting off his hands and feet. He just needs to buy a week or two. How long might it take to do an identification? I'm assuming it would take some time to locate his old medical records and that crime labs don't whip through autopsies these days. I'm also assuming the removal of the hands and feet would slow things down and that the decay of the body after about a week in the water (and being nibbled by marine life) would be pretty considerable. Please let me know whether this would work.

Dana Cameron
Author of the Edgar Award–nominated short story "Femme Sole"
Beverly, Massachusetts
www.danacameron.com

The water in New England even in summer is cold, thus the body would not decay much in a week. It could, however, be damaged by marine life. Most likely the ME would have a fairly intact corpse to deal with. Except for the missing parts, that is.

In this situation, the ME would have both a corpse

and a suspected identity. This is much easier than simply a corpse and no idea who it might be. In the latter situation he would have nowhere to start and would have to canvass missing persons reports in the hopes of narrowing down his search. This can be difficult, time consuming, and not always profitable.

His best and most rapid methods for answering these questions are through fingerprints, dental matching, and DNA analysis. Or the victim could have an implanted medical device such as a pacemaker or hip replacement, both of which have traceable serial numbers. Or he could have a distinctive tattoo, surgical scar, or malformation.

In your scenario, there are no fingerprints and I assume no devices or identifiable marks. So the ME will use what he has.

A problem arises with the head of the victim. If the police find the head and have dental records of the killer (the suspected victim), they can compare them and determine that the corpse is not the killer's. This can be done very quickly. A day or two. Even if the gunshot blew out his teeth and damaged some of them, they could still make the comparison with only a few teeth available. But if no records are available, a dental examination is worthless. Also, if the killer removed the head as well as the hands, none of this would come into play.

If DNA from the killer was available, then a comparison with the corpse would show no match. If none of the killer's DNA was available, all is not lost. If the killer had a close relative, they could match DNA or mitochondrial DNA from the corpse with that of the relative and might be able to determine that the corpse is unrelated and not the killer. This can be done in a few days to a couple of weeks. If the killer has no known close relatives, then identifying the victim from a headless, handless corpse is typically a long process.

If your killer cut off the head and hands and had no close relatives around, he could hide out for months, years, or maybe forever.

COULD MY CORONER DETERMINE THAT A YOUNG GIRL WAS ALREADY DEAD BEFORE BEING BURNED IN AN ARSON FIRE IN 1912?

Q I am currently working on a scene where a young girl has been found dead in a factory fire in the north of England. I want the coroner to discover or at least suspect that the girl was dead before the fire. How would he have been able to determine this in 1912?

C L-H

A In a fire a living person and a corpse will burn the same way. The body will be charred to varying degrees but is almost never completely consumed in a house or a factory fire unless large amounts of highly flammable materials are in the area.

The key to determining if the person was alive or not at the time the fire burned the body is finding evidence that the victim was breathing. Today the level of carbon monoxide (CO) in the blood and tissues can be measured. If high, the victim breathed in CO, a by-product of the fire, and was thus alive as the fire burned. At least for a while. If dead beforehand, then no increase in the normal level of CO is found. This wasn't available in 1912.

The other thing the ME would look for is soot and burning within the lungs, bronchial tubes, and throat. If these are burned or if soot is present, the victim must have been breathing during the fire and inhaled the flames and soot. If dead before, none of this would be found.

Also, if the victim was not unconscious but rather trapped within the structure, there might be evidence that she tried to escape the fire. Claw marks on the door or splinters in her fingers. Maybe some of her fingernails ripped off as she tried to claw her way to freedom.

Your coroner could use the soot and burning of the lungs and the damage to her nails to determine that the victim was alive during the fire. In the absence of any of these he might conclude that she was indeed dead before the fire occurred.

COULD MY ME IDENTIFY AND DETERMINE THE CAUSE OF DEATH IN A CORPSE FROZEN FOR THIRTY YEARS?

 My murder victim is found in a freezer thirty years after she disappears. The freezer was on all that time. The cause of death is a heroin overdose. She had consensual sex shortly before her murder. What condition would her body be in? Would it be possible to take fingerprints for identification? Would the medical examiner be able to determine a cause of death by drug overdose and gather enough evidence to determine that she had sex shortly before her murder?

LC

A frozen corpse is an ME's dream. If the freezer was of the commercial variety, the body would be completely preserved. These freezers hold temperatures around 0 to 10 degrees, so if the freezer remained functional and powered for the entire thirty years, the corpse would be well preserved. The body might be somewhat desiccated (dried out). If failures occurred from time to time that allowed the body to completely or partially thaw, the corpse might be decayed to some degree. The degree would depend upon how long, how often, and how completely the body was allowed to thaw.

With uninterrupted freezing, the corpse would be preserved, fingerprints would be available, semen could be obtained, and even her last meal could be determined if she ate within a few hours of death. The last meal might fix the time of death very accurately. For example, if she dined with someone just before she disappeared and if this person testified what that meal was, the ME could determine the approximate time of death by examining the stomach contents. In general, it takes two to three hours for the stomach to empty, so finding food materials in the stomach would mean that the person died within about two or three hours of eating.

Since all body processes stop at death, the heroin would be present. Actually not heroin but monoacetylmorphine and morphine. After injection heroin is almost immediately broken down into monoacetylmorphine and then to morphine. The toxicologist will test for these. If he finds both monoacetylmorphine and morphine, the victim used heroin.

The semen would also be frozen and preserved, but it would be useful only if a suspect was identified or if the killer was in the national DNA database CODIS. After thirty years the killer could be long dead. Or not.

COULD THE ME DETERMINE THE TIME OF DEATH IF THE CORPSE REMAINED IN AN AIR-CONDITIONED OFFICE BUILDING FOR THREE DAYS?

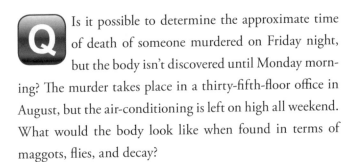 Is it possible to determine the approximate time of death of someone murdered on Friday night, but the body isn't discovered until Monday morning? The murder takes place in a thirty-fifth-floor office in August, but the air-conditioning is left on high all weekend. What would the body look like when found in terms of maggots, flies, and decay?

Catherine Maiorisi
New York, New York

After the approximately sixty hours between the actual time of death and the discovery of the corpse you outlined in your scenario, body temperature, rigor mortis, and lividity would be of little help. A corpse loses about one and a half degrees of body temperature per hour until it reaches the ambient temperature. Here the ambient temp would be about 72 degrees, which means the corpse would reach room temperature after about eighteen hours.

$$98.6 - 72 = 26.6/1.5 = 17.7 \text{ hours}$$

The body temperature would then remain unchanged, so this determination is of little help.

Rigor mortis becomes full after twelve to twenty-four hours and then resolves over the next twelve to twenty-four hours, so by sixty hours rigor will have come and gone. Again, of little help. Lividity becomes fixed after about eight hours, so this also offers no help.

Your ME could use stomach contents and the degree of putrefaction (decay) to assist with his estimation. At death all bodily functions cease, including digestion. After a meal it takes two to three hours for the stomach to empty and about twenty-four hours for the food to complete its passage through the body. This is general but a good ballpark. If it was known that your victim had a dinner of spaghetti at 7 p.m. on Friday night and the ME found spaghetti within his stomach at autopsy, he could state that the death occurred somewhere between 7 and 11 p.m. on Friday evening.

Under normal circumstances putrefaction follows a predictable pattern, which the ME can use in his estimation of the time of death. The rate at which this process occurs is almost never normal because conditions surrounding the body are almost never normal. But in your scenario, the environment is known and constant. This would help the ME make an educated guess. Coupled with the stomach contents information, your ME could narrow down the time of death to a few hours.

There would not likely be any insect activity in such a closed environment.

WHAT WOULD A CORPSE LOOK LIKE AFTER TEN YEARS IN A SEPTIC TANK?

Q The victim in my story is bludgeoned to death, and his clothed body is dumped into a partially full five-hundred-gallon septic holding tank in central Alberta, Canada. No one lives at the location or uses the tank. Ten years later new owners have the tank emptied in late summer and the remains are discovered. I'm expecting that the remains will be disarticulated bones and that some small bones and teeth might be lost when the tank is emptied. Would this be correct? Would any clothing be identifiable? The victim is wearing a poly-cotton T-shirt, cotton blue jeans, leather belt, and leather steel-toed work boots. I used some of the elements of the 1977 Septic Tank Sam case from Alberta for my story, but Sam's remains were discovered after only a few months in the tank.

Jena Snyder
Clear Lake, Alberta, Canada

A There are several possibilities, but most likely you are correct that the corpse would be reduced to skeletal remains. After ten years the ligaments and tendons would also have decayed and the bones would be disarticulated or separated from one another.

The bacteria that cause decay in most corpses come from the gastrointestinal tract. The body basically decays inside out. In a septic tank there are many nasty bacteria floating around, and a body in that environment would decay both inside out and outside in. One caveat is that some septic tanks are filled with antibacterial chemicals that could greatly slow the decay process. Could this allow some tissue to survive after a decade? Possible but not likely. I would go with only skeletal remains since that is by far the most likely.

Clothing is tricky. Sometimes it survives these types of circumstances, and sometimes it doesn't. If any remained, it would be severely damaged, friable, and difficult to handle. It would easily fall apart and would probably do so during the pumping process. It is possible that some fragments could be found and analyzed. Leather products such as belts and shoes would be more likely to survive and if so would also be severely damaged. Or they might be destroyed completely. If the shoes had rubber soles, these would be more resistant to destruction, so the size, tread pattern, and manufacturer could possibly be determined.

Metallic objects such as belt buckles, jewelry, and buttons could survive this environment for ten years. They would be corroded but still should be identifiable. It might help identify the victim if a belt buckle or a piece of jewelry was unique and recognizable by friends or family. The steel-toed boots would survive and might indicate the size, model, and manufacturer, and this might help identify the victim too.

WHAT WOULD A CORPSE LOOK LIKE AFTER TEN YEARS IN A SILAGE PIT?

Q In my scenario, a female corpse has been buried in a silage pit for ten years. She was wearing black vinyl boots and chunky metal earrings when buried. When my protagonist digs up the silage, what would the body look and smell like, and how would the earrings and boots appear? Also, what condition would the silage be in directly around the remains?

Beth Montgomery
Author of *The Birthmark* and *Murderer's Thumb*
Victoria, Australia
http://aelanstori.blogspot.com

A In the production of silage, anaerobic bacteria (those that thrive in an oxygen-free environment) ferment plant materials such as corn. A by-product of this is the production of acetic and lactic acids, which tend to help preserve the silage for long-term cattle feeding.

When a corpse decays it does so through the action of bacteria. Most of the bacteria responsible for this are also anaerobic and come from the corpse's gastrointestinal (GI) tract. Heat and moisture favor bacterial growth and thus putrefaction (decay).

What would happen to a corpse in silage? There are several possibilities. The heat (a by-product of the fermentation process) and the presence of bacteria both within and around the corpse could lead to a rapid decay, so in a week to several weeks, depending on the actual silage temperature, only a skeleton might remain.

On the other hand, the fermentation process could produce enough acetic and lactic acid that the growth and activity of the bacteria were slowed. The body could be very well preserved. Similar to Bog People, where the acidic nature of the bog kills the bacteria and preserves the corpse for many, many years.

And anywhere in between. The body could be moderately decayed but not completely. A portion of the body could be severely decayed, even skeletal, while other parts are more well preserved.

If the body was skeletal, there would be no body odor since the odor comes from decaying tissues. If tissue remained, the odor would be that of a decaying corpse plus the smell of the silage.

The earrings would be intact. The boots could be intact also, but they would likely be discolored, stained, and frayed a bit.

WHAT WOULD A CORPSE LOOK LIKE AFTER SIXTY YEARS IN A MINIATURE SUBMARINE?

 Here's my scene: A body is trapped inside a perfectly sealed, unflooded miniature submarine for sixty or so years. What would it look like? Smell like? Skeleton or mummy or something else?

Grant Blackwood
Author
www.grantblackwood.com

The corpse's condition at the time of discovery depends on the conditions within the sub, mainly the temperature. If the sub is stored or dry-docked or in harbor or in shallow water where the temps are warm, then the remains would be skeletal. But I suspect your sub is in deep water, where the temps might run in the mid-30s to low 40s. If so, the decay process would be greatly delayed. It could still decay to only bones, or it could dry out and mummify. It could also partially decay and partially mummify. For example, a leg or arm or torso or half the body could mummify, and the rest could be skeletal.

Whether the remains were mummified or skeletal, there would be no active decay and thus no odor of decay. It would probably smell musty with an undercurrent of death.

WHAT DEVICE MIGHT DETECT THE RESIDUAL ODOR OF A CORPSE IN A CAR TRUNK?

Q I recently read in my local newspaper about a test that was done by the investigators on a suspect's car trunk. They used an air-modulator to determine if a corpse had been in the trunk in the last few months. What is this test?

A Whether the fragrance of a flower or the stench of a decaying corpse, we sense odors when molecules released from the object contact the olfactory (smell) nerve endings in our nose. The brain then searches its files and attaches a name to the odor. It is our most primitive sense. When a corpse or anything is left in an enclosed space such as a car trunk, the molecules concentrate in the air and attach to things such as the trunk's carpet. These molecules are slowly released over time, so the air within the enclosure will contain a few molecules at any given time. More if the place remains sealed and less if it is repeatedly opened or ventilated in any way. Just like odors dissipate over time and do so faster if the room or object is aired out.

The instrument you describe is an "electronic nose." It is basically a gas chromatograph, an instrument for separating and often identifying the types of molecules contained within an air sample. The "nose" searches for and identifies the molecules known to be associated with a decaying body. If these are found, they suggest that a decomposing body has been in the trunk at some time in the past. Such a device was employed in the Caylee Anthony investigation. Whether this new technique will be admissible in court or not hasn't been determined.

WHAT WOULD MY PREGNANT DROWNING VICTIM LOOK LIKE AFTER TWELVE HOURS IN THE OCEAN, AND CAN AN ACCURATE TIME AND MANNER OF DEATH BE DETERMINED?

Q I'm a South African suspense novelist. In my new story, the victim is a nineteen-year-old woman of slight build, four months pregnant, and of mixed Caucasian/Khoikhoi descent. It is summertime, the temperature about 20 degrees Celsius (68 Fahrenheit), and the seawater is approximately 16 degrees Celsius (61 Fahrenheit). Fishing net is thrown over the victim's head when she is picking mussels, and she is held underwater in a shallow pool while being strangled with the net. Her body is thrown into the sea from an outcrop of rocks. She is found faceup twelve hours later in shallow water amongst rocks on the other side of the small bay. The seagulls have had a go at the corpse. The net is still tangled around the victim's face and neck.

My questions: What would the body and face look like? Can a relatively accurate time of death be established? How can strangulation be established? Could there be doubt about the manner of death? Accidental drowning versus homicide? Can my detective spot petechial hemorrhages before the autopsy is done? Can the autopsy reveal there is too little water in the lungs to point to drowning? How long would DNA paternity testing take?

Chanette Paul
Stanford, South Africa
www.chanettepaul.co.za

A After only twelve hours in water of this temperature there would be very little evidence of decay, so the body would be only slightly swollen, and there could be some pruning of the hands and feet just from contact with water. The major visible injuries would be cuts and scrapes that occurred from the rocks and other trauma and from the seagulls pecking the body. Also, there could be marks from the net that was thrown over her as well as signs of drowning. The signs would predominantly be petechial hemorrhages in the eyes and the nasopharynx (the back of the throat) and perhaps debris in her mouth and throat from inhalation of the water while she was dying. Petechiae are more associated with strangulation, but in a violent drowning where the victim struggled a great deal, they can also be present. Petechiae are easily seen as bright red dots in the sclera (white part of the eyeball) and the conjunctivae (the pink part around the eyeball). The petechiae in these areas should be visible to your detective.

Time of death could be fairly accurately determined since the medical examiner would use the body temperature, the stage of rigor mortis, and the pattern of the lividity. A corpse loses heat at about 1.5 degrees per hour, though this might be faster in water of this temperature. Here the body temperature would be in the range of 75 to 80 degrees, and this would allow the medical examiner to estimate that the death occurred roughly ten to fourteen hours earlier. Rigor would be full in that the entire body would be stiff. Typically full rigor takes about twelve hours to develop, but in the case of drowning with the extreme struggles that go on during this, the rigor often comes on much earlier. The pattern of lividity is a little trickier since it would depend upon how long the body tumbled around in the water and how long it lay in one position. A body must be in one position for six to eight hours for the lividity to become fixed.

The scenario you laid out does not seem to be one of strangulation but rather one of her being trapped in a net and held underwater to drown. Unless I misunderstood your setup. But if part of the net was wrapped around her neck and used to strangle her, there would be blue-black bruises visible on her neck. These are simply the bruises that occur during the strangulation process. If the net was rolled in some way and used as a strangulation device, it is possible the bruises could mirror the pattern of the net.

There could easily be confusion regarding the cause of death if she wasn't strangled as I discussed above. If she was simply trapped in the net and held underwater, there would be no strangulation marks, and it could look like an accidental drowning.

One of the most difficult things to determine at autopsy is whether a drowning occurred or not. The amount of water in the lungs has little to do with it. The lungs of people who die for other reasons and are then thrown in the water will passively fill with water over a few hours. Also, some drowning victims have what is known as dry drowning where their lungs are actually free of water. The initial inhalation of water causes the vocal cords to spasm and slam shut, which prevents air movement, and the person dies from asphyxia. This vocal cord spasm also prevents water from entering the lungs, and therefore, the lungs are dry. The medical examiner would look for inhaled debris deep in the airways and lungs, and finding this would suggest that the victim inhaled water and thus drowned. Not definitive but highly suggestive.

DNA testing for paternity requires DNA from the mother, the fetus, and the prospective father. Two out of three will not work. If all three are available, paternity testing is quite easy. How long it would take to get the results back depends upon the sophistication of the jurisdiction. I'm unfamiliar with how things are in South Africa, so I can only speak for how it is in the US. If it took place in a major city where there was a well-equipped crime lab that had a sophisticated DNA lab, they could get the results in twenty-four hours. Unless they were backlogged weeks or months as is often the case. If it was a smaller jurisdiction and they had to send the samples out to a regional, state, or the FBI lab, it might take several weeks.

BEFORE THE INVENTION OF THE STETHOSCOPE, HOW DID A PHYSICIAN DETERMINE IF SOMEONE WAS DEAD?

Q I need some medical advice for my historical novel set in 1815. According to my research, stethoscopes were not yet invented at this time, so how did physicians determine if a person was dead or alive (besides obvious things like decapitation)? Did they know of the pulse points in the wrists and neck, or did they simply put their ear to the chest of the victim?

Diane M. Downer
Shallotte, North Carolina

A The concept for a stethoscope came to Rene Laennec in 1816 when he was asked to examine a young woman who was suspected of having a form of heart disease. The typical method of examining the heart was for the doctor to press his ear against the patient's chest, but in a young woman this was not allowable. Therefore, other means of determining heart disease, such as percussion (tapping on the chest), were employed. Percussion was not a very accurate or effective tool, however. The young woman Laennec was examining was apparently overweight, which made percussion difficult and of little value. Since necessity is the mother of invention, he came up with the novel idea of rolling a piece of paper into a cylinder, then pressing one end against the girl's chest and the other against his own ear. This amplified the sound, and he was able to hear the young woman's heart. Subsequent to that he invented the stethoscope, which originally was a solid hollow tube and not the rubber tubes we see today. He first reported on his invention in 1819. So in 1815 there would've been no stethoscope to listen to the heart.

Physicians as far back as ancient China understood that pulses were important for life, and they were able to locate them in various areas of the body. The problem with pulses is that people who were severely dehydrated or in some form of shock would have pulses that were so weak that they could not be felt, and they were pronounced dead when indeed they were not. As you can imagine, this led to some very frightening situations. Dead folks are not supposed to sit up and gasp for air, but unfortunately that happened. So determining that someone was dead in 1815 was not easy. Very often the body was left in an observation room for several days, and once the odor of decay appeared, they knew the individual was indeed dead. The stethoscope helped avoid these errors. Not always, though, because sometimes even the heart sounds are too weak to readily hear, but its invention was a step in the right direction.

WHAT MATERIALS WOULD THE ME USE TO IDENTIFY A MURDER VICTIM IF ONLY A LIMB WAS FOUND?

Q I'm writing a murder mystery and need to know how DNA is used to identify a missing person. If only a limb is found, will blood alone be used to make the match? Or tissue, fingerprints, or something else? If the police suspect the arm belonged to a particular individual, what will they take from that person's home to try to match the arm to the missing person? Maybe hair from a brush known to belong to them?

DW

A The police will use any and all means available to establish the identity of a missing or deceased person. In the situation you describe, they would have fingerprints and DNA. They might also have birthmarks, tattoos, and jewelry.

Let's dispense with the latter three first. Jewelry could have an engraving or be so distinctive that the owner or the manufacturer could be located. Birthmarks, such as a port-wine stain (like Gorbachev's), are very distinctive as are many tattoos. If the victim had had a previous brush with the law, these could have been photographed and stored. A match would lead to the ID of the victim.

Fingerprints might be obtainable from the limb, depending upon the degree of putrefaction (decay). Again, if the victim had ever been fingerprinted, the prints could be part of the national print database known as the Automated Fingerprint Identification System (AFIS). Your cops could run an AFIS search and ID the victim. If he was in the system, that is.

DNA is present within the nuclei of all cells that possess a nucleus. Red blood cells (RBCs) have no nuclei and thus no DNA. But white blood cells (WBCs) do. It is this DNA that yields the DNA obtained from blood. Skin, muscle, and other tissue cells contain DNA. Thus, the arm would yield much usable DNA unless it was extremely decomposed. The ME could then match this against DNA known to be from the missing person. This could be obtained from many household items such as stamps or envelopes the victim had licked, a toothbrush, and yes, hair from a brush. Hair has no cells and no DNA, but the follicles do. The hair would yield DNA only if it had attached follicles, which is often the case with hair taken from a brush where some hair is pulled out during brushing.

CAN THE ME DETERMINE WHERE A DROWNING TOOK PLACE?

Q Would an autopsy in 1965 be able to distinguish the type of water in which the victim was drowned? For example, in a bathtub as opposed to a river? If so, how specific, as to the source of the water, might the determination be?

SU

A When people drown, they inhale water and whatever is in the water into their mouth, nose, throat, and lungs. This includes leaves, insects, seeds and pollens, and other debris. In a river or other natural body of water, the plant and animal materials found in the victim's lungs can be specific for an area. For example, if pine pollen or bits of pine needles are found in the lungs, the victim drowned in an area where pine trees grow near the water. Same can be true for all types of trees and other plants. Insects also have specific areas where they live, so finding these in the lungs could point to a particular locale.

In addition, when victims drown they grab for anything they can get a hold of in an attempt to survive. Drowning victims are often found with dirt, pebbles, plants, etc., clutched in their hands and beneath their nails. These can also be used to pinpoint the location.

If a corpse is found in a swimming pool but at autopsy the ME finds debris in the victim's lungs or beneath her nails that is not present in the pool water, he might conclude that the person drowned elsewhere and was dumped into the pool to stage the death as an accidental drowning. If he can match the debris (pollen feathers, seeds, etc.) to a particular location, then he might say that the drowning took place at that location.

In a pool the water is typically fairly clean but does contain chlorine, which can be tested for. Chlorine is not found in a natural body of water. Even in 1965 this testing was possible but not common. In a tub the water would be clean and free of chlorine but might contain some soap or oil, and these too could be tested for.

So the things that are present in the inhaled water can often help determine the location of the drowning.

WHAT TYPES OF BUGS VISIT A DECOMPOSING CORPSE, AND HOW DO THEY DEVELOP?

Q I am doing a project for school and would like to know the name of some bugs that arrive at decomposing bodies. How long does it take them to get there? How long does it take them to reproduce?

AL
United Kingdom

A A dead body attracts numerous insects. These are typically flies and beetles that feed off the corpse's flesh. They tend to appear at predictable times and in a predictable sequence, and the ME will use this to aid in his determination of the time of death. Unfortunately, these patterns vary greatly, depending upon geographic region, specific locale, time of day, and season. Because of the complex nature of the bug world, the ME will often request the assistance of a forensic entomologist. Entomology is the study of insects.

Numerous species feed on the dead body, feed on the insects that are attracted to the body, or both. Each has a preferable time and order of appearance and a different life cycle. This subject is simply too big and complex to address completely here, so let's confine ourselves to the most common species, the fly. An understanding of this insect will give you a feel for the problems the forensic entomologist faces.

When a body is left exposed, blowflies appear early,

often within the first hour after death. They seek out the moist areas of the corpse to lay their eggs. The nose, mouth, armpit, groin, and open wounds are favored locations. The eggs hatch to larvae (maggots) within hours. Over the next six to ten days the larvae feed, grow, and repeatedly molt, finally becoming pupae when their outer covering hardens. Approximately twelve days later adult flies emerge. This entire cycle takes from about eighteen to twenty-two days. The mature flies will then lay eggs, and the cycle repeats.

Under normal circumstances, if the ME or entomologist finds only eggs, the death likely occurred less than forty-eight hours earlier. If he finds maggots but no pupae, the death occurred between one and ten days earlier. The finding of pupae means that six to ten or more days have passed, while the presence of mature hatchlings indicate that death occurred two to three weeks earlier.

As you might suspect, it's not really that easy. Blowflies do not deposit eggs at night and are less plentiful in winter. If the victim was murdered at midnight, the blowflies might not appear until dawn, and if it is cold, they might not appear at all. If conditions are unfavorable, the maggots might go dormant for extended periods of time. For example, if the body is in an area where it is warm during the day and very cold at night, they might be dormant half of each twenty-four-hour period. If it turns cold for several days, the developmental process may be put on hold for that time period. These situations must be considered when insect activity is used to determine the time of death. To help with calculating a developmental timeline, the entomologist may consult a climatologist. He can provide information regarding weather conditions over the past few days and weeks, and that might aid the ME with his time of death estimation.

It is important to note that insect studies can only give a *minimum* time since death occurred. If pupae are found, the corpse must be at least six to ten days old. It can't be less since the pupae would not have had time to appear. But if the weather is inhospitable to the fly or the larvae, it could be much longer. Another compounding factor is that the insects appear in waves and new generations appear all the time. The adults produced after two weeks will themselves lay eggs, and these eggs will follow a similar cycle. A three-week-old corpse may show fly eggs, maggots, pupae, and adults. Sorting all this out is no easy task.

The criminalist must obtain samples for the entomologist to review, so the entomologist can evaluate the types of insects present, where each is within its developmental cycle, and estimate how many cycles have occurred. He should collect live maggots and pupae as well as empty pupal cases. Some maggots should be placed in alcohol or in a KAAD solution (a mixture of alcohol, kerosene, and other chemicals). This will preserve them in a state that reflects the scene.

HOW WOULD AN ME DETERMINE THAT A ROCK HAMMER CAUSED THE WOUNDS ON A CORPSE?

Q My main character (a crime scene tech) and a detective attend an autopsy where the ME examines a victim's wounds, which were caused by a rock hammer. The murder took place the evening before the corpse is found in the desert where it was dumped. It is February, which can be quite cold at night. How would the ME describe the wounds to the tech and the primary detective? Could the ME tell that the instrument was a rock hammer and that both ends were used?

BER
Tucson, Arizona

A A rock hammer has two distinct ends. One is similar to a standard hammer, and the other is pointed or chisel-like. When used as a weapon each end would produce different wounds. The hammer end would produce blunt traumatic injuries that could result in bruises, abrasions, and fractured bones. Individual bruises could be in the shape of the hammer face, which could be square, round, hexagonal, or almost any other shape the manufacturer gave it. The coroner would describe the bruises and abrasions and comment on their number, location, and shape. If he had the suspected weapon at his disposal, he could compare the shapes of some of the wounds and might be able to conclude that either this hammer or one very similar in size and shape produced the wounds.

The other end would produce penetrating wounds. The length, width, and depth of wounds would be measured, and the coroner could use these measurements to state what type of weapon made them. He could give a fairly accurate cross-sectional description (width and thickness) of the weapon and could state its minimum length. This is similar to stab wounds from a knife. The blade, or in this case the pointed end of the hammer, would need to be at least as long as the deepest wound. It could be longer but not shorter. If he had a weapon to compare with the wounds, he could determine if this weapon or a similar one produced the wounds.

The only way he could state that it was this hammer and not simply a similar one would be if blood or tissue from the victim was found on the hammer. Here DNA testing would be crucial. Even if the attacker cleaned the weapon, traces of blood could have soaked into a porous wooden handle or seeped into the crease where the head and the handle join.

In describing these wounds the coroner would state their size, shape, location, and general severity. This would be true of each bruise, abrasion, or penetrating injury he saw. He would then state what type of weapon likely made the wounds and if he had a suspect weapon whether this weapon was consistent with having produced the wounds he saw. If he found blood and matched the DNA on the weapon to the victim, he can say that it was this exact weapon that caused the injuries.

WHAT WOULD A CORPSE LOOK LIKE IF THE PERSON DIES FROM INJECTING A COMBINATION OF HEROIN AND STRYCHNINE?

Q I have a question about a death caused by strychnine-laced heroin. Several college kids show up at a shooting gallery and make a heroin buy. The heroin has been cut with strychnine. I would like the death to be very quick, too quick for anyone to summon help. I understand that strychnine causes severe muscle spasms. Does this happen even if the dose is high? What exactly causes death?

When found, they've been dead long enough for there to be noticeable decay. Would the bodies be contorted or have visible pain on the faces? How would the way they looked differ from a true heroin overdose? I understand rigor is almost instantaneous when the death is caused by strychnine. Would it be immediately obvious to the ME or a homicide detective that this wasn't a heroin overdose but something else?

P.A. Brown
Author of the L.A. Shadows series
Ontario, Canada
http://www.pabrown.com

A Heroin, like all narcotics, kills by depressing the brain's respiratory center. The victim falls asleep, stops breathing, and dies from asphyxia. Strychnine causes spasm (contraction) of all the body's muscles, including those used for breathing, and again the victim dies from asphyxia. As long as the dose is enough to cause this reaction, it makes no difference how much more is given. The lethal dose of strychnine in humans is typically between 100 and 200 milligrams.

Strychnine causes the body and face to contort. The body is drawn into what we call opisthotonus, which is a severely arched position. The eyes will be wide open, and the mouth is drawn into a broad grimace called risus sardonicus. However, most of the time this is lost at death when all the muscles relax. It is true that instant rigor, sometimes called cadaveric spasm, can occur in some circumstances, including strychnine overdoses, and if so, the body might be frozen in that posture and with that facial expression. Even if it does happen, the posture and facial expression will resolve when the body begins to decay, which depends upon the temperature of the environment. The warmer it is, the faster the decay process moves along. In your scenario where the corpse displays noticeable decay, the body and the face would be flaccid (relaxed). If you want the posture maintained until investigators arrive have the bodies found within hours of death.

There is nothing specific about a heroin overdose other than needle marks, and virtually no poison leaves behind any visible abnormalities. Toxicological testing is required to prove a drug OD. The corpse in your scenario would look like any other partially decayed, dead body.

HOW WOULD THE IDENTIFICATION OF A CHILD ABDUCTED AT THE AGE OF ONE MONTH BE ACCOMPLISHED WHEN HIS CORPSE IS FOUND SEVEN YEARS LATER?

Q I am writing a screenplay in which an infant is kidnapped a month after birth. Seven years later the police find a seven-year-old boy dead. They suspect it is the missing infant from seven years prior. The mother died in childbirth. There are no dental records. How would they identify the child?

RG
Chicago, Illinois

A Identifying an unknown corpse is often very difficult. As you pointed out, there would be no dental records since the child disappeared as an infant before he had teeth much less dental records. With the mother gone, there would be no direct way to get DNA from her. Her corpse could of course be exhumed, but even if this isn't possible, all is not lost.

The fact that the police believe they know who the dead child is helps immensely. Rather than simply having a John Doe corpse, a strong suspicion as to his identity guides their investigation and points them in the right direction.

The only sure way of proving paternity, and in this case proving that this child belonged to the mother in question, would be to have DNA from both the mother and the father.

If the father is known, obtaining his DNA is possible, and of course DNA could be taken from the child's corpse.

Getting the mother's DNA could be more problematic but not impossible. Perhaps someone had an old hairbrush or toothbrush that belonged to her. Maybe she had sent letters to friends and relatives and in doing so had licked the envelope and the stamp. DNA can often be obtained from these items even after many years. If DNA is acquired from the child, the father, and the mother, then it can be proven with certainty that the child was the offspring of these two parents.

There are other options. Mitochondrial DNA (mtDNA) is passed down the maternal line generation after generation essentially unchanged for many thousands of years. This means that the child would have the same mtDNA as any of his siblings (if there were any), the mother, the maternal grandmother, and any maternal aunts. The finding that the mtDNA of this child matched mtDNA from a known child of the mother (a sibling of the dead child), from the mother herself, from the grandmother, or from a maternal aunt would be strong evidence that this child was indeed a child of the dead mother. Who else could it be? This is not as absolute as using nuclear DNA, but it is powerful evidence since not that many children are abducted and their bodies found seven years later.

Since your child is male, there is another option. If the father was known and DNA was obtained from him, it could be matched to the child using Y chromosomal DNA. It's similar to mitochondrial except that it is found solely on the Y chromosome and is passed down the paternal line.

This child would have the same Y chromosomal DNA as his father, his grandfather, any male siblings, and any paternal uncles.

One or more of these methods could be employed to identify your unfortunate child.

HOW WOULD MY INVESTIGATORS IDENTIFY A CORPSE THAT HAD A PACEMAKER?

Q In my next novel, a limbless, headless torso is all that remains of the victim. Because the torso is unremarkable and lacking DNA for comparison, I assume that identification would be difficult. I am planning to have my victim be a pacemaker recipient. How would the patient's files be tracked down for identification purposes?

Robert Scott
Author of the Jack Elton Mystery series
Assiniboia, Saskatchewan, Canada

A Without DNA, fingerprints, or dental records for comparison, investigators will use things like clothing, tattoos, scars, and, as you pointed out, surgical devices such as pacemakers, artificial joints, and a few other things. Tracing a pacemaker is very easy. It has the manufacturer's name and the device's serial number etched on its surface. Companies keep meticulous records of every device: who got it, what doctor implanted it, where and when the implant was done. The recipient's name, address, and contact info would be part of this record. Same is true for joint replacement hardware.

COULD MY CORONER IN 1946 ENGLAND DISTINGUISH A HEART ATTACK OR STROKE FROM A BLOW TO THE HEAD AS THE CAUSE OF DEATH?

Q My victim, a sixty-six-year-old female, has been struck on the head by a ceramic teapot, falls, and is found unconscious some time later. The immediate assumption is that she had a stroke or a heart attack. There is no external evidence of the blow to the head.

She is transported to the hospital where she dies without regaining consciousness. When hospital staff find evidence of the head injury, it is assumed that, on falling, she struck her head. The stroke or heart attack would be considered the precipitating event that caused her to fall.

Would an autopsy in 1946 England be able to discern whether the blow or the stroke/heart attack occurred first? I'm not as concerned with what killed her as I am with making her death initially appear accidental, only later to be determined to be the result of homicidal malice.

HvH

A The initial confusion you need is already built into your plot. With no obvious cause of death visible at the scene, the real cause of death will not be revealed until the autopsy and that might not be done for days, even weeks. There is a backlog at most coroners' offices, so you can have the autopsy done anytime you wish—the day of the event, weeks later, or anywhere in between.

A blow to the head that causes unconsciousness is called a concussion if there is no brain injury involved. These folks wake up in a minute or up to five or ten minutes. To be out longer and to cause death, the injury would have to be more severe, and usually an intracranial bleed is involved. This is bleeding into or around the brain and is often fatal, particularly in 1946 when surgical techniques for this were less sophisticated than now. The time interval between injury and death could be almost anytime you need—immediately to weeks later. Brain injuries come in many flavors.

At autopsy the ME would see that there was no clot plugging one of the coronary arteries (supply blood to the heart) or one of the cerebral arteries (supply blood to the brain) and would know that neither a heart attack nor a stroke had occurred. He would see the brain injury and the bleeding and know that the cause of death was blunt head trauma with an intracranial bleed. The question then becomes whether the blow was delivered by another person or whether she slipped and fell, striking her head. The former would be a homicide and the latter an accident. If paint or chips from the pot were found in her hair or embedded in her scalp, the coroner might conclude that she was struck by the pot rather than suffering an accidental fall.

There is nothing about a blow to the head that would predictably cause a heart attack or a stroke, so if the coroner found evidence for either of these as well as blunt head trauma, he might conclude that the victim suffered a heart attack or a stroke, fell, and hit her head, causing the bleed. That would rule out foul play since there is no way to make someone have a heart attack or a stroke.

This should give you several ways to construct your plot.

HOW DOES THE CORONER LOCATE NEEDLE MARKS ON A CORPSE?

Q During an autopsy where the victim is suspected to have died from bad drugs, what does the coroner look for to determine the presence of needle marks? I understand they can be hard to spot. Is there some way to scan the body, or would it be strictly an eyeball search? Once the needle mark is located, what would be done with it? Would it be excised and if so what then?

P.A. Brown
Author of the L.A. Shadows series
Ontario, Canada
http://www.pabrown.com

A Injection marks are located by visual inspection. There are no scans or other tests for this. Though injection marks are sometimes difficult to see, sticking a needle through someone's skin leaves a mark that is usually pinpoint and brownish red. The color is from a small drop of dried blood that clots in the path left by the needle.

Drug users often try to hide their needle marks by injecting themselves in places other than their arms, and this can make the search more difficult. Sometimes along the inner thighs, between the toes, and even under the tongue. A murderer could do the same thing if the victim was compliant, restrained, or severely sedated.

The location of the injection site might tell the coroner whether the individual could have injected himself or not.

This is critical since an injection site along the back or in the crease of the buttocks or somewhere else the person could not have reached himself rules out a suicidal or accidental overdose and makes a homicidal overdose very likely.

The lab would do toxicological testing to uncover what drug was injected. This would at least include blood, urine, and liver tissue. It is also possible that the coroner would remove the tissue around the needle mark and test it since some of the injected material always leaks into the tissues surrounding the needle track. He would need to take only a small plug of tissue perhaps the diameter of a drinking straw.

CAN MY KILLER REPOSITION A STIFF CORPSE?

Q I have a woman murdered sitting in a chair in the evening. The killer leaves her in the chair until he dumps her body early the following morning. I would like lividity to be in her buttocks and rigor to have set in when she's found around 6 a.m. Would she still be pliable enough after the lividity sets in for the killer to position her when he dumps her?

Michelle Thouviner
Arnold, Missouri

A Lividity is the settling of blood in the dependent areas of the corpse as dictated by gravity. It begins within a couple of hours and becomes fixed by six to eight hours. Your corpse would have lividity along the buttocks and the backs of the legs as well as the lower legs. On the buttocks and the backs of the legs, where these areas contacted the chair and supported the body, there would be whitish areas of no lividity. This is due to the body weight compressing the capillaries and preventing blood from leaking into the tissues in those areas. After six to eight hours much of the lividity would be fixed, so the ME would know that the corpse had been moved if the lividity pattern did not match the victim's position.

Rigor typically follows the 12-12-12 rule. It takes twelve hours to become complete, remains for twelve hours, and then resolves over twelve hours. This is very general and there are many exceptions. But if your victim remained in the chair for around twelve hours after death and was then found shortly after being moved and dumped, the corpse would be locked in the sitting position and the lividity pattern would be as described above. Unless he repositioned her, which is what you want. Rigor can be broken by the forceful bending of the joints, and once done your killer could reposition the corpse any way he wished.

HOW WOULD A SEMEN STAIN BE
REVEALED IN 1906?

Q My story is set in Toronto in 1906. How would a semen stain on a petticoat be identified? How long after its deposition would such an identification be possible? If this was an attempted rape, what other legal issues should I consider?

Whitney Smith
Author of *Lucy Speaks*
London, England
www.whitneysmith.ca

A The first test for semen was the microscopic detection of sperm. This was established in 1839 by H.L. Bayard and was improved by W.F. Whitney when in 1897 he discovered a stain that is currently called the Christmas Tree Stain. This chemical fixed and exposed semen for easy viewing under a microscope. The first chemical test would come in 1896 with the discovery that teriodide of potassium caused a reaction with semen, but the first reliable chemical test for semen was the acid phosphatase test discovered in 1945.

This means that your sleuth has a couple of options. If the stain is fresh, maybe twelve to twenty-four hours, he might examine the material under a microscope and see intact and even motile sperm. If it is several days old, he might stain it with the Christmas Tree Stain and see dead sperm or sperm heads, remnants of the sperm. If he was aware of the teriodide of potassium test, he might also employ that.

Each of these would allow him to say that semen was indeed present. Then it would be up to the judge and jury to decide if there was an innocent reason for the suspect's sperm to be on the young lady's clothing or if a rape occurred. *Rape* is a legal term, not a medical one. These tests only prove that semen is present but not how or why it was placed where found.

COULD MY FORENSIC ANTHROPOLOGIST DETERMINE FROM SKELETAL REMAINS THAT THE VICTIM'S CAROTID ARTERIES HAD BEEN SEVERED AND HER HEART REMOVED?

Q In my novel, the skeletal remains of a young woman are found buried in the wilderness. By examining these remains, is it possible for my forensic anthropologist to know or suspect that the woman was killed by transection of the carotid arteries and that her heart was removed postmortem for ritualistic purposes? My killer used a razor-sharp obsidian knife for the killing. He also severed the victim's feet postmortem. Would he use another tool such as an ax for this?

Jennifer Froelich
Boise, Idaho

A Since there are no soft tissues left in skeletal remains, there will be no direct evidence for the slicing of the carotids. And if the perpetrator removed the heart by cutting into the abdomen and then removing the diaphragm, lungs, and heart that way, there would be no evidence of this, either.

But if the blade that cut the carotids also cut or nicked the cervical vertebrae (neck bones), then these nicks and cuts would be visible. This would require a very deep cut (basically a near decapitation) since the carotids lie toward the front of the neck and the cervical bones in the back.

If he cut through the rib cage to remove the heart, nicks and cuts on the ribs and sternum (breastbone) might be visible. Same is true of the feet and ankle bones.

Different types of blades and instruments make different types of cuts. A sharp knife blade, as in your scenario, would make narrower cuts and nicks than an ax blade. The examiner might be able to estimate the type of weapon used by looking at the nature of the bony damage. Also, if the blade itself was nicked or the tip broke off during the attack, these small pieces might be found embedded within or lying near the bones. If so, the fact that an obsidian knife had been used would be more apparent. Even better, if the weapon was located and the missing piece found with the remains matched it in a jigsaw fashion, the ME would know that this was the exact knife that did the deed.

WHAT WOULD THE CORPSE OF A CIVIL WAR SOLDIER LOOK LIKE WHEN UNEARTHED 130 YEARS LATER?

Q How intact would the skeleton of a young soldier buried in a West Virginia backyard during the Civil War be if it was unearthed in 1994? The terrain would be mountainous, the weather wet in spring and cold and snowy in winter. Would the depth of the burial make a difference? I need the skull to be somewhat intact.

LB

A The bones would be white, chalky, and as brittle as a dry twig. A fingernail could easily indent the surface, and if one was snapped in two, the fracture line would be straight and there would be some crumbling of the bone along it. Fresh bones tend to be heavier and sturdier because the protein matrix (the framework that holds the calcium) is intact, and this makes the bone stronger. A fresh bone will bend before it breaks, and when it breaks it does so in a greenstick fashion.

I should point out that the bones themselves would not be connected like the skeleton that hangs in the corner of most high school science classes. As the tissues of the body decay, so do the tendons and ligaments that hold the bones together. This means that the bones will no longer be attached and the teeth might even have fallen from the skull. The remains would simply be a collection of bones and perhaps some loose teeth.

The depth of the grave is only important if it is so shallow that predators have gotten to the body and carried off parts of it. If this has not happened, it makes very little difference when you're talking over one hundred years later. The skull could be intact, but the mandible or lower jawbone would not be attached, again because the ligaments would have decayed. Or the skull could be crumbled or broken into pieces. It could go either way, so have it intact or shattered as you need for your story.

DO TEETH AND THEIR FILLINGS REMAIN IN A SKULL TWENTY YEARS AFTER DEATH?

Q I think I know the answer to this, but I want to be sure: teeth remain in a skull. I assume, therefore, that metal fillings in those teeth would also still be present in a skull found twenty years after burial.

Chris Grabenstein
Agatha and Anthony Award–winning author of mysteries,
thrillers, and middle grade chillers
New York, New York

A Actually, the teeth often fall from the skull and jawbone. This is due to decay of the gum and the socket tissues that anchor the teeth in place. It depends upon the degree of decay and how long after death the skull is found. You can construct your story either way (teeth in place or not), and it will work. Also, some teeth might be in place, others scattered near the skull or grave site, and still others missing altogether.

It is probable that any fillings, crowns, etc., would be intact. They help the forensic odontologist (dentist) match a skull to old dental records or X-rays. If he has all the teeth, this is usually easy. If he has only one or two, it is more difficult but still possible since the fillings in each tooth would be individual. What are the odds that two people would have identical fillings in the same two or three teeth? Very unlikely so even with only a couple of teeth he might be able to make a match.

COULD THE ME DETERMINE THAT A VICTIM'S TATTOOS HAD BEEN APPLIED POSTMORTEM?

Q If a killer tattooed his victim, would the medical examiner be able to tell whether the tattoo was applied after death?

Julie Kramer
Author of *Stalking Susan*, *Missing Mark*, and *Silencing Sam*
Winner of Minnesota Book Award,
RT Reviewers Choice Best First Mystery
Finalist for Anthony, Barry, Shamus, Mary Higgins Clark,
Daphne du Maurier Awards
White Bear Lake, Minnesota
http://www.juliekramerbooks.com

A Most likely he would have no problem making this determination.

Imprinting a tattoo into someone's skin is a traumatic injury. The body will then react as it does to any trauma by rushing certain types of blood and tissue cells into the area. We call this an inflammatory reaction. The same thing happens if you cut your finger or burn it on the stove or slam it in a car door. The cells that are attracted to such injuries begin the repair process and remove damaged cells.

If the tattoo was placed prior to death, microscopic examination of the tissues would show the infiltration of these cells, whereas if it occurred after death there would be no such reaction. After death, the blood stops flowing and the cells of the body quickly die, so no reaction is possible. These cells arrive almost immediately, so even if the tattoo was done in the final few minutes before death, there would still be at least some evidence of this inflammatory reaction.

PART V
ODDS AND ENDS,
MOSTLY ODDS

COULD MY KILLER COMPLETELY DRAIN A HUMAN BODY OF BLOOD AND MAKE IT APPEAR AS IF A VAMPIRE WERE THE CULPRIT?

Q I am currently working on a book that includes a murder scene involving a nineteen-year-old female college student who has died from puncture wounds to her carotid artery. I would like readers to initially believe the injuries are due to supernatural forces such as a vampire. Is it possible to drain an entire body of blood through the carotid artery? If so, by what means could it be done? If it is not possible to bleed out naturally, what medical equipment might be needed? One of the murderers used to work in a mortuary and acquired two canine teeth from a dead middle-aged man, which he has hollowed out. Could any medical equipment needed be filtered through these, and if so, could a forensic test detect this?

CC

People can easily bleed to death after an injury to the carotid artery. It would gush and spurt until the victim lost a great deal but not all of her blood. The victim would die after losing roughly half of her total blood volume. Bleeding would cease at death because the heart stops and the blood no longer circulates. Your victim could lose half of her blood "naturally," but the remainder would require specialized equipment such as an embalming setup. Here the embalming fluid is forced into the vascular system under pressure by way of a trochar (large needle) and is removed through another at a separate site. But even the loss of half the blood volume could still raise the specter of a vampire if that fits the overall milieu and tone of your story.

One point: Most respectable vampires bite the jugular vein and not the carotid artery. Much less messy and accomplishes the same goal. But your "vampire" could easily attack a carotid artery.

If you want to create the illusion that a vampire might have done the deed, then the wounds need to be round punctures and not slashes and cuts as with a knife or an ax and not a large ragged wound as might occur with a bullet. A round tube or large bore needle (embalming trochar) would work. The victim needs to be alive during this, or your killer needs some embalming equipment to apply pressure to wash out the blood. Of course, the trick in this circumstance is getting the victim to hold still. If she was drugged to the point of losing consciousness, the needles could be inserted into her carotid, and most of her blood could be drained that way. If two needles were inserted side by side, it would take on the appearance of tooth marks. The stolen teeth could be used, but that might be technically more difficult.

At autopsy the ME would likely be able to determine that the punctures were made by sharp round objects but little more. This should fit your needs.

HOW LONG COULD A MAN SURVIVE CHAINED TO A WALL IN A SUBTERRANEAN ENVIRONMENT?

Q My students are studying short stories by Edgar Allan Poe and have some questions about how long someone could survive chained to a subterranean wall. The victim is an average-sized, middle-aged man, and he is chained to a catacomb wall. The nitrate levels in the chamber are high. How long would he be able to survive under these conditions without water, nourishment, and a sufficient amount of air?

MF
Euless, Texas

A There are several things that could lead to the victim's death in the circumstances you describe. First would be hypothermia. This would likely kill him before the lack of food, water, and air came into play. Catacombs tend to be damp and cold, and he would not be able to curl up to conserve heat. He could become very cold in a matter of hours and could die from hypothermia in the next twenty-four hours or so. Maybe less since many people are more susceptible to hypothermia than others. His inability to reach food and water would hasten his slide into hypothermia.

Another factor would be the crucifixion syndrome. When someone is locked into an upright position, whether from being nailed to a cross or chained to a wall, his body will eventually sag downward. His legs would give way to fatigue, his arms would be stretched upward, and he would hang by his wrists. This sagging occurs both externally and internally. As the body sags the shoulders droop, the chest cavity becomes smaller, and the heart and lungs are pressed down toward the diaphragm. This compresses the lungs, and the victim can die from asphyxia.

If he managed to live for several days, lack of water and food could be an issue, but I doubt your victim would last more than thirty-six hours under the conditions you describe.

The nitrate in question would most likely be potassium nitrate (KNO_3—saltpeter or niter) found in the walls, dirt, and stones of the catacombs. His exposure would be minimal since what little absorbed through his contact with the wall would be of no importance.

HOW LONG COULD MY CHARACTER SURVIVE IF BURIED ALIVE?

Q How long could a person survive buried alive in a coffin? What stages would a character go through due to the lack of oxygen? What long-term physical problems could the victim experience after being rescued?

Angie Lockett
Ontario, Canada

A How long the person survived would depend on the size of the coffin and the size and activity of the victim. A small person who remained calm in a large coffin would last longer than a large person in a small coffin who panicked. It is highly variable, but the person would not likely last more than fifteen to sixty minutes. The victim would become hypoxic (low oxygen content in the blood), which would make him giddy, then fatigued and short of breath, and finally disoriented. He might even hallucinate. He would ultimately slip into a coma and die from asphyxia.

If the person was rescued, the long-term effects would depend on how long and how severe the hypoxia was. The victim could be normal or suffer mild to severe brain damage. This could range from chronic headaches to loss of memory to all types of psychiatric problems (depression, anxiety, anger, acting out) to chronic confusion to loss of some motor functions (weak or paralyzed arms or legs) to a long-term coma. The scope of problems is large and unpredictable.

This unpredictability is good since you can craft your story almost any way you want.

HOW WOULD A SNOWPLOW BLADE DAMAGE A FROZEN CORPSE, AND WOULD MY CORONER BE ABLE TO DETERMINE THE CAUSE AND MANNER OF DEATH?

Q My murderer hides a nearly decapitated male corpse behind a large haystack. It is late February in western South Dakota at an elevation of four thousand feet during a cold snap where the air temp is below zero and the ground is frozen. The body is covered with three feet of snow. A week after the body is hidden, the body is hit by a tractor with a snowplow blade.

Would the frozen corpse snap in half like an icicle, or would there simply be gouges and chunks removed by the blade? If the body was close to the haystack, would the warmth/insulating factor of the hay make the body more pliable, and if so, could predatory animals eat some of the flesh? For whichever one of the above holds true, would the plow blade have the potential to wreak enough damage that the initial cause of death would be undetectable?

Lori G. Armstrong
Shamus Award–winning author of *Snow Blind*
Rapid City, South Dakota
www.loriarmstrong.com

A Icicles crack and break cleanly because when they're frozen water molecules align in a crystalline manner, causing them to shatter or snap in shards or clean lines. Tissues are more like a frozen side of beef. Sinewy in nature. The corpse wouldn't shatter or snap like ice, but rather the blade would cut and gouge it in almost any manner you want for your story. The coroner might think the decapitation was due to the blade and not know that it was the cause of death. He might think the person simply froze to death and was then damaged by the blade. This could lead him to sign off the death as natural or accidental. Or not.

A competent ME might discover this is not the case. Once the corpse has been slowly thawed (most likely over a few days in a refrigerated room), he would be able to examine the neck wounds more carefully. If he saw bleeding into the tissues around the wound and clotted blood within the throat, mouth, and lungs, he would know that the wounds occurred while the victim was alive and the blood was still flowing. If he saw none of this, he might assume the wounds were postmortem. So you can have your coroner figure it out or not as you wish for your story.

HOW WOULD MY SCIENTISTS ANALYZE TISSUES OBTAINED FROM AN UNKNOWN LIFE-FORM?

Q I am writing a novel where an unknown, shapeless creature is responsible for several mysterious deaths. A small fragment of this creature is found in a city full of corpses and must be analyzed. Which lab tests would be done? Would its DNA be compared with known DNA strands? Would this testing be done in a BSL-4 facility like the CDC?

Sandro Fazzi
Firenze, Italy
www.sandrofazzi.com

A Testing biological tissue from an alien or unknown creature would definitely be best in a BSL-4 type facility to prevent contamination and spread of any unknown toxins or biological organisms associated with the tissues. The Centers for Disease Control and Prevention (CDC) in Atlanta, Georgia, has such labs.

The first step is to identify the type of tissues present—muscles, skin, scales, organs, whatever. This requires slides prepared from slivers of the tissue that would then be viewed under a microscope. It would reveal any cellular or other microscopic structures. Chemical testing determines if the tissue was protein or some other known or unknown material.

Biological examinations would follow. Attempting to grow bacteria or viruses or parasites or any other biological species from the tissue fragment would be important to see if the material was infectious. Also, if cellular structure was found in the material, the scientist might attempt growing the tissues in cell culture mediums, so he could see how it multiplied on a cellular level and also to produce more material for future testing.

Gas chromatography is typically used when looking for drugs, toxins, or other chemicals in tissues, and this could be done to see if the tissues were contaminated with or produced some toxin. Another reason to do this in a sterile and controlled environment.

DNA sequencing and testing for various enzymes and hormones would also be done. This could take many months to complete, but much would be done in a few days or weeks. This of course assumes the creature has DNA.

What other testing followed would depend upon the nature of the tissue and what if anything was found with the above testing. Since this is sci-fi you can be very creative about what is uncovered during these investigations.

COULD DNA FROM SPONTANEOUSLY COMBUSTED VAMPIRES REVEAL THEIR AGE?

Q My detective hero is investigating a series of apparent arson homicides. It turns out that the victims were vampires who underwent spontaneous combustion after exposure to sunlight. Assuming bone fragments and perhaps other materials survived the fire, could DNA be extracted, and if so, could it reveal exactly how old the individuals were? They are centuries old. Could there be anything to indicate they had been vampires?

A Fires only rarely completely destroy a body. Usually the corpse is severely damaged but tissue remains. In the real world. Whether this is the case with your vampires or not is up to you. Your corpses could be completely consumed and there would be nothing left to analyze, or there could be bones or tissue fragments as you wish. So your assumption works and is believable. DNA could be extracted from these tissues, bones, and particularly from the teeth, where the enamel offers some protection to the interior pulp and its DNA.

Could the age of the deceased, vampire or not, be determined from DNA alone? No. There is nothing in the DNA profile that tells the age of an individual. Vampires are basically humans with some form of altered physiology that allows them to live for many centuries as long as they get the blood they need and avoid sunlight. So there is no marker in the DNA that would scream vampire.

That said, your story is by definition science fiction and fantasy, which means you can do what you wish. If you want your vampires to have specific genetic markers that could be discovered and indicate that they were vampires, then go ahead. If you want them to have a marker that reflects their age, then do that too. Who's to argue?

IS A MUTANT GENE THAT CAUSES HOMICIDAL BEHAVIOR BELIEVABLE?

Q In my fictional work *SK-1, The Killer Gene*, my protagonist, an internationally recognized female molecular biologist, attempts to discover a mutated gene that is responsible for homicidal behaviors. She is driven by the fact her mother was brutally murdered by a serial killer. If such a mutation did occur, where would it likely be located in the chromosomal configurations?

TH

A Since you are writing speculative fiction you can do anything you want. We have forty-six chromosomes arrayed into twenty-three pairs. Forty-four (twenty-two pairs) are called autosomal genes, and two (one pair) are our sex chromosomes (XX or XY). You can place your mutant gene on any of the forty-four autosomal genes or on the X chromosome if you want it expressed in both sexes (since both males and females have these) or on the Y chromosome if you want it expressed in males (since only males have this one).

CAN MY MARINE BIOLOGIST NAME A NEWLY DISCOVERED SPECIES AFTER HERSELF?

Q A question has popped up in the book I'm working on. My marine biologist has discovered a new genus of deep-sea worm. Does she get to name it, and if so, would she use her own name or some version of her name in both the genus and species?

Cynthia Riggs

A The answer is no on the genus and maybe on the species.

The accepted scientific nomenclature for every known organism follows a specific pattern. Each category is subdivided into others. Much as an outline is. They go: kingdom, phylum, subphylum, class, order, family, genus, and species.

Humans are classified as follows:

Kingdom: Animalia
Phylum: Chordata
Subphylum: Vertebrata
Class: Mammalia
Order: Primates
Family: Hominidae
Genus: Homo
Species: Homo sapiens

This means humans are animals that possess a spinal

cord (Chordata and Vertebrata) and are mammals. In the class of mammals, humans are classified as primates (as are chimps and gorillas) of the hominid family, meaning we walk more or less upright. See, it's simple.

Species names are binomial (meaning two-part names) and include both the genus and the species. It might seem redundant, but the genus is repeated in the species name. In this binomial naming system first is the genus and second the species. Humans are Homo sapiens since we are of the genus Homo (*man* in Latin) and the species sapiens (*wise* in Latin). So we are supposed to be wise men. There are other species in our genus such as Homo erectus, Homo neanderthalensis, and others. They are mammalian primates that also walk upright (hominids) but are not exactly like us.

The genus and all the classifications above it (family, order, etc.) tell us where on the tree the organism belongs, and the species tells us something about its particular characteristics. For example, the genus of oak trees is Quercus. A white oak is Quercus alba, and a red oak is Quercus rubra. Albus is derived from Latin for *white* and rubra from Latin for *red*. So the species is more descriptive, while the genus places the particular organism in its proper place in the accepted standards of scientific nomenclature. This means that the genus isn't negotiable, but the species might be.

There are several genuses of sea worms. One is Osedax. If her worm was in this genus—and that would depend upon its anatomical and physiological characteristics—she could apply to name it Osedax Sally or whatever her name is. It might or might not be accepted. She could not call it simply Sally Jones, however.

COULD MY YOUNG GIRL, WHO IS BOTH VAMPIRE AND VAMPIRE SLAYER, EACH WITH ITS OWN BLOOD TYPE, DEVELOP MEDICAL PROBLEMS FROM THIS BLOOD MIXTURE?

Q In my scenario, a girl wonders if she could be both vampire and slayer. If so, the problem is that the two bloods fight each other and could eventually kill her. I have heard that this is similar to what could happen with a fetus if the parents are of two different blood types. Is this true? How can the death be prevented, and what are the odds that the infant would die without treatment?

Robin Connelly
Boise, Idaho
www.robinconnelly.com

A What you are referring to is hemolytic disease of the newborn (HDN). It's an extremely complex physiological situation and comes in many varieties and degrees of seriousness. It occurs when the fetus has a blood type that is different from the mother's.

During pregnancy, the maternal and fetal blood do not mix as they are separated by the placental membrane. This membrane allows oxygen and nutrients to pass but not blood, so the two circulations (mother and fetus) don't truly mix. But this separation isn't perfect, and a few red blood cells (RBCs) from each slip back and forth. The child's immune system is too immature to recognize the mother's RBCs as foreign, so nothing happens on that side of the membrane. But the mother's immune system might recognize the fetus's RBCs as foreign and construct antibodies to attack the "foreign invaders."

This most commonly occurs with the Rh (rhesus) factor. When we say someone has A positive blood, we mean they are type A with a positive Rh factor. Type A negative would be type A but with no Rh factor. The problem arises when the mother is Rh negative and the baby is Rh positive. Here the Rh negative mother recognizes the Rh positive antigens from the baby's RBCs and builds anti-Rh antibodies that then cross back to the baby and begin to destroy the RBCs. This process is called hemolysis (hemo means blood; lysis is to break up or destroy).

This can also occur with ABO blood type differences. For example, if the mother is type O but the baby is type A, then type A RBCs sneak into the mother and her system builds anti-A antibodies. When these antibodies drift back across the placental barrier, they attack the baby's RBCs and destroy them.

Regardless of whether the mismatch is in the ABO or Rh types, if only a small amount of these antibodies are made, then only a small number of fetal RBCs are destroyed and the child is fine. If large amounts are built, the stage is set for massive destruction of the child's RBCs and the release of bilirubin, a breakdown product of RBC destruction. This can cause anemia, brain damage (called kernicterus), kidney damage, and fetal death. And it can occur anywhere between these two extremes.

This doesn't tend to happen with the first pregnancy

but will worsen with each subsequent mismatched pregnancy. It takes time for mom to build enough antibodies. The first pregnancy starts the process, and those that follow make it worse.

The treatment for a baby born with this problem is often an exchange blood transfusion and exposure to UV light, either the sun or an artificial UV source. The UV light breaks apart large bilirubin molecules and helps prevent kernicterus.

The preventive treatment is to give the Rh negative mother a substance called RhoGAM, which blocks the mother's ability to produce the antibodies that damage the baby's RBCs.

This is just the very, very basics (told you it was complex), but hopefully you can incorporate some of it into your story.

WILL FLIES DEPOSIT EGGS ON AN INJURED
BUT LIVING INDIVIDUAL?

Q Here's a grisly scenario for you. A man has been seriously wounded by a gunshot to the gut. He's alone in a mountainous North American forest in summer, and insects are plentiful. I know flies would be attracted to the blood, but would they begin laying eggs before the victim's death? The man is delirious and beyond chasing them away.

P.A. Brown
Author of the L.A. Shadows series
Ontario, Canada
http://www.pabrown.com

A Absolutely this can and does happen. Flies look for any place that is warm and moist to lay their eggs and carry on the next generation. They don't really care whether the chosen site is living or dead. It's a matter of survival and species propagation for them.

Ask any emergency room physician, and he will tell you that he has seen what we call "maggot people." Not exactly a flattering term but it is highly descriptive. It is usually older people or people who are mentally infirm who have diabetes or some other chronic disorder that has resulted in ulcerated lesions on their legs. Flies will deposit eggs in these open sores, and they will hatch into maggots, which then feed on the tissues and often on the infected pus that can be found in some of these lesions. Not a pretty sight but the presence of fly maggots doesn't create any extra discomfort. In fact, the maggots might actually help with the healing process because they remove dead and infected tissues.

The treatment in this circumstance is to wash away the maggots, clean and dress the wound, give the individual both topical and systemic antibiotics, and treat the underlying illness whether it be diabetes or chronic congestive heart failure, two very common underlying diseases in this situation.

Your character's wound could easily be populated by such maggots, and he could be unaware it has occurred.

COULD MY CHARACTER HIDE A KEY BENEATH HIS SKIN?

Q If my fit ex-Marine wanted to hide a key under his skin and cut it out later, what would be the best location? I'm thinking the upper body area. How deep would it need to be placed?

Richard J. Brewer
Sherman Oaks, California

A It could be placed anywhere he could reach and that would be out of sight. The chest, belly, inside an arm or leg. The incision would need to be only half an inch wide and deep since the key would easily slide just beneath the skin. He would then need to suture it closed and let it heal. Later he could open it and remove the key.

He should sterilize the key and any instruments used to avoid introducing an infection. This could be accomplished by simply boiling them for a few minutes.

WHAT EFFECT WOULD FACIAL IMMERSION IN MOLTEN BRONZE HAVE ON MY CHARACTER?

Q In my story, a bronze sculptor is pouring molten metal into a mold when she is hit on the back of the head. She slumps forward and the 2010 degree metal covers her face. If she is dazed from the blow, would she be able to move out of the way, or would she instantly be incapacitated? What would the molten bronze do to her face? Would it cool enough upon contact to form a mask, or would it actually burn into the flesh and eyes and mouth? If she died, would the cause of death be suffocation?

TM
Holyoke, Colorado

A The scenario you lay out would be almost uniformly fatal in very short order. We are not talking candle wax or even a hot stove burner here. To add perspective, cremations are done at temperatures of approximately 1500 degrees. Your unfortunate lady would be facedown in molten metal of over 2000 degrees. This would immediately destroy her entire face, including her nasal passages, mouth, and throat. She would likely inhale some of the molten metal into her throat and lungs. The pain alone would cause her to collapse and perhaps lose consciousness, and the destruction of her face and airways would prevent her from breathing. She would die from asphyxia quickly.

The only way to save her would be to perform an emergency tracheotomy, which would have to be done within a couple of minutes.

WHAT WOULD HAPPEN IF A PARASITOID INSECT ATE A HUMAN FROM THE INSIDE OUT?

Q My fictional victims have fallen prey to a colony of parasitoid insects. The female parasitoid lays her eggs inside the body of her host. The eggs hatch, and the larvae eat the hapless host from the inside out while it is still alive. They eat everything except the nervous system, saving it for last in an effort to keep their prey alive and fresh as long as possible. Could a human body be eaten alive from the inside in a similar manner? If so, which system(s) could be eaten so the host (person) remains alive?

Susan Gallagher
Weatherly, Pennsylvania

A Yes, this could happen with certain restrictions. Muscles and tissues and organs such as the kidneys and the spleen could be eaten and the victim live. For a while anyway. Hours to a couple of days. But surviving weeks or months in this circumstance isn't likely since the damaged areas would bleed or become infected and this would lead to death. If the vital organs—the lungs, heart, and brain—are attacked, death would follow very quickly. If any of the major blood vessels were damaged, the victim would bleed to death in a few minutes. Use these general guidelines and time frames, and your scenario will work.

The excellent 1979 movie *Alien* was based on a similar scenario. I believe they used the life cycle of a parasitic wasp as the model for the alien.

WHAT HAPPENS WHEN SOMEONE SWALLOWS RAZOR BLADES?

 My killer makes his victims swallow six double-edged razor blades. What internal damage would this do, and would it be enough to kill them?

RS
Houston, Texas

The injuries would be what you probably imagine. The blades would lacerate the mouth, tongue, pharynx (back of the mouth), esophagus, and stomach. The bleeding could be severe but maybe not life threatening at first. The victim would spit and cough blood, and if the esophagus was severely damaged, he would bleed profusely into the stomach. This would lead to vomiting large amounts of blood. If no major bleeding occurred, the blades would then move down the intestine, continually doing damage. Bloody diarrhea would follow. An esophageal, stomach, or intestinal perforation (where the blades cut through the entire wall) could occur, and if so, the bleeding would be severe and into the chest or abdomen. The victim would then bleed into shock and die.

WHAT PHYSICAL CHANGES AND SENSATIONS WOULD MY CHARACTER EXPERIENCE AS HE TRANSFORMS INTO A JAGUAR?

Q I am writing a paranormal urban fantasy book where my character will transform into a jaguar. I know this sounds crazy, but if this were to happen what would need to change, and would there be physical pain? Would it make sense for the transformation to start with a severe headache or maybe spinal pain?

Andi Callahan

A You have a great deal to work with here. This process could be painless or painful as you wish. Or rather than pain your character could experience warmth, electric shocks or tingling sensations, a burning discomfort, aching, cramping, or any other sensation you want.

Regardless of what sensation or combination of sensations you decide to use, these areas would be the most affected.

The head and face as the structure of the skull, face, and jaw changed to the feline form.

The mouth as the two large canine fangs grew from the gums.

Neck, shoulder, and back as the body changed from two-legged to four-legged locomotion.

The end of the spine and buttocks as the tail began to protrude and form.

The hands as the fingers became shorter and broader and the claws extended from the ends of the fingers.

Since this is science fiction you can have almost anything you want to happen in almost any order and in almost any severity.

Good stuff. Have fun with it.

HOW LONG COULD MY VICTIM SURVIVE
WHILE BEING SKINNED?

Q In my story, a serial killer kidnaps victims and subdues them with ketamine. He then skins them while they are still alive. How long would a person survive (conscious or not) while being flayed?

Connor Bryant
Coos Bay, Oregon

A Ketamine is a powerful general anesthetic that has been around for forty years or so. Whether the victim is awake and capable of feeling anything or not would depend upon the dose of ketamine given.

Your killer could tailor the dose to the desired effect. A little bit would sedate the victim, but he would still respond to the discomfort. He could take the victim a little deeper where he could be completely out but still respond to the pain by trying to move, withdraw, or cry out. Even more ketamine would put the victim into deep anesthesia, and he might not respond at all. This scenario would require some form of artificial ventilation since at this level of anesthesia the victim would not breathe on his own. If there was no method for doing this, the victim would die from asphyxia.

Ketamine is short acting and must be repeatedly given in a prolonged procedure such as this. Your killer would need to give small repeated doses to maintain the victim at whatever level of anesthesia he chose.

Early in this scenario the things that would lead to death are fluid loss and hypothermia. This procedure would cause blood loss, but even more importantly the exposed tissues, now without the protective coating of the skin, would weep fluids dramatically. Ultimately, the victim would slip into shock and die because the body was depleted of fluids.

The skin serves as our thermal barrier. It helps control heat loss by controlling blood flow through the skin. Higher blood flow leads to greater heat loss and lower blood flow to less. This is why people appear flushed when they're hot and pale when they're cold. In this scenario, the protective layer is lost and body temperature could deplete rapidly.

There is no way to determine exactly how long this individual would survive this ordeal but it could be anywhere from one to two hours and up to a day.

If your killer was completely diabolical, he could start an intravenous line and give the victim fluids throughout the procedure. This would help with fluid loss, and if he covered the victim with a thermal blanket or some other barrier, he could lessen the heat loss. The victim could be kept alive for many days.

If your killer decided to do this, the victim would become infected after about forty-eight hours. Without the skin as a barrier, bacteria would settle into the moist tissues and grow rapidly. As the bacteria grew they would seed the bloodstream and lead to what we call septic shock, which would result in death.

A FEW FINAL WORDS

Now that you have completed this book, I hope you have learned something from the questions and answers inside. Some questions were straightforward, others complex, and still others downright bizarre.

Yet each question reveals the incredible imagination, curiosity, and dedication to getting it right that is essential for credible storytelling and fiction writing. As I said in the introduction, I believe these questions provide insight into the creative process and demonstrate the depth of commitment to craft that is found in successful writers of fiction.

I hope you found these pages interesting, informative, and stimulating. It is my sincerest wish that this information will improve your own writing and reading and stir your creative juices.

Thank you for your time, interest, and curiosity.

D. P. Lyle, MD

Visit my website and blog:
The Writer's Medical and Forensics Lab at www.dplylemd.com
The Writer's Forensics Blog at http://writersforensicsblog.wordpress.com

SPECIAL THANKS

To the writers: As with *Murder & Mayhem* and *Forensics and Fiction*, *More Forensics and Fiction* belongs to many people but mostly to the writers who submitted the amazing questions that make up this text. I thank each of you. I encourage readers to visit their websites and read their books. You will be greatly rewarded.

To my wonderful agent, Kimberley Cameron of Kimberley Cameron and Associates: KC, you're the best.

To my keen-eyed editor Lorie Popp Jones: You found the many things that slipped past my eye and made this a much better book.

To all the outstanding folks at Medallion Press: Thanks for your professionalism and support. Love you guys.

OTHER BOOKS BY D.P. LYLE

FICTION

Stress Fracture
(Dub Walker Series, Book 1)

Hot Lights, Cold Steel
(Dub Walker Series, Book 2)

Royal Pains: First, Do No Harm
(The First *Royal Pains* Tie-In Novel)

Royal Pains: Sick Rich
(Another *Royal Pains* Tie-In Novel)

Devil's Playground
(A Samantha Cody Novel, Book 1)

Double Blind
(A Samantha Cody Novel, Book 2)

NONFICTION

Murder and Mayhem: A Doctor Answers Medical and Forensic Questions for Mystery Writers

Forensics for Dummies

Forensics and Fiction: Clever, Intriguing, and Downright Odd Questions from Crime Writers

Howdunit Forensics: A Guide for Writers